3-17-70

SOLDIERS

of Compassion

By URIE A. BENDER

HERALD PRESS
Scottdale, Pennsylvania 15683

To Alexander Mavrides
with warmest affection
and the deep thanks of 674 Paxmen*

1533505

*Up to June 1968

♊ DEDICATION

We sat across the table from each other. Coffee, bread, cheese, meats, and Greek sweets were set before us. It was my last hour with Alexander Mavrides, the faithful interpreter who had midwifed the Pax program in Greece—first at Panayitsa, then at Tsakones, and finally at Aridea.

For a few days he was my constant companion. We had talked, eaten together, and visited coffeehouses. We had met peasant and government official, doctor and lawyer, shopkeeper and tradesman, professor and villager—all his friends, and thus mine—as we traced the trail Paxmen had left everywhere across the lives and in the hearts of countless Greeks.

Alex reminisced about "his" Pax boys, the changes they had brought to three Greek towns and a large number of villages, his fifteen years of service from 1952 to 1966. "They were fine boys," he said. "Christians. We are glad they came. We wish they would have stayed."

In his modesty, he said nothing about the part he played in the success of the Greek projects.

An interpreter is often an unsung hero. Wherever

Paxmen have gone, until they have learned the language, the interpreter has made their service possible. And many times he has made their service meaningful.

When Pax began in Germany, a common ethnic origin simplified the crossing between cultures. But when Paxmen moved to Greece, not only were the field crops and demonstration programs experimental; the whole concept of short-term overseas service was being tested.

Alex helped it to succeed. "He not only interpreted our words. He interpreted our lives, our motivations, even our fumbling efforts."

"He kept us from making serious mistakes. He tempered our hot reactions and our American impatience. He helped to channel our youthful exuberance. He covered for us when, in ignorance, we offended our Greek friends."

"He stopped us sometimes and said, 'I'm not sure you want to say it that way. If you do, this will be the result. Why not try it like this?'"

A citizen of the country, Alex had the native's insight into Greek culture, life, and emotion. He had personal sensitivities that helped him understand the deprivations of the poverty-stricken villagers in Northern Greece. And he knew how to share these insights with young, inexperienced American farm boys so that their gift to the Greek people was transformed into something more than material; it grew into a contribution with spiritual and lasting dimensions.

Alex served as a teacher also. In his teaching of the language he helped Paxmen to build their own bridges, to begin their own reaching across cultures. In this he also excelled, limited only by the myriad demands on his time.

In a sense, Alex symbolized each Pax interpreter to follow, in country after country. Aggressive in his support of Pax objectives; yet yielding in his willing-

5

ness to see his personal contribution submerged completely in overall program. Forward in those early days when his presence and understanding were crucial to each development; retiring as each Paxman found his own channels of communication opening up. Firm in his insistence on recognition of Greek cultural patterns; flexible as program took on life, changing constantly to accomplish the greatest good.

To Alex and his kind, these pages are dedicated. Without their faithful service, Paxmen would be severely hampered. And Pax, as a way of life overseas, undoubtedly would not have grown to its present stature and level of usefulness.

Probably Alex holds the Pax record for length of service. He gave the good years of his life to the Pax program, to the Mennonite Church which sought to serve his fellows, and to his country. Many are in his debt, especially those of his own countrymen who reaped the benefits of his singular service and whose thanks he may never hear, simply because they have never been told of the significant role he played in Pax Greece.

It was night in Salonika. The coffee cups were cold. For a while we sat in silence. That hour was packed with a final remembering. Emotion rimmed the edge of each minute and brushed each word with a twinge of warmth and sadness.

Finally, Alex looked up at me and sighed. "Sometimes I feel like a tree which has cast its fruit on the ground."

I nodded. "I understand. But in the casting, seed has sprung up in many places. Today, there is much fruit."

Neither of us spoke again. We shook hands. And I went down a long flight of stairs into the driving rain.

♊ ACKNOWLEDGMENTS

This book cannot claim a single author. Its pages have been written by persons in more than a score of countries—Paxmen, refugees, doctors, government officials, farmers, teachers, community leaders, matrons, villagers, file clerks, administrators, nurses, children, secretaries. All of them have had their part in telling the story of Pax. From activity reports, correspondence, memos, booklets, and studies have come significant gleanings. Through interviews, hundreds of them, the Paxman's profile began to emerge. Amassed, a myriad of details flowed together to sharpen the picture of Pax Service. The author's by-line is only symbolic. It represents the combined interest and commitment of many. This is their book.

Mennonite Central Committee, the organization which fathered Pax, has contributed immeasurably in the long research procedures. Its Executive Secretary, William Snyder, in his willingness to help in every way, exemplified the gracious and generous assistance given me in every overseas contact and in the home office, by staff and field personnel alike. He and others provided invaluable assistance as the idea took shape and became an outline for probing questions.

Last but not least, special thanks is due Ann Detweiler. Her singular loyalty to the success of the project carried her and other typists through tedious transcription and almost endless manuscript typings done gladly after full days spent in office responsibilities. Without her valuable help, given unstintingly, the work could not have been completed.

The writing itself has been a mission of discovery. Discovery of one of the principles of Pax Service. What began as a desire to tell a story and thus share something of value with others has opened a door instead into such a wealth of experiences and insights and relationships I cannot escape the conclusion that I have become the principal beneficiary of this effort.

June 1, 1968   *Urie A. Bender*

𐓷 FOREWORD

This book is neither a counterpart to *The Ugly American* nor further documentation of *The Quiet Battle*. It is true that in the first book the image of an American serving abroad is not exactly commendable, while in this book the Paxman certainly seems to make the grade. And though the other book argues that the alternative to violence is nonviolent resistance, this book on Pax in effect insists that the Christian answer to violence is not to resist, but when compelled to go one mile, be willing to go gladly two miles.

This is the story of men who refuse to take up the gun, choosing rather the tools of agriculture and other peaceful pursuits for their fellowmen, mostly in the Third World. While some served in Europe in reconstruction after World War II, most of the Paxmen served two or more years in underdeveloped countries.

During World War I, conscientious objectors (CO's) in America were often regarded as traitors. Some were tarred and feathered; others suffered worse fates. During World War II, CO's were not considered traitors but often regarded as second-class citizens. The Civilian Public Service camps were definitely an improvement over anything World War I had to offer.

And now there is Pax—a positive program of service abroad in church-related projects instead of military service. History offers no precedent for this either in the church or in the state. The government of the United States, however imperfect it may be, needs to be commended for this practical and positive solution. Few governments of the world permit their citizens to be conscientious objectors to war. Even enlightened and otherwise democratic Switzerland has no alternative but the jail for its CO's. Other European countries, like Germany and the Netherlands, have legal provision for CO's to do alternative service, but at home and not abroad. America sends its soldiers and allows its conscientious objectors both to go to Vietnam. This poses tremendous problems, both for the church and government, but it also contains the seeds of a solution to a better way of ending conflict.

Of all the hopes and high aspirations of man, none seems to be more desired and more elusive than peace. In their desperation, men have killed and are killing each other to obtain peace. Much depends on the church and on our homes as to what we make of the Pax alternative. Many can now practice the Christian way of life and at the same time fulfill their national obligation.

It has been my privilege to work with many Pax-men. I have accompanied General Lewis B. Hershey, Director of the Selective Service System, on an inspection tour of Pax projects and heard his comments. As pastor of a church in Kansas, I had opportunity to observe firsthand the I-W program. I have also experienced war, notably in England when the German Luftwaffe bombed the British cities. In Manchester, England, I twice faced the judge for refusing to serve in the military. If I were a young American of draft age today, I would go the way of Pax.

Peter J. Dyck

10

✿ TABLE OF CONTENTS

ꙮ LIST OF ILLUSTRATIONS

12

1 INTRODUCTION

A silver thread of peace is spun wherever human resource touches human need. And when that slim strand is wound about with divine compassion and guided by divine purpose, one sees the torn fabric of life made whole again. Frayed ends are caught up; naked spirits are covered by the warmth of caring; the wounds of war and strife among men are sutured and bound.

To mend and stitch and weave, men of Pax have gone to Baghdad and Paris; to Hong Kong and Jericho; to Asuncion, Bechterdissen, Camel's Neck, Djakarta, and Espelkamp; to Halmahera and Henchir Toumghani; to Jerusalem; to Kaiserslautern, Karachi, Kinshasa, and Kolymbari; to Panayitsa; to Quang Ngai in Vietnam and Quatro Ojitos in Bolivia; to Tansen and Timor and Tournavista.

Paxmen have gone to Muslims of Algeria, to their own Mennonite kin in Germany and to the Simbas in the Congo. They have gone to their spiritual cousins in Israel and to Hindus in Pakistan. They have gone to emperor-worshipers in Nepal and to their Christian brothers in Greek Orthodox Crete. They have gone to unbeliever and religious fanatic alike.

Never have they stopped to ask—who are you? Only —what is your need?

Conscripts in their own country, they have volunteered to serve in places where ignorance and oppression and greed had chilled the spirit and crushed hope. From communities of plenty and quiet they traveled to share in hunger and turmoil.

For decades conscientious objectors deserved that name. For reasons of conscience they objected to participation in violence and destruction. In many cases, their understanding of commitment to Christ blocked enlistment in the military with its designs of force. Their concept of brotherhood did not allow a man to take the life of his brother. Their loyalty to God claimed a primary response.

They rejected the extreme provincialism of some nationalistic attitudes. They denied that doing battle was the only way to reflect patriotism. They deplored the carnage and dislocation and futility of war.

So they objected. And were called objectors. Conscientious objectors.

The term was correct in light of the observable patterns. Nevertheless, its implication was fragmentary. It cast a negative hue on a people whose essential commitment had always been positive in character. It distorted a witness of peace which the world needed badly. It hid from view a significant ethic of love with its active involvement in the ills of people and countries.

Conscientious objection came to be known as a wartime term. Among others, Mennonites came to be known as those who refused to bear arms. And young men with this ethnic and spiritual background came to be known as CO's.

During the American Civil War a CO, along with anyone else, could purchase his freedom from service.

In World War I, both the United States and Canada tolerated CO's but their dealings with these men committed to peace were sometimes marked by shameful episodes.

When Hitler gave the command that plunged the nations into World War II, Mennonite churches and others supported a massive and more or less passive Civilian Public Service program. More than 12,000 conscientious objectors were assigned by United States Selective Service to work of national importance. Camps were set up and men were deployed across the country. From the inception of this program to its end in 1947, six million man-days of labor were contributed. To finance this extensive effort to protect a principle various religious denominations raised a total of seven million dollars.

Canada also established an alternative service plan. But its period of conscription was shorter and the policies and procedural patterns of the Canadian plan led to much less disruption than came with the wholesale movements of men in the United States.

In the decade beginning with 1940, four hundred years of history began to catch up with the Mennonite Church. In this decade, the heritage of love and concern began to find expression in a new way beyond the islands of isolation Mennonites generally had lived in. Many of the Civilian Public Service men then were assigned to mental hospitals for orderly service. Here they discovered pockets of desperate need. Most of them brought to their assignments a quality of compassion which resulted in meaningful and meritorious service. Arising partly from the insights gained during CPS, a new concept of voluntary service for young people developed in various areas of the Mennonite Church.

So, when the Korean conflict touched the horizon of history in 1950 and the prospect of new draft laws became real, Mennonites began to ask among themselves,

"Why must we always wait for our government and some international crisis to nudge us into an expression of our love ethic?"

With that insight plans were laid, before conscientious objectors became subject to draft, for a Builders Unit to go to Germany and assist a residue of refugees from World War II to acquire homes and reestablish normal living patterns. Pax Unit I arrived in Europe April 1, 1951. As they stepped ashore, unknown to them, the first Paxmen carried with them the seed of a flower that has bloomed around the world.

Those blooms have begun to dispel the old negativism of refusal to bear arms. In its place has come a new understanding that the way of love, if it is to survive, must be a way of life. And as a way of life, loving concern must touch and transform every aspect of living—from the most exalted to the most menial and lowly.

In this, men of Pax have led the way.

The story given here is far from complete. Hundreds of Paxmen are missing from these pages not because their contribution was insignificant but simply because the objective of discovering the spirit of Pax would not have been served by a lengthy listing of names and dates and places and sequence of service assignments.

So only a few stories are told. These persons were selected not because their service was more illustrious than that of others but rather because they were typical of the spread of interests and abilities and, sometimes, of youthful inadequacies. Or because their efforts often reflect the excitement and adventure of untried ideas and the exuberance of untested energy.

Nor is the story complete in terms of international coverage. Only some of the countries Paxmen have served are mentioned in the text. Glimpses of several more are caught in the photo sections. The names of other countries appear only in the appendixes, again not because these countries are less important or because Paxmen there have served with less distinction; rather, because a labored attempt at scholarly completeness might well have overwhelmed the reader. But more particularly because the mass of both routine and exciting detail would have hidden from view the essential character of the Paxman's service.

That service did not represent an escape from military obligation or a running from danger. It was not a bid to become, in underdeveloped countries, either an arrogant lord or a condescending servant. Nor was it primarily a *telling* mission or ultimately even a *doing* ministry. Perhaps the essence of every Paxer's contribution was his willingness to *be with* people in need, to live in relationship with deprived persons, to sit where they sit.

"Then I came to them of the captivity at Telabib, that dwelt by the river of Chebar, and I sat where they sat, and remained there astonished among them seven days" (Ezekiel 3:15).

This, then, is not a book for the scholar or historian. Except for the appendixes, no attempt to be exhaustive or complete was made in the research procedure, or in the reporting of research results. Although the material is factual in every respect, only those segments of experience are used which contribute most precisely to the overview of Pax intended. This intention, simply stated, was to paint a picture of Paxmen in their natural habitat: responding to human need, serving as agents of reconciliation, reflecting the ultimate in peacemaking—helping man to be at peace with himself, his environment, his fellowman, his God.

Men of Pax are human. They possess limitations and inadequacies which reflect both their humanity and their lack of experience. But most of them also constitute exhibits of how undreamed-of resources and potential rise to respond to a variety of needs in other human beings. And in these responses, the Paxers themselves become truly men, men of maturity and judgment, sometimes a little awed and even puzzled by their own commitment in the face of hardship and sacrifice.

Commitment is not rare in this day of causes and of inhuman demands on the human spirit. And yet to find commitment in a young man or a group of young men, voluntary, unselfish, and dedicated unreservedly to peace and compassion, is to find a quality of living and giving which thrives on its essential purpose of concern for one's brother—properly defined as anyone in need. This quality seems to be especially rare in our time when history is being marked by arrogance and selfishness and destruction.

Men of Pax have said no to involvement in military answers to man's dilemmas. But they are more than conscientious objectors to pulling a trigger. They are more than passive pacifists who stand on the sidelines while others stride bravely into danger. They are more than nonresistant individuals who are opposed to the principle of force and violence used to gain certain ends. And definitely, they are more than neurotic negativists who refuse to participate in the affairs of state.

Paxmen are not just "no" men. They are persons whose commitment to God and the way of life Jesus taught has drawn them deeply into the redemptive mission of Christ. This mission, first and last, is life-giving, not life-destroying. To be part of any machine designed for destruction is to deny simply but profoundly his participation in Christ's earthly purpose, as the conscientious objector understands it. So he says no to those situations which would lead him into that denial but only so he can fulfill his primary calling—to be an emissary of God's peace.

The Paxman is *for* much more than he is *against.* The objector image has saddled him for decades, many times completely hiding the extraordinary courage required to face ridicule, physical tortures, extreme danger, capture by hostile peoples, and even death. All the way from the sordid treatment accorded some CO's in the United States during World War I to service under fire and other extreme conditions in the seven-year Algerian struggle for independence, to the boiling tribal cauldron in the Congo and more recently the fateful vendetta in Vietnam, the so-called CO has sought service. But always service with a difference—a service which reflected caring and in some way could lead to betterment and health and well-being for persons caught in need.

In no century have there been more opportunities to prove courage and commitment. And never before have men of Pax acquitted themselves so extensively and valiantly and selflessly in defense of the principle of love to all men in every situation.

These pages tell that story. If you look, you will find the drab routine of daily detail which demands dedication and self-discipline. You will discover errors in judgment, proof of humanity and ordinariness. You will see contributions which betoken unusual skills or even flashes of brilliance. You will share in the uncovering of insights which come only to those whose loyalty is single-minded. And you will meet hometown boys who grew to manhood in short months, not because they traveled to another country, but because they learned the lesson of service—the importance of *being with* a person in his need. The word is involvement.

2 MEN OF PAX

GERMANY

Howard Landis

The machines of war, grinding their way across a country, leave in their wake more than a memory of the whine of bullets, the acrid smell of powder, and the crunching leaping crash of exploding bombs; more than a bleeding landscape gashed by rape and lust, blackened by the fires of revenge; more than shattered cities and broken bodies and plundered lives with their tomorrows crushed into oblivion.

More than all the destruction, the wretched residue of war is made up of those who have been sentenced to life amid the rubble—the refugee. Haunted by his memories of a better day and numbed by fate's trip-hammer blows, he hunches against still other terrors. Torn by the wrenching away of hope and faith, his bloodied spirit shrivels into despair.

Stripped of purpose and meaning, shivering in the horrible aloneness of neglect, the refugee sits and waits for the release of death.

World War II was no exception. As armies seesawed across the nations of Europe, they left a trail of ruined businessmen, dispossessed landowners, and splintered families. By the end of war in 1945 some of the mass

21

of refugees had already found their way home. Others, in the years that followed, made new lives elsewhere. But for many thousands, herded together in camps, huddled in barracks, and crowded into abandoned factories, the new decade beginning in 1950 pointed only toward more black uncertainty.

More than 12,000 Mennonite refugees were among these, a part of the seemingly endless stream of displaced persons flowing into West Germany from Russia, Poland, Prussia, Danzig, and East Germany. Some camps were set up as staging areas for resettlement projects in South America, Canada, and the United States. But both in these camps and elsewhere, many remained for reasons of age, health, or other problems which rendered the refugee unacceptable to the country of his choice.

Conditions in the camps varied little from place to place. The December 1954 issue of *Euro-Pax News* describes one such situation in an area served by Paxmen as early as 1952.

"At the South German city of Backnang the government is using a large school building to provide temporary housing for approximately 1,000 persons. Although it is a substantial structure, extreme overcrowding makes the place hardly livable. In one case, fifteen persons—five families—were living in a space about twenty feet square. Very few families have a whole room to themselves.

"Living units packed to overflowing, with not a single curtain partition anywhere, make privacy impossible. Double-deck beds, pushed together end to end, fill the rooms and leave only narrow paths. Adding to the impersonal austerity of settlement life, the central kitchen prepares meals for everyone and dispenses the food in simple line-up fashion. Each takes his portion to his quarters where there is often no table on which to put it.

"In the same vicinity, about sixty refugees have been living for eight years in a low wooden barrack. Little better than a shack, the bleak building fails to provide even moderately adequate accommodations. Inside, one family's single, poorly lighted room must serve as their kitchen, bedroom, and living room. Outside, the cluttered ugliness of the dusty yard depicts carelessness born of despair.

"But children are the greatest tragedy. They wander through the echoing halls and poke about the rubbish heaps. They flock together in shouting groups and run aimlessly here and there. Educational facilities are often poor, giving them little to do. These children have never known anything else. . . ."

To alleviate the pressing needs of these refugee communities the Mennonite Central Committee arranged for a Builders Unit to provide building assistance so that these people could become settled permanently. Comprised of twenty young men, the first unit left the United States for Europe in March of 1951.

Dr. Howard Landis, now Dean at Messiah College, Grantham, Pennsylvania, was a member of the first unit. He was born in the year 1927 at Souderton, Pennsylvania, and graduated from high school in 1945. At that time he began full-time work in his father's construction firm, looking forward to a business relationship.

In his own words, Howard tells part of the story:

We went over on the Dutch liner, *Leerdam.* This in itself was quite an experience for the fellows. I suppose one could say it was a continuation of the orientation begun at Mennonite Central Committee headquarters in Akron, Pennsylvania.

We had a number of discussions on board ship with other passengers. I'm afraid there was a certain defensive attitude about our peace position, perhaps aggravated by the fact that by then the Berlin cold war was getting pretty hot, feelings were running rather high, and there was an element of danger involved in travel.

Many of the passengers with whom we spoke couldn't believe young men would give an entire year to a reconstruction project and actually pay $900 for the privilege. Even the people in Europe were skeptical of our story.

My teens had been a time of turmoil. At no point during later adolescence did I have a significant faith. So I became another young person searching for meaning. I did a lot of reading, including the Bible.

Of course, I never really broke away from church life, but neither was I getting any satisfaction from it. Not even after I made a public religious commitment. However, some months later—I was 22 at the time— the content of this commitment to God began to make sense and the reality of my new spiritual experience came into focus.

When this happened, life took on meaning and I began to see some direction and purpose.

Very shortly after, I saw a note about the Builders Unit program planned to help refugees in Germany. The idea struck a responsive chord, so I applied.

Since the program was so new, really only experimental, I was the first person accepted by MCC from the Brethren in Christ Church. At the time none of us knew if this service might fulfill our draft obligation or not. Because of impending legislation we were almost certain conscientious objectors would be drafted. It was not until just before I came home, at the end of three years, that I discovered my service had fulfilled Selective Service requirements.

I suspect the men in the first Builders Unit were indulging an urge for adventure and change; they were frontier personalities. Certainly the same may have been true of later Paxmen as well. But the first group went into a completely new situation, indefinite and unknown. Few precedents had been established. Policies were still basically unformed; and where formed, untested. These first men were true pioneers.

Of course, more than adventure was involved. A number had already been in other kinds of voluntary service; this was more of the same. There was a sense of personal commitment to help people in need. In spite of a rural, largely nonacademic background, many of the fellows reflected considerable ideological content in their discussions. I became aware very soon that most of the fellows had been doing a lot of thinking.

For me, the Builders Unit opened the door to a significant opportunity. Since all of these men were conscientious objectors, the unit objectives gave me the privilege of taking the peace position and also of doing something positive. I had become a little disgruntled with the stifling negative flavor of the nonresistant ethic. For me, my faith and convictions stood for more than a matter of nonparticipation in war; they issued in a strong desire to do something worthwhile. I welcomed the building unit experience in Germany.

Most of us were relatively untrained. However, this did not mean we were without skills. Farm experience, mechanical aptitudes, or relation to the building trades were elements in the process of selection of the first unit of twenty from a considerably larger number of applications.

That first group, the one I knew best, also reflected a high degree of spiritual maturity. The General Conference Mennonite fellows were top quality.

A funny thing happened during orientation, on the trip across, and during the first months of working together. We fellows came from different Mennonite or Mennonite-related groups and from a variety of areas, all of us with preconceived conclusions of the superiority of the groups or areas we represented. It didn't take long, though, for lessons of understanding and tolerance to take effect. Those who perhaps had felt their viewpoints were right discovered greater spiritual depth and perception in others about whom they had entertained questions or doubts.

This was good for all of us.

We traveled by bus to Espelkamp-Mittwald, Germany. This was to be our first location. Heavy rains had softened the roads in the area. Before we got to our lodging our bus became mired in a mudhole and the Pax unit had to push it to solid ground.

Triple-deck bunks had been set up in a storage shed, part of a deserted munitions factory complex. We trekked in the first night with only the lights from a truck parked outside shining in to show us the dim outline of our quarters.

Our arrival and first weeks were not without frustrations. In spite of previous arrangements, not all the red tape had been cut so that we could begin our work. One example of this related to the area where the buildings were to be erected. This land was still covered by trees. Understandably and commendably, Germans are slow to cut them. Although the project had been cleared, permission for the tree removal had not yet been granted. Finally, after a week of waiting, Dwight Wiebe, European Pax Director, gave the order to begin cutting. He felt starting to cut the trees might also snip some of the red tape and that the authorities would be out shortly. He was right. Before noon they came to ask what we were doing and why, then granted permission. Shortly the trees were down, stumps were pulled, and digging for basement foundations begun.

That's the way it began, *said Howard as he finished talking. But his comments don't tell the whole story.*

Pax construction units worked in close cooperation

with Mennonitische Siedlungshilfe, the German Mennonite agency in charge of the refugee resettlement
program.

A unique part of the Pax work had to do with its
involvement in the mortgage arrangement set up to
make home ownership possible for the penniless refugees. Specific details varied from place to place.

The Federal German government had offered loan
funds to refugees on a second- and third-mortgage
basis repayable over a period of 34 years. But it was
required that each refugee provide 10 percent of the
cost of his apartment as a down payment and also
provide a substantial amount of labor in lieu of a first
mortgage. For a refugee father barely able to earn
enough bread for his family, this was impossible. In
effect, the Paxmen, through their donated labor, served
as proxies for the refugee. And the American Mennonite Central Committee, with its German counterpart,
Mennonitische Siedlungshilfe, assisted refugees with the
necessary cash payment through the establishment of a
revolving fund.

Current German records show that Pax labor constituted an average of 10 percent of the total value of
the housing at Enkenbach. This represented 3,300 hours
of work on the multiple-dwelling housing.

In a recent letter (March 12, 1968) from Germany,
Richard Hertzler and Fritz Stauffer, representing
Mennonitische Siedlungshilfe, confirm emphatically
the significance of Pax service, "The real and indispens-
able help of the Paxmen will not be minimized. But
we know and repeat very clearly, today as we have
before, that none of the Mennonite settlements could
have been established if the Pax boys had not contributed the last notch in the financing, that is the
Eigenhilfe (comparable to down payment) which none
of the refugees could have supplied. . . ."

Very early the first Builders Unit was divided. Twelve

fellows stayed at Espelkamp to carry on building. Eight fellows transferred to Neuwied at Niederbieber. Here there were pumice deposits, a kind of light volcanic ash material which formed an excellent aggregate mixed with cement for the manufacture of blocks and bricks.

The Paxmen set up an arrangement with a local man, August Heineman, who owned a number of acres of this pumice running as deep as nine feet. They sold him a continuous-run cement mixer and a block machine. He provided the aggregate and cement. Paxmen provided labor and agreed to operate the plant for one year. His return was four fifths of the output which he sold. The Paxmen received a one-fifth share as payment for their labor. Their share of production was used to build five four-apartment houses at Espelkamp during the first year.

The "bims" or blocks were transported, 400 blocks weighing from nine to ten tons in each load, by a British-made Chevrolet truck and a German trailer to the building locations—13 loaded hours away.

In spite of primitive living conditions—farm granary at Neuwied or converted ammunitions storage shed at Espelkamp—morale was high. The units had found purpose in their mission, and progress could be measured. Each day was filled with hard work but at these and succeeding locations, Paxmen found meaningful extracurricular activities as well.

In the October 1956 issue of *Euro-Pax News* a Paxman outlines his schedule, fairly typical of all the European units engaged in construction.

"Those of us who've been to college can draw similarities to dormitory life. But here with the ten to twenty fellows of a unit rooming, working, eating, and playing together every day, the associations are much closer and the atmosphere quite different from a college dorm.

"Breakfast downstairs at 6:15 means rolling out of

28

the sack sometime between 6:00 and 6:14, depending upon your early morning efficiency and the distance of your bunk from the table. (Some get to enjoy the early fresh fog during a jaunt to the Pax apartment from their room in a different house.)

"Nobody knows what time the matron's day begins, but those pancakes are usually hot, ready, and eaten with no questions asked.

"Morning devotions—Scripture reading, prayer, and singing together—are held around the tables following breakfast. Each unit member takes a regular turn in leading this daily activity.

"Things begin buzzing on the project at seven o'clock. After getting a good start on our 8 3/4-hour workday, we call a 15-minute halt at nine for a customary *zweites Fruhstuck* or second breakfast—quite a pleasant German habit. German workers usually carry theirs with them to work in their leather briefcases. We have our milk, bread, butter, and cheese brought out by the unit leader or matron.

"From 12 noon to one o'clock, trowels, hammers, picks, shovels, wheelbarrows, and the mixer get a rest while we eat dinner, read our mail (if and when), and glance at the latest newspaper or magazines.

"Then if no rainstorm interrupts—and has it ever been wet this past summer—we work until 5:00 p.m.

"Supper is at 5:30 after which two or three lucky fellows get to help the matron with the dishwashing. This necessary assistance is efficiently arranged by weeklong assignments of personnel to the task as determined by an alphabetized listing of our respective family names.

"We then manage to keep busy with a weekly evening schedule including: chorus practice with the German youth; German language class; neighborhood boys' club led by several Paxers; unit Bible study; organized unit recreation of softball, volleyball, or basketball;

social and Bible study evenings with German youth; refugee camp visitation.

"Besides these scheduled events, we like to find time for some photography work in our basement darkroom, for visiting the settlement families, reading, and, of course, the inevitable late-hour 'bull sessions.'"

The off-time activities are pretty important to Paxmen. In fact, as one person wrote, "The good use of this off time helps to make Pax an educational experience, as well as a unique opportunity for spiritual growth and witnessing."

Units often arranged their own worship and Bible study activities in English, as well as participating in the church life of local congregations. And in some locations, Paxmen organized quartets or choruses which shared in special occasions or took tours to various parts of the country. An 18-member chorus traveled to Berlin, singing at refugee camps, a large prison, and the Mennonite church in the city. An octet, organized later, also traveled to Berlin, singing for refugees in various camps.

One of the more impressive camps was in an old factory which held about 2,000 refugees. Individual rooms were very few. When the Pax octet first arrived within the gates of this camp a few curious children started to gather around to watch the men. The octet began to sing American Christmas carols. Soon they and a hundred or more children were all singing *deutsche Weihnachts-Lieder*. As they went through the camp singing and inviting the people to their music program, the children followed them. Some enjoyed walking hand-in-hand with the *amerikanische* Pax boys. After the program the children gathered around the car. A few even wanted to go along in the car.

One of the men reported, "In talking with the people in camps we found that they were all very human; they all had a story to tell.

"When they hear about our pacifism many of them will say, *'Ja, das ist viel besser als Soldat spielen.'* *(What you are doing is much better than playing soldier.)* But, when they start talking about Russians or any soldiers who may have killed some of their family or driven them out of their homes, one can see the hate in their eyes and hear it in the tone of their voices."

But perhaps one of the most touching and meaningful extracurriculars was the distribution of MCC Christmas bundles prepared by American Mennonite children for refugees. Each Christmas season, Paxmen entered into this activity with real joy. Why is best described in the December 1954 issue of *Euro-Pax News*.

"The hall was dark. Picking their way through the clutter of boxes and broken furniture, the three Paxmen found the door at the end of the crowded passageway and knocked. A shabbily dressed woman, appearing older than she was, opened the door to the single room where the family of seven had been living since 1946. The eyes of five children gazed forlornly at the intruders. Hanging crazily and seeming to symbolize the broken lives of its owners, a shattered mirror gave a dozen distorted reflections of the primitive kitchen, the jumble of beds, and the scarred table.

" 'You see us in our misery,' the woman said as she invited the three Americans into the room. 'We've been here for a long time and don't know when we'll get out. Sometimes,' she added hopelessly, 'I think it would be better to end it all.'

"After talking with her about the family's welfare, the Paxmen told her of their own experiences of the power of prayer and personal faith in God. The news that Christmas bundles would soon be given to her children brought a smile to her lips. 'Yes,' she responded, 'do what you can for the children.' "

Activities like this helped to dispel the earlier skepti-

cism with which some of the first Paxmen were greet-
ed.

Howard tells about their first experiences:

It was interesting to watch. When we first came to
Espelkamp, we went to local shops to get mechanical
or repair work done. After the second or third visit, the
owner would say to us, "Go ahead and do the job
yourself. Anything in the shop is yours."

This was true in building also. The Germans have a
highly developed system of masters and apprentices in
each speciality. Naturally, they were suspicious of a
group of young men, none more than apprentices in
age or experience, who were attempting major construction including a number of specialties—carpentry,
block laying, interior decorating, among others. But
after observing our work, the German masters would
let us go without the close supervision they were certain earlier would be necessary.

Of course, as projects were completed in our area and
men began elsewhere, the harvest of confidence grew,
and succeeding jobs became easier and relationships
closer.

Fascinating thing to see—the rapid growth of confidence, *Howard smiled as he finished.*

The whole matter of supervision was a puzzle not
only to the Germans but to the American military as
well. In 1956, Dwight Wiebe, Pax director, received a
call from the *Stars and Stripes*, asking if they could do
a feature on Pax.

The reporter said, "We'll let you proofread the
script."

Dwight said, "That won't be necessary."

The reporter reacted. "This is very unorthodox."

But Dwight didn't want to influence him in any way,
so he arranged for one of the Paxmen to show the
reporter around.

The basements in Enkenbach needed to be hewn out of rock shale.

The reporter looked around and asked for the man in charge.

"He's not here," was the reply.

"Well, why are the men working?"

"Because that's what we are here for," was the answer.

"Well, I'll be damned," said the reporter. He simply couldn't believe there were men who could keep working without a boss.

Both Enkenbach and Backnang constituted major projects. Both towns were located in the hilly, wooded area of South Germany, Backnang about 18 miles from Stuttgart in Wurttemberg province and Enkenbach near Kaiserslautern in the Palatinate, from which region many Mennonites immigrated to Pennsylvania over two hundred years ago. Paxmen moved to Backnang on May 15, 1952, to help the refugees who, under the leadership of one of their own men, Richard Rupp, had actually begun the work in January, digging out one basement and leveling a street. The refugees there had come from Silesia and gathered at Backnang temporarily where they found an empty refugee camp. It was their hope to emigrate to Paraguay, Canada, and the United States. But by 1948 when the major groups had moved out, it was clear that for some, for political or physical reasons, emigration would be difficult.

This group of 130 persons in thirty families requested the privilege of working toward permanent housing and settling near Backnang. As a result of C. F. Klassen's yeoman efforts this was arranged. These thirty families, along with an additional thirty refugee families resettled from Schleswig-Holstein, a northern province of Germany, were to comprise the community.

In the May Pax group ten men came from Espelkamp and Neuwied. Later they were joined by ten more. At first they lived in a renovated Backnang hotel, but in December of 1952 moved into several apartments in the first dwelling completed by that time.

Original plans called for ten six-apartment units to house these sixty families. But this plan was doubled in size later in order to accommodate refugees from Russia, Poland, and Danzig. Later units were built with four apartments in each.

The units were built almost entirely of concrete blocks. So there was little carpenter work involved except on roof construction and in the final trim. Each apartment included three rooms, a kitchen, and a bath.

Although unit building plans varied from occasional single-dwelling houses to multiple-apartment dwellings with room for two, four, or six families, the structures had many similarities—block walls, sand plaster finish inside, concrete decks, and tile roofs. A composition with a hardening finish was poured on the decks.

In Espelkamp the Paxmen began a pattern of work which was used to some degree elsewhere as well: they had working with them unemployed men from the German refugee community.

This was good in that it provided an opportunity for direct sharing. But there was also quite a chasm between recently dispossessed older persons with traditional European viewpoints and young, energetic, idealistic Americans. This was not always bridged with understanding.

Fortunately, the local German communities had skilled persons who did the basic planning and engineering. Usually some area construction firm supervised construction, supplying the German foremen or *Meisters* to give Paxmen direction in the various trades. Paxers worked largely at excavation, pouring concrete, laying blocks, putting up rafters, and plastering. Later some helped on finish and interior decorating crews.

Tile roofing, electrical work, and most of the plumbing were done by German tradesmen.

Generally, relations with the German *Meisters* were excellent. Of course, on occasion, Paxmen, accustomed to American methods which seemed more ingenious and efficient, became disgruntled at traditional German ways. And sometimes *Meisters* would wring their hands over a blundering *Lehrbub* or beginner (not all of the men had had previous building experience). But there was a good spirit of comradeship. Many times *Meisters* were amazed at the versatility of most of the Paxmen, especially since few of them had served as apprentices or journeymen in the trades they were learning quickly to do well.

One example of a bridge built between the Paxers and their *Meisters* took place in the crew building outside scaffolds for the masons to work on. For months a spade had been used to dig holes for the poles placed in the ground to support the scaffold cross members. Then one of the Paxmen wrote his father asking him to send a post-hole digger. He gave it to his *Meister* who was extremely proud of this gift from "*his* Pax boys" and delighted in showing off his new machine. Not the least of his satisfaction came from the speedier work that was being done.

Living accommodations varied from place to place. Usually, the fellows who began at a location roughed it a bit. Later the Pax builders would move into the first one or two units built unless other adequate housing was available. 1533505

In Espelkamp, the first regular living quarters were barracks—one large room about the size of a small ranch house. In the room 25 to 35 people slept on triple-tiered bunks. At one end a small bedroom was enclosed for the cook, Erika Klaasen, and her husband.

Frau Klaasen's assignment was cooking but unofficially she served as matron also. She added an interesting and necessary feminine touch to both living quarters and group living.

The cook's job was never easy. The fellows felt free to make comments about the food. Sometimes these comments, although not intended in this way, sounded personal and caused some misunderstandings.

Later, in Germany, matron-cooks became almost permanent Pax fixtures. Usually they were American or Canadian girls chosen for their versatility and ability to big-sister lonesome Paxers—young enough to be interesting but too old to be interested (in the Pax age category).

At Neuwied, A. Lloyd Swartzendruber, an American pastor, "fathered" the fellows. He visited Espelkamp every second week. During the last half of his one-year term, Mrs. Swartzendruber was with him.

In Backnang, "Pop" Short and Rosie, his wife, another U.S. pastor couple, provided spiritual and temporal leadership for the unit. His jovial good nature is remembered by Paxmen and refugees alike.

"Jesse Short was a diplomat," said Heinrich Warkentin, one of the refugees who found a home at Backnang and is now a pastor in the Mennonite church there. "When the Paxmen moved into the house, they didn't want any overcrowding, so they planned to have two fellows in each room. 'Pop' took them to the barracks and showed them how the refugees had lived for five years. At that point the fellows offered to double up, put four in a room, so the refugees could have additional space.

"He'd take a problem boy and put him on the committee of five that worked with 'Pop' administering the unit.

"The Paxmen often visited us. We enjoyed them. They'd make themselves at home—even put their feet up on the desk or table. This made us feel good.

"Of course, sometimes there were differences. The

Paxmen sang a little faster than the Germans and they didn't fold their hands to pray. The Paxmen didn't have all the form but they did have the inner life.

"But the differences were not important.

"We have no bad memories of Paxmen. They were excellent."

Mrs. Warkentin added, "They lived Christ's service among us."

The Warkentin family is typical of the kind of person helped by the Paxmen. And typical also is their generously grateful spirit. The October 1956 issue of *Euro-Pax News* tells a little of their story:

"Without a home, with little food or possessions of any kind, living much of the time in fear, uncertainty, and separated from loved ones partly describes the ten-year experience of one of the Mennonite refugee families now settled in a new Pax-built house at Backnang, Germany.

"The Heinrich Warkentin family of Liebenau, Ukraine, in Southwest Russia, had been fortunate in 1941 when German armies first invaded from the west. A one-night evacuation order was effected by the Russians and hundreds of families separated as persons, loaded atop open freight cars, were transported to Siberia. German forces gained the area before Warkentins were taken and they were able to return to their farm.

"However, in fleeing ahead of the returning Russian front in November 1943, Mr. and Mrs. Warkentin with sons of two years and five weeks plus Mrs. Warkentin's mother left their home farm and most possessions behind.

"They reached a displaced persons' camp in Poland in early '44 but Heinrich was drafted into the German army later that year, leaving his family to move farther west with the mass of refugees, mostly women and children.

37

"Overtaken by the Russian army in January of '45, Mrs. Warkentin says she cannot adequately describe the suffering which so many humans endured during 1945 and '46 in those Polish DP camps. She thought at first that they, being of German descent, would be shot by the Russians, and later almost wished it had been so when inhuman treatment, disease, and starvation worsened, claiming dozens each day.

"Filth prevailed as the camps had no sanitary facilities or privacy. Women had to work on the roads with no more to eat than a bit of thin soup. Mrs. Warkentin counts it a miracle that she, for one period of five weeks, had a job where a little bread could also be gotten.

"Later when, against terrific protests, all children were taken away to a different camp (hers were then ages two and five), she lost all will to live and lay sick for days. She recalls another 'miracle' at that time of someone finding an old familiar hymnbook which helped give her courage to go on. She also found her boys among 240 other starving youngsters and managed to get them back.

"The war ended in May 1945, but Mr. Warkentin was hospitalized in Germany with a wound. He heard no word about his family until January 1946, when a friend wrote that he knew of them still alive in Poland. Warkentin later heard that they would be trying to come out to Berlin with one of the large DP transport trains in December. He spent a very anxious Christmas wondering if they might have been caught by the freezing weather or perhaps by the Russians and sent back as prisoners.

"When they arrived safely in Berlin in January 1947, Mrs. Warkentin, the boys, and Grandmother received their first assistance from MCC in the form of food, clothing, and transportation to West Germany.

Life in a series of camps followed, usually together with other Mennonite refugees.

"In February, Warkentin met his wife for the first time in 2 1/2 years and later joined his family at a transient refugee camp in Munich.

"After six years in the old camp barracks at Backnang, during which time a third son was born and Grandmother emigrated to Canada, the Warkentins moved into a Pax house in April 1953.

"Now owning their own apartment in house No. 14 on Mennostrasse, their happiness and thankfulness for what they have is very apparent. Mr. Warkentin is employed by one of Backnang's many leather factories and 16-year-old Heinz is an apprentice machinist.

"Their apartment, similar to the other 109 in the settlement, includes a living room, kitchen, bath, and two bedrooms."

Howard compares the two parts of his Pax service:

Germany and Greece were quite different in terms of Pax involvement with the community. In Greece, there were fewer of us fellows, so our contact with the people tended to be more direct.

In Germany we had an excellent involvement in local church life. But our day-to-day contact was greatest with other Paxmen. We built American islands in which English served as the camp language. Our group was quite cloistered and perhaps rather uncosmopolitan in attitude. I'm sure we could have capitalized much more on the opportunities we had for learning experiences—in language, in cultural insights, even in our unit life.

In one sense, we missed it, *said Howard.*

Nevertheless, Pax as a program opened up significant doors. Not the least of these was the door to understanding between people. Living and serving those whose needs were great illustrated to the refugees a kind of dedication and unselfish service that reawakened hope. And, seeing for themselves the devastations of spirit and nation that war can accomplish, the Paxmen found basis in reality for their essential commitment to the way of peace and reconciliation.

Pax service took the idea of peace out of the abstract air of theory and put it to work in the grubby ground of daily reality. For this the demands on Paxmen were great.

It's possible that only a certain kind of person enters Pax—the adventurer, the individualist. But perhaps the demands of some kinds of service require this: a willingness to risk total involvement, to enter the uncertain unknown, to give up the security of familiar things and patterns of work and a comfortable culture.

Dr. Landis sums up his three years in Pax:

"For me Pax was a positive experience. The negative elements were far outweighed by the good in it.

"In Pax I learned a completely new attitude toward people, I saw them from a different perspective. I saw them as distinct individuals rather than categories.

"This has colored my life. Were it not for the horizons Pax opened for me, I don't know where I'd be or what I'd be doing."

Paul Hershberger

Kleine was our dog. Big and fat, she was later sentenced to death for wreaking havoc in the refugee gardens. But while she lived, Kleine (German for small) was our dog. Pax mascot perhaps. On the job, after hours, in the unit shack, everywhere—there was Kleine.

Unknown to them, Kleine honored the choir from Bethel College (Newton, Kansas) on their trip through Germany. They were touring the country singing in

Mennonite churches. One of their stops was at Wedel, the Pax location near Hamburg. Our hospitality to the choir included a meal. And the meal included soup.

The soup was good—delicious, in fact. Even though it was made in Kleine's bathtub.

When Kleine needed a bath the old boiler out back of the shack served the purpose. And when the entire busload of choir members arrived for dinner, there was only one container large enough to contain soup for the group. So, scrubbed and scoured, it served double duty.

Not once during the entire meal did Kleine give away her secret. She sat benignly watching the students enjoy their soup, happy to make her small contribution to the visitors; in fact, honored that she could help.

With or without Kleine, we had a good unit. Smaller than most and somewhat isolated, the fellows were close to each other, *says Paul Hershberger, one of the Paxmen who, during the last half of his term, also served as unit leader.*

Paul was born in Iowa City, Iowa, December 7, 1934, but lived in Goshen, Indiana, where his father, Guy, was professor at Goshen College. With sabbaticals and special assignments moving his father about, occasionally Paul's school experience was dotted with year-long absences from Goshen—second grade at Bluffton, Ohio; high school sophomore year in Switzerland; high school senior year at Hesston, Kansas. Then there were two years of college at Goshen before Pax.

Paul went on:

I suppose I thought more about the CO position after Pax than I did before. The CO position was more or less automatic: age and church make it easy. Then there is the social pressure of the group or family.

Of course, it's the same for guys of non-Mennonite

41

(nonpacifist) background. Their background and circumstances and social pressure make the army the thing.

It's probably a little unusual for a fellow of 17 to make independent decisions where deep ideological content is involved. That is to say, the person who thinks and acts in a way opposite to his social group tends to be most honest and an individualist. And 17 is not a particularly individualistic age.

At any rate, I accepted the CO position with more or less thought.

However, as a CO, going into Pax was a different matter. I did a lot of thinking about this, and discussing. And I came to some conclusions.

I hadn't decided on a major in college, so doing my service at that point seemed right. I didn't want domestic voluntary service or I-W work. I didn't particularly want to be a hero. I did want to do something worthwhile and constructive.

The Pax program appealed to me as being more constructive than emptying bedpans.

So I applied and was accepted. *That's when it all began for Paul Hershberger of Goshen, Indiana.*

Paul went to Wedel, a small industrial city of nearly 20,000 inhabitants located northwest of Hamburg on the Elbe River. The unit there came into being in August 1953, largely through the efforts of Otto Regier, formerly of Danzig who with a Mennonite banker, Herr Peters, purchased a former artillery range for one third the normal price.

Five men transferred from Backnang to Wedel. Ten new men arrived a few days later.

The entire area was crisscrossed with embankments and bristled with scrub trees, brush, and weeds. A few squatters' huts lay at the end of narrow paths. One of these was empty. So the unit moved into the two-room shack with a kitchen, bedroom, and open porch. The first fellows found a wood stove and made a table.

Within a week there were benches to sit on and bunks for 15 men.

Within two weeks town leaders came through with the tools that were promised—picks, shovels, wheelbarrows. Later they brought sections of track and small mine cars which were used to haul the ground. The big job was leveling the long hillock or mound of earth running through the entire area and the protective embankments. But there were also trees to cut, brush to clean up, and the extras which unit life in primitive conditions required. Within three months the major land leveling was completed, as well as excavations for three basements.

Paul describes a little of the work:

We put up twelve apartment houses—enough to house 48 families. We worked under a German contractor but the Paxmen did practically all the building here except inside plaster and outside stucco.

I had had little background in construction. My work experience was limited to a bit of painting and some months in a boat factory. So manual labor required considerable adjustment for me.

Since our unit was small—as few as three and never larger than 15—everybody did everything. We really helped each other. I dug ditches, worked as a hod carrier, did carpentry and painted, among other things.

As soon as the first house was finished, the unit moved into half of it, leaving the other half for refugees.

The completion of a house always seemed like a milestone to us fellows, *said Paul. And well it might, for each new house marked measurable progress toward the unit goal.*

When Wedel began in August 1953 Backnang was already well along. All of the Backnang refugees had moved into their new homes and others were being moved down from northern Germany as rapidly as apartments were completed. In May 1954 construction on a church building was begun and a second section of ten houses planned to accommodate more refugees from the Prussian and Danzig areas. By September 1956 the Paxmen left behind in Backnang twenty large apartment houses, a church, and a host of friends.

Enkenbach also represented another site of major Pax activity. In January 1953 Paul Kliewer, refugee from Prussia and administrator of the Mennonitische Altersheim there, began work on the project by buying five acres of land. From the beginning of construction in June 1953 until the project was completed in September 1961, 150 Paxmen worked in Enkenbach, building 44 houses with 140 apartments housing 450 people.

Of course, statistics only hint at the real drama of Paxmen at work in construction. They don't show the men at work in winter picking frozen ground out of basement excavations. They cannot provide the flavor of unit life, community relations, or cultural interchange. They're incapable of illustrating the manhood these experiences brought to untried volunteers. But they can represent accomplishment. They do point to a monument of concern which marked the service of each unit in Europe and specifically of most Paxmen.

Perhaps the clearest reflection of this monument is seen in the comments of Frau Ewert who lives in the Enkenbach Siedlung or Frau Rexin who lives in the Home for the Aged and whose husband gave strong community leadership after Paul Kliewer, the original founder, passed away.

"We were sad when they went away. They sang with our young people and played with our children. They had such friendly personalities.

"They were always taking photographs.

"And always taking baths; every evening they took a bath.

"Whenever they finished a house there would be a celebration. We would invite the Paxmen, the laborers, and anyone who helped. There would be coffee and cakes and singing.

"Evenings too they would visit us. One evening every week the boys brought their musical instruments to the different families and sang and played.

"They did good work here. Our concern now is that this community which was helped does not ignore other countries like Greece or Algeria where people also have needs."

The attitude of Enkenbach residents was well illustrated one day when the unit leader stopped in at the local bike shop for repairs. When he arrived the owner was in the middle of a tirade against Americans and all the evils they had brought to their community.

After listening quietly for a while, the Paxman spoke up. "You know I'm an American?"

The reply was quick, "Oh yes, I know. But you're a Pax-American. I was talking about the American-Americans," and he pointed to the nearby air base.

Perhaps one of the greatest contributions Paxmen have made is to weld a new link in a growing chain of reconciliation which extends from person to person, and from country to country. Wherever this has been true the pathway of peace has been marked a little more surely.

Another view of the monument of concern erected by men of Pax came from Preacher Johann Plett in the Siedlung (settlement) of Bechterdissen, near Bielefeld and about 50 miles west of Hannover. "Here the Paxmen gave us a Christian voluntary service. The people are grateful and remember those who gave themselves to help us."

Pastor Plett was 15 when he fled from Russia in

1948 and went to Paraguay. In 1956 he returned to Europe and settled in Germany.

Spring of 1955 marked the beginning of the project. Now 450 Mennonites live in this settlement of 1,600 former refugees. Paxmen worked for a local contractor. Pay for their services went to establish equity for the residents. In all, by the time the unit closed officially in 1958, they had built 49 houses and given more than 40,000 hours in labor.

In 1959 Paxmen returned to build a church for the community. In 1961 they built a parish house. And in 1963 they built an education wing on the church.

One of the unique features at Bechterdissen was the international flavor of the work force. From beginning to end Paxmen and heads of families who would live in the houses labored side by side. This proved to be both culturally and spiritually rewarding.

At one time all of the area now covered by houses was farmland—in wintertime it was actually under water. The first big job the Paxmen had to do was dig canals for drainage; some of them were nine feet deep.

Now, where water-covered open fields had been, there stands a community, typically German in its neatness and order. High-gabled two-story houses nestle close to each other along the narrow streets. Low hedges line the walks and boundaries. Inside, the furnishings are Spartan but adequate.

Wedel, Paul's home for almost two years, had its own unique features. He describes them:

In Wedel we had some interesting extracurricular activities—some organized, others not. Our matron, Nettie Redekop, taught girls in Sunday school and carried out other activities with them. I did the same with boys, also showed films to people in the community.

Along with this, members of the unit visited in the homes of various families. One day a week each of the men had two meals with a German family. This was a deliberate and successful attempt to break down the "island" mentality so easy to develop within an English-speaking unit.

Within the unit we had weekly Bible study. Also devotions each morning before breakfast. To help our matron, two fellows were assigned each week to do dishes. And every morning one of the Paxers would be on early call to make a fire.

Unit members also traveled during vacation days. On one occasion a fellow Paxer and I took a two-week hitchhiking trip as far as Andorra and Spain. We carried our own sleeping bags with us. The entire trip cost each of us $28.

But probably the biggest deal of each year for a number of years was the Pax trip to Palestine. Usually it was well planned and very educational. Each Pax-man paid his own way. However, the tour cost was quite low since groups ranged in size from forty to sixty. Dwight Wiebe, one of the European Pax directors, gave birth to the idea in an attempt to use our time to the best advantage.

Especially in the north of Germany, construction came to a standstill during the coldest weeks in winter. To shift entire units to a warmer climate for a short period seemed impractical, so in reward for long summer days when building was pushed at an accelerated pace several weeks of wintertime were opened up for this travel.

Normally the tour lasted a full three weeks. Reading lists were circulated in advance so that tour members would be prepared. Lectures were planned along the way. In Beirut a professor from the American University gave a lecture on Arab-Jewish relations. In Israel, another professor presented his view of the same subject. Daily worship experiences were planned using Scriptures from the areas being visited.

A typical tour took the group from Munich, Germany, to Athens, Greece, by train. Then on to Cairo, Egypt, by plane for a two-day bus tour. After five to ten days in Jordan and Israel the group would cross the Mediterranean by boat or plane to Italy, spending several days there, then return to Germany by train from Rome.

Another unique Pax extracurricular was the annual Pax conference. This was set up on a two- or three-day schedule at some central point. The sessions offered inspirational messages, practical how-to talks, and plenty of time to learn to know each other. The conference days also provided a convenient context in which to air gripes, make suggestions, arrange job transfers, and place incoming Paxers from America. For most of us the Holy Land Tour and the Annual Pax Conference marked high points in our two- or three-year overseas assignments.

Unfortunately, when job patterns shifted away from seasonal work and especially after the Pax program merged more completely into the total MCC program, neither the tours nor the conference were continued.

A few months before I left for home, I was assigned to Vienna, Austria. (See photos on pp. 111-134.) Work had been begun here by the Brethren Service Commission and consisted largely of rebuilding the entire inside of a five-story Lutheran school building. During the war it had been used for munitions storage and the Germans had destroyed all but the outside walls which were a full meter (almost 40 inches) thick. The major project, before building could begin, was hauling out massive amounts of rubble.

The two-year experience in Pax was good; I'd do it over again.

But coming back to the States was rough. Our affluence here seemed almost to be a sin, so utterly unjust. In Pax we had learned to live simply. Now to have things in such unnecessary abundance bothered my conscience.

I don't think of it much anymore; probably I'm becoming calloused.

Of course, being in another culture changed me as a person. However, I suspect the chief benefit was the new ability I had acquired to stand back and look at my beginnings—where I came from—and my objectives in life—where I was going. This was extremely valuable.

The Mennonite Church has a history of 400 years which I'm proud of. But it's so important to discover what has to be done today.

The Anabaptists are known now because they faced their mission as Christians as realistically and relevantly as they knew how. But their vision isn't enough for us. We can learn from the Anabaptist vision, but then we have to take that lesson and start all over again with today.

I don't think I could start with the Anabaptist vision. Rather, I'd start with the New Testament. I suspect we've put too much emphasis on the wrong starting point. This has led to hero worship, and hero worship distorts both our objective and our understanding of resources.

I'm impressed with the stature of the individual in God's economy. Each man is personally responsible for his own life—how he lives it, what he does with it.

In Pax, our contributions to people were both group and individual, of course. There has to be a balance.

But ultimately the gift of a self or love or concern comes from and through an individual. Here is where we go astray in Pax or MCC or Mission Board service. Hundreds of people in the comfort of their home communities think they're serving by proxy. And they're missing the point.

Who got the greatest good out of Pax service? The people at home who were happy about a nice program? Or the refugees for whom we built houses? Neither, really! We did. We Paxers who became personally involved with people in their need.

That's all there is to it.

Arnold Roth—Panayitsa

The Yugoslav countryside was quiet in the morning mist. Over the small village, the chill of dawn hung heavy, waiting for the April sun to push it back across the rolling land. A few cowbells tinkled nearby and a stray shout cut across the calm.

At the edge of the village there was parked a 1948 Chevrolet Carryall and attached to it was a two-wheeled army trailer. Both were heavily loaded. Near the vehicle, in a grassy depression, lay four cloth-covered mounds. Occasionally one or the other stirred; then, again all was still. Around the mounds stood a few villagers, curious. The circle grew. Seldom did these Slavs see a motor vehicle pass through their rutted streets, and never had they seen what turned out to be sleeping bags.

Suddenly, one of the mounds moved abruptly.

As Arnold opened the sleeping bag zipper from inside and stuck his head out for a breath of morning freshness, he was hardly prepared for the audience of onlookers. Nor were they quite prepared for the appearance of one tousle-headed young man, then three more, from the cloth mounds at the side of the road. The four received an unusual reception not only here, but in the remote villages in Southern Yugoslavia through which they were passing. It had been years since any of these people had seen foreigners.

These four Paxmen had offered themselves for service in Greece. A year before all four had come from America to Germany to help in construction of refugee housing at Espelkamp, Neuwied, and Backnang. Now an opening in Greece had challenged them. They were

51

on their way to Thessalonika where their director, Ivan Holdeman, the fifth member of the team, would meet them.

Travel from Frankfurt, Germany, through Salzburg, Austria, had been easy. But roads in Yugoslavia in April 1952 were hardly designed for cross-country trips, especially south of Belgrade. Only six months earlier, Yugoslav borders had been opened to foreign travelers. From the Austrian border to the Greek border, the trip took five days. In the south much of the travel was done in low gear—at ten to fifteen miles per hour. Their food supplies were limited, since they expected to purchase food as they traveled. But bread was the only staple they could buy in the stores. So for five days, five men lived on bread and a gallon of apple butter.

At the southern border Yugoslav customs formalities stretched from 8:00 a.m. until after noon. Greek customs and a short 75-mile drive took the remaining part of a 12-hour day. At 8:00 p.m. the Chevy Carryall arrived in Salonika.

To each of the men, coming to Greece was an uncertain adventure. None of them could know they were blazing a trail over which dozens of Paxmen would travel as they served the Greek people. Nor could they have guessed how their experiences there would bring profound change into their own lives. They knew only that their assignment was to take them to a hinterland Greek village called Panayitsa, located so close to the Yugoslav border that police permits were required of all residents.

When Paxmen came to the village in April 1952, Panayitsa was only beginning to come to life again. The history of its people is full of suffering dating back to the Greek-Turkish population exchange thirty years before. These residents, descendants of Greeks and formerly living on prosperous farms near the Black Sea,

52

became refugees in 1922 and moved to Northern Greece.

The Greek people have a history of hardship. For 500 years they were subjects of the Ottoman sultans. During these centuries the Greeks suffered greatly. In 1912-1913 they were embroiled in the Balkan wars, against the Turks and then the Bulgarians. From 1914-1918 World War I raged. In 1922 the Turks and Greeks were battling again and as result many Anatolian Greeks were removed to Greece and became refugees. World War II from 1940-1945 brought German occupation and from 1946-1949 communist guerrillas ravaged much of the area in their fighting against nationalistic forces.

For more than twenty years, from 1922, these displaced farmers had been struggling to eke out a living from the depleted soils in the foothills along the Yugoslavian border. Then came the German occupation forces plundering at will. This was followed by the guerrilla warfare between communists and nationalists. Draft animals were taken by marauding forces, and other stock was slaughtered. Some nearby villages were largely evacuated during this period when communist guerrillas moved down from the north. But Panayitsa villagers resisted the communist aggression, remaining firmly nationalistic.

Even though their homes were burned, their animals destroyed, and many among them killed, Panayitsa never fell to the communists. As one Greek said, "It became like a wedge in the lines of the enemy." This was the village that was chosen by the Ministry of Agriculture and the Holy Metropolis of Thessalonika (Salonika) as being in need of help from the Mennonites.

It is not clear how many Paxmen saw the gentle irony in their presence at this place or understood the paradox of Pax service being given to the villagers of Panayitsa as a reward for their loyalty to the Greek government during the Civil War, their faithful and successful resistance against communist guerillas. This irony simply emphasizes the dilemma faced by helping agencies and highlights a fundamental question: whether it is ever possible to serve a people or an area with complete freedom from the taint of political manipulation or having such service constitute some form of reward or favoritism. Whenever a government—national or regional—is in a position to grant the privilege to serve needy persons it is also usually in a position to utilize or shape that service to accomplish its own ends.

The first Pax plan had been to engage in reconstruction, but when the unit studied the needs more carefully it was agreed that assistance should be given in more necessary areas. The most urgent lack was not housing but draft animals for cultivation of the ground. And even where these were available, land had been left idle for so long, the hard soil barely yielded to the homemade wooden plow pulled by an emaciated mule left over from the Marshall Plan.

The rocky hillsides at Panayitsa were far different from the lush farmland around Wayland, Iowa. This was where Arnold Roth was born and where he was graduated from high school in June 1950. His dad owned and operated a garage and Arnold worked for him as a mechanic and helped to drive a school bus route.

Arnold reminisces:

If it hadn't been for Pax, I'd be back in Wayland, Iowa, managing a garage.

I suppose publicity about this new program came to Wayland as soon as to any other place. But no one paid much attention to it. At least I didn't, not until Boyd Nelson, a schoolteacher at Wayland, asked if I had seen information about Pax. His comment that a year in Europe was worth two in college sort of got under my skin.

Then someone else spoke to my father about it and the matter became a family discussion.

When I wrote to the Pax office, my application was accepted but I couldn't get a draft release—that was a release from the impending draft—necessary to leave the country. At the point it appeared I'd be staying home, the draft release came through—on the day "my" group sailed. But within two weeks I sailed—the twentieth man in the first group.

I disembarked at Antwerp. David Shank, missionary from Brussels, met me at the port and we drove to Amsterdam. I spent Friday to Monday there, then left for Espelkamp, Germany, where I was assigned to vehicle maintenance—a 1941 Chevy pickup with 250,000 miles on it, a 1941 Ford car, and a 1946 Dodge power wagon.

The first Pax Builders Unit was located there. In addition to vehicle maintenance—there was plenty of that—I worked with the winch on the power wagon pulling stumps and later, when the building began in late summer, I hauled lumber, blocks, and sand.

A second Builders Unit arrived in August—again a mixture of men from various Mennonite and Amish groups. Both the Pennsylvania Dutch flavor and a hint on motivation was reflected in the announcement one man made upon arrival, "I came over to enchoy [sic] myself and I am going to enchoy [sic] myself."

One other thing happened during my Germany experience that probably influenced my decision to serve in Greece later and certainly changed the whole course of my life.

A number of us fellows traveled to Amsterdam for a few days. The first night we went to a concert, *Beethoven's Ninth*, sung with a 300-voice choir. I shall never forget the point where the 300 voices came in

"Joyful, joyful, we adore Thee." For me it provided an awakening in a number of ways—aesthetically, spiritually, emotionally. Something happened. I was sort of opened up. I think I made a new kind of commitment to God that evening. In the telling it sounds so insignificant but somehow that phrase of worship symbolized a response in my own heart.

About January 1952 we were told the Pax program would continue and we could volunteer for one or two years in Germany or two years in Greece. I'm not sure anyone was really excited about Greece because that country was an unknown factor and the Germany experience had been good. But finally five of us were chosen to go.

I spent two years and four months in Greece in order to provide some overlap for new men coming in.

The first order of business at Panayitsa was housing. A widow offered us the upstairs of her house which had been gutted by the ravages of war. We repaired the house at our own expense and in return had the use of the second story for two years. This seemed to solve the difficulty we had been warned of—our choice of housing or location could have implications within the village political structure. Until our living quarters were ready, we rented two rooms.

After the decision was made to forego construction and work instead on getting land back into production, plans were laid to bring in equipment. Within a month, the Mechanical Cultivation Service of the Ministry of Agriculture loaned us a Massey-Harris 44 tractor and some implements. When we got the tractor, we pulled a four-wheel trailer with implements on it the 120 kilometers from Salonika. It took us from 3:00 p.m. one afternoon to 3:00 a.m. the next morning.

The plow was the basic piece of equipment. But our tractor couldn't pull a 3-bottom plow through the Panayitsa ground—it was like heavy red Oklahoma soil. So one plow was removed and we had to be satisfied pulling a 2-bottom plow. A year later we bought the tractor and still later we were able to get a Ferguson tractor with attached implement. This was much better in the small plots of ground, some of them less than a quarter-acre in size.

Two of us rode the tractor—one to do the driving and one to handle the plow levers. This was exhausting work—with rocks and roots to make it still more difficult. Our tires were filled with spring water to provide more weight. We wore out a set of tires in one season of plowing. Where possible we plowed on contour, using a transit made from a wooden level. We'd sight across the bubble, set our stakes, then strike a furrow.

At first, farm owners were apprehensive. But soon our Pax unit house became a thoroughfare. In season, the farmers stood in line waiting for the Paxmen to come and work in their fields. Also at first they came and watched us carefully—all day. It was incredible to them that a fellow would do good work without supervision. Later, when we'd leave the house in early morning six or eight farmers would go with us to show us where their fields were located, then would leave us to go home.

Villagers paid for this service, although it took most of a year to get the idea across that ours was not a giveaway program, that we had come to help them help themselves.

Plowing and harrowing were the only tilling operations. Then the seeding was done by hand except for corn. We had a planter for that—pulled by Alex, our interpreter, and Ivan, our director. We had no draft animals.

Our beginning work centered in two areas. The first was getting villagers' land back into cultivation so that they could farm it themselves. The second was finding various plots of our own so that we could set up experimental projects.

These field experimental plots were difficult to find. The farmers refused to participate on their land, understandably. No sane head of a family would risk his only source of food for an unknown result.

Finally the village gave us church land. In each local economy the church owned a certain amount of property. When the land was divided, the church received as much as the average family, located also within the same pattern of land distribution.

East of the village the soil was rocky and hard; west it was easy and loamy; the rest was heavy and dark. Each family received its share of each kind of soil, usually about 30-40 *stremma* total. (Four stremma are almost equal to one acre.) The church plots matched this division.

Obviously, this was an equitable plan for dividing the available land resource. And for our purposes of experimentation and demonstration it was excellent. But this pattern severely limited the size of fields, scattered a farmer's work over a large area, increased the opportunities for misunderstandings, and generally inhibited the agricultural improvement so desperately needed to raise the standard of living above an uncertain subsistence.

But we were here to help them, not to upset them. So we learned to fit in. It wasn't easy though to make the adjustment from working in fields in the Midwest with an acreage of 20 or 50 or 200 acres to a little rocky corner of less than an acre in size or, if we were lucky, perhaps an acre or even two. *Arnold was no exception in his reaction to this pattern of field work. However, such adjustment was basic to the success of the Paxmen's service.*

Experimental field work was done with fertilizers,

corn, sorghum, and alfalfa. Some testing was also done with relation to the limited rainfall potentials. In corn, with hybrid seed, a moderate amount of fertilizer, and a different method of cultivation, yields were doubled.

But perhaps the major initial contribution, apart from restoring farmland to production, was the work done with wheat. Patterns of seeding and beginning growth showed an overuse of seed which inhibited individual plant development and prevented proper stooling. This problem was discussed with the villagers but the words of one farmer reflected general community reaction, "Our ancestors have always planted wheat this way. This is the only way it will grow."

So demonstration plots were arranged to prove the thesis that less seed would yield a better harvest. Considerable care was taken to block off the two-stremma area in an equitable way.

Normally, villagers in this area seeded wheat at the rate of 15-20 okes per stremma. The experimental field was divided into equal-sized plots in which seeding was done at the rate of 12, 9, and 6 okes per stremma. The 12-oke seeding produced 89 okes in two thirds of a stremma or 144 okes per stremma which was at least equal to and in most cases better than the average yield from seeding at the rate of 15-20 okes per stremma.

While the grain was growing one reluctant farmer looked at the plots and said, "That will never do. It simply won't produce heads."

When the heads began to appear he said, "It looks good, but the heads won't fill."

When the full-kerneled wheat was threshed and taken to his house, he said, "That looks like good wheat but it won't make good bread."

So the wheat was ground into flour, and a loaf of bread brought for his taste inspection.

Soon after the wheat experiment results became common knowledge, the villagers began coming to the Pax-men with other problems: poor poultry production, bloated cows, toothaches.

One of the interesting sidelights to the wheat experiment was the calculation made of possible savings if each farmer followed the new seeding pattern. The director, Ivan Holdeman, did a careful analysis of costs using both the experience of Greek farmers and the demonstration plot tests to highlight the contrast.

At that time, Panayitsa had about 2,500 stremmas seeded to small grain. If each farmer reduced his seeding by six okes per stremma, the saving of grain at prices then current would have been almost equal to the purchase price of a new Ferguson tractor. A second year of saving seed grain would have covered the cost of the tractor and a full line of implements.

The implications of such a simple discovery certainly affects the welfare of the Greek peasant and could reach into the economy of the entire country.

Arnold describes the side effects of this discovery:

Once we had gained their confidence, the people came in a steady procession asking for medical help, even though none of us had medical training. Toothaches sometimes yielded to peppermint oil, a home remedy Bill Yoder knew of. Minor cuts were treated with iodine and Band-Aids. Aspirins were all that others needed. And for the more seriously ill or injured, the Chevy Carryall was used for an ambulance or for taxi service to the doctor's office in Edessa, two hours away. Sickness and accidents were not always arranged to fit into the early morning once-a-day bus schedule.

One Sunday evening about five a man came to the house and asked if we would take his wife to the hospital. Questioning revealed she had been in labor since morning. We got ready immediately, only to wait for almost an hour while the father-to-be received certification from the village president of his inability to pay the hospital bill. Finally, we picked up the patient and started.

Since Paxmen are unmarried, neither Bill Stucky nor I knew what kind of driving was customary in a case like this. Should one drive fast and arrive sooner? Or was it better to drive slowly over the bumps and hope to retard the process by a smoother ride? Finally, we decided on the slow easy ride—for a little more than half of the trip. Then one of the midwives in the middle seat leaned forward and said in Greek, "Faster. As fast as you can."

We did. Over rocks, through potholes, around sharp curves, until we made it to Edessa and the hospital. With a lady on either side, our patient was hustled off upstairs.

Bill and I walked the length of the car and back when we heard a baby's cry overhead. We had made it. *Arnold smiled. Of course, not all our days were this exciting.*

People were not the only needy creatures in Panayitsa. Each of the fellows was called on occasionally to help with sick animals. Some of them, with more experience, were called on frequently.

Dean Zehr tells of one solution to a problem that probably few trained veterinarians have ever encountered. The problem was not unusual—a cow having trouble delivering a calf because the calf was upside down in the womb. But the attempted solution is not likely to be found in the better texts.

When Dean arrived to help he discovered the cow hanging by its two hind legs from a rope tied to the ceiling. The reasoning was rational—if the calf was upside down when the cow was in a normal position, then this new posture for the cow would place the calf right side up and birth could proceed normally.

"I directed the cow to be taken down," said Dean,

"and we attempted gentler procedures—successfully."

Because land and stock were plundered recklessly during the German occupation and the guerrilla fighting, there was not only a shortage of draft animals but also of milk stock. And what cows were there were undersized and poorly fed.

So after grain production was upped, and the feed situation had improved, a stock development program was begun. This took two forms. First, a Jersey bull and heifer were brought in. The bull was used in crossbreeding with existing stock and the heifer's offspring demonstrated the improvement possible with better foundation stock.

But this was only a beginning. In 1956 a significant contribution was made to the health of the people in the area. The July issue of *Euro-Pax News* reports the occasion in some detail:

"Presentation of twenty choice U.S. heifers to poor Greek farmers on May 9 launched a new dairy promotion phase of the Mennonite Central Committee Pax rehabilitation program in Northern Greece.

"It was a memorable occasion for the isolated mountain community of Panayitsa and a significant milestone in the Pax agriculture and livestock improvement services there.

"Nearly the entire population of the village gathered for the presentation ceremonies opening the dairy project which will mean a better life for the impoverished small farmers of the region.

"The twenty Brown Swiss heifers, donated by Eastern Mennonite Board of Missions and Charities, had arrived just the day before at the port of Salonika, Greece, after a 25-day voyage from New York. The gift of these animals represented sizable contributions of cash, time, and services by various American Mennonite groups and individuals, plus other church, welfare, and government organizations.

"Upon arrival, the heifers were housed in a new Pax-built dairy barn where they will remain for at least a year, enabling the Paxmen to demonstrate proper animal husbandry.

Purchased in Wisconsin

"It was a long and varied operation that brought the twenty heifers from Lake Mills, Wisconsin, U.S.A., to Panayitsa, Greece. Making this livestock donation a material aid project, the Relief and Service Committee of Eastern Mennonite Board of Missions and Charities purchased the two-year-olds, with full health certification, at $210 a head through the Brown Swiss Breeders Association of Wisconsin. The cattle were trucked to Lancaster, Pennsylvania, where Benjamin Stauffer (father of Paxmen Bob and LeMar in Greece) stabled them without charge until the date of sailing.

"The Greek cargo ship *Hellenic Wave*, equipped with twenty cattle stalls, transported the heifers from New York to Salonika, on the northeastern coast of Greece. Amos Mellinger, Lancaster, Pennsylvania, cared for the animals en route. Mellinger, who donated his time for the job, reported a fine voyage, with the cows showing no ill effects.

"Ocean freight of $7,000 was paid by the U.S. government foreign aid program. Boat passage was secured through Heifer Project, Inc., and World Council of Churches. Heifer Project, Inc., also arranged for duty-free entrance of the animals into Greece. Feed for the trip was donated by Eastern States Cooperative of the Lancaster area and Eastern Mennonite Relief and Service Committee.

"After lengthy customs procedure at Salonika, a 3 1/2-hour drive by truck brought the heifers to Panayitsa where the last was put safely into the Pax dairy barn at 11:30 on the night before the presentation. 'What a relief when the twenty fine Brown Swiss heifers were finally standing in their stalls,' said D. C. Kauffman, European MCC Director, who was present for the project's opening.

"Director Kauffman's home community, West Liberty, Ohio, contributed $1,000 to build the model barn, completed in March. A wooden barrack, furnishing material for the structure, was sold to MCC at one fourth its value by the Public Power Corporation of Athens. Five Paxmen from Germany went to Greece on short-term assignments to help in the construction.

Ceremony at Pax Barn

"Held at the new barn, the presentation ceremony attracted most of the community people. Don Schierling, Pax leader in Greece, opened the program with an explanation of the project. In the presentation address, D. C. Kauffman credited the long list of persons and organizations that made the project possible.

"Other speakers were the *Nomarch* (governor) of Macedonia, Greek Agriculture Agent Veros of Edessa, and Peter Kruger of Heifer Project, Inc., Athens. Amos Mellinger spoke on behalf of the Eastern Mennonite Relief and Service Committee, the donor organization.

"After an acceptance speech by the village secretary, the Greek Orthodox bishop of the province spoke a few words of appreciation, as is customary in Greece, and pronounced a blessing upon the entire project.

"Each of the twenty previously selected farmers then received a heifer by having a small boy and girl draw names and numbers from two boxes.

"Reports indicated that since the herd exhibited outstanding quality and uniformity of size and appearance, all recipients and promoters were very pleased with the animals.

"According to observers, the new heifers are undoubtedly one of the finest possessions the Panayitsa farmers have ever had, since the Brown Swiss are nearly twice as large as the typical cattle of that region. Upon hearing a description before the heifers arrived, one villager reportedly commented, 'Only elephants are that big!'

I-W's Supervise 'School'

"Some months earlier, Paxmen had selected the 20 recipients from a group of 52 applicants. They based their choices upon the villagers' ability and resources for providing sufficient feed, their willingness to cooperate with the Pax unit in promoting the project, and in their reliability shown by previous experience with the individuals. To help further dairying in the village, each recipient paid the equivalent of $67 to MCC.

"The project operates as a type of 'dairy school' with each participant pledging cooperation. Each houses his heifer in the common barn and cares for it under supervision of Paxmen who teach proper feeding and sanitary handling of cows and milk. Pax is also responsible to keep daily records, check on individual care, and make suitable arrangements for milk sales.

"After at least a year under this arrangement, the owner may, if he has provided adequate facilities, move the animal to his own barn. In each case, the first heifer calf will go back to the Pax unit at the age of two months. It will in turn be given to another of the farmers, chosen on approximately the same basis as the first twenty.

"With the cows due to freshen this summer, Paxers expect villagers' enthusiasm to grow as they realize paying results."

By 1959 people in most parts of Greece had heard about the dairy program at Panayitsa. Many farmers came to buy calves and learned stock care and feed improvement techniques. For a period of time the project was singularly successful in this.

But the second step—marketing milk in Edessa—

eventually failed. For a time Paxmen took care of deliveries and developed a burgeoning demand. However, at the point where a co-op was set up so that the Greek farmers could be responsible, serious problems emerged. Added to this was the distance from a market for the product. Breeding problems also developed. The government had begun an artificial insemination program but the facility wasn't regular. At the same time, farmers who had now taken their cows to their own barns were running into feed difficulties. With a collapse of the milk-marketing plan, and thus no income to buy sufficient feed, some of the families sold their animals.

One of the lessons the Paxmen learned was that you can't do things for people and then pull out. With special reference to the milk route to Edessa, one must do things with people instead of for them.

Of course, there were marked interim benefits, not the least being improved patterns of stock care, higher feed production, as well as better health for families who were drinking milk regularly. And certainly, both cattle and offspring contributed to stock improvement at Panayitsa and in other parts. However, the original hope that this herd should grow into twenty herds, and then multiply again, providing income and healthier living for an increasing number of families simply did not materialize.

Poultry, swine, orchards, pea crops for ensilage, and canning projects claimed a lot of time and attention on the part of Paxers, and interest on the part of villagers.

Field peas became a significant part of the local economy. A legume, this crop helped to build up the depleted soil. But at the same time it provided additional income.

This new crop proved to be much more than a substitute for a second wheat crop. In fact, pea hay has a market value more than twice as high as the average wheat yield.

One of the Paxmen built a baler to bale the pea vines. Manually operated, it could turn out a high quality bale every six minutes. Another built a silo and experimented successfully with pea vine ensilage.

Paxmen often used their ingenuity to introduce techniques and to improvise simple tools or machines the Greeks could make for themselves. In addition to the baler, the Paxmen built an animal-drawn cultivator which served well to till the increased acreage of corn. And although long obsolete with American farmers, the "cradle" and scythe method of harvesting grain was a great improvement for Greek villagers accustomed to sickles.

A meat-curing project grew out of the canning program at Tsakones. This may well have been one of the most significant projects in terms of long-range effects. As was true in most aspects of the Paxmen's work, a project began with an insight into a need and a special application of interest and know-how on the part of at least one person. Simon Miller was that person in this case.

At the end of the first year, Bill Yoder, one of the original five, returned to Holland. In his place came an Amish young man from Kalona, Iowa. Simon was different, but he fit in—from the village streets in Panayitsa to the socials held by the consular officer in Salonika to which Paxmen were invited.

Simon was assigned to the kitchen as cook. From the beginning, he went to the store to do his own shopping, without an interpreter. He helped with first-aid work; he spent time with the villagers learning to know them and their language.

In short, he made a tremendous contribution to the unit and to the village. One area in which he was skilled was butchering hogs. To skin the hog he slit one of the legs slightly, inserted a tire pump hose between skin and flesh, and pumped air until the skin became a large balloon around the carcass.

In a special class, he taught the local women how to cut up the meat. He trimmed out the hams deftly while the women watched. Finally, when the lesson was over; Alex Mavrides the interpreter asked, "Are there any questions?"

A woman's hand went up. Alex said, "Yes, what is your question?"

Without a moment's hesitation the woman said, "Is Simon married?"

But marriage was not to be for Simon. Short months after his arrival, but not before Simon had endeared himself to unit and villagers alike, tragedy took him.

In June of 1954 Devon Schrock, Simon, and Eli Miller had been out working with the villagers, harvesting peas and lentils. The whole plant was pulled out, each seed separately. Then the peas were threshed separately (by flailing) and the results weighed.

There was a large lake near their project. They had worked there for several days; each evening the men went out for a cooling dip in the water. Although they were just learning to swim, they had been out four or five times.

On this particular evening the three went swimming with a friendly police officer from Panayitsa.

Whether from lack of knowledge about the lake, currents, or prevailing winds, no one is certain, but both Simon and Eli lost their lives that day by drowning.

This accident cast a pall over the Pax family and, indeed, touched the village deeply. In one brief hour, villagers and Paxmen alike saw how intertwined their lives had become. And they began to understand, perhaps more clearly than ever before, that no institution or ongoing program or new technique could ever become a significant monument to the efforts of a man or a group. Only the memory of a personal presence and the residue of meaningful relationships could serve truly to mark the pouring out of a life.

Arnold picks up the story of growth from the small beginnings in Panayitsa:

In 1954 we began to think of expanding our work. A small village in the Aridea Valley was selected from a number of needy areas, largely because housing was available. Five additional men came to Greece from Germany to allow development of this new location at Tsakones.

This expansion showed me still more graphically how great were the needs in just this one country. And even the humble work we were doing seemed to be packed with challenge.

In fact, Greece became a turning point in my life. When I graduated from high school, I had no idea what I wanted to do—work in a garage with Dad or go on to college. But before I had spent six months in Greece I began to have some idea of how big the world was and how much needed to be done. This led to a decision later to attend college and seminary.

My thinking about people has changed also. I'm afraid before Pax I was pretty narrow. I even had questions about other branches of Mennonites, only to discover they were teaching me spiritual lessons. I found the teachers at Anatolia College service-oriented. This was a revelation to me, since I rather thought Mennonites had a monopoly on this characteristic.

In short, I grew. I get a bit shaky just thinking about what my life might have been like had I not gone into Pax. *Arnold's confession mirrors the experience of many other Paxmen.*

The work at Panayitsa continued until late 1959. At that time, the unit closed its program formally in order to concentrate on the needs in Tsakones.

In a touching farewell to the Greek village which had become home to so many Paxmen, the Pax unit distributed Bibles to the townspeople. Larry Eisenbeis reported the occasion in *World Pax News*, January 21, 1960:

"The Bible distribution idea was first cleared with the bishop in Edessa who is responsible for the area. After getting his approval and recommendations the local priest was contacted. He was thrilled with the idea. Our approach was that Bibles were a farewell gift to each family, and since Christmas is a time of giving we chose it as the proper time to give our farewell gift. The priest made an announcement on Sunday that on Tuesday, December 22, Pax would give each family a farewell gift. The town crier also made the announcement on Monday night. People were speculating whether they would receive clothes, food, or something else.

"The time set for the presentation was nine o'clock. Nine came and went without a soul in sight. One very old man, Barb Spiro, who spent at least two hours each day in our house arrived shortly. He had the honor of receiving the first New Testament given in Panayitsa. Greatly pleased, and instead of sitting by our stove comfortably warming himself and dozing off as usual, he left to show the gift to others. Within 15 minutes the house was full of people. The priest came and sat through the presentation. We were very happy for his presence. In two hours 220 of the 240 Bibles were presented. By the time evening came around only six families remained that had not come for their Bible.

"Many upon receiving the Bible pledged to read it faithfully. Little speeches were made by both the president and a former president thanking Pax profusely for its presence in their village, telling us of

70

the sadness in their hearts to see us leave, and begging forgiveness for the times they were contrary and hard to deal with. As Alex, our interpreter, sat in the coffee shop that afternoon and evening, time and time again he observed that the conversation came back and dwelt on the New Testaments many had received. Everyone was so pleased that there was a modern Greek translation of the ancient Greek text alongside it.

"They were grateful that we had chosen the New Testament as a farewell gift to them. One coffee shopper observed that had we given them food it would have been consumed and that would have been the end of it. Had we given clothes, they would have worn them out; and likewise, they would not have had a lasting remembrance of Pax. New Testaments were truly the most appropriate gift which Pax could have given, said he, because it is something all families will cherish the rest of their lives and, furthermore, as they read the words of love, peace, and faithfulness in the New Testament they would be reminded of the reproachless lives lived in their midst by the Paxmen."

No less touching was the response of the people of Panayitsa in the words of their priest, reported in the same issue of *World Pax News:*

"We always bear in mind the remarkable and praiseworthy philanthropic work done by you in our village. Your work showed us and proved by example the progress of cultivation, the improvement of all kinds of products for a better income, and the systematic and proper plowing of the fields with the cost of gas only paid by the villagers. We remember the help you gave to every seriously sick person and the transportation of them to Edessa or Salonika free of charge, in the night and in any time after midnight. We remember the good and expensive gifts, the cows, and your care for them the last two or three years. We also remember your various and good vivid Christian examples: your politeness, meekness, forbearance, patience, love in Christ, prudence, humility, charity, and benefaction. You are the great benefactors of our village.

"We feel and understand your concern and sincere love and are moved with today's godly and precious gifts of the Word of God which is the New Testament. You introduced into each home of our village the divine will which is the greatest of all the gifts. We will never forget, as long as we live, the eagerness and the godly zeal you portrayed to decorate our holy church with the icon of the Annunciation of the Archangel Gabriel to the holy mother. We consider it our duty to express our warm thanks for your pains and efforts, the good presents, the one you will donate to our church, and for all the rest of the gifts and benefactions you contributed and caused the progress and the embellishment of our village. 'Glory, honor, and peace to all those who work for the good. We must grant justice and praises, honor and gratitude for all the above. We assure you that your names will remain ineffaceable in our memory and that it will pass to future generations."

Arnold sums up his experience in Greece:

Our relationship with the Greek Orthodox Church was good. The priest, after observing us two or three months, supported our work. In fact, again and again he told his people to pattern themselves after the Pax boys.

I'm afraid that was a little thick. We fellows were far from perfect. But his comments emphasized the importance of our presence and our service.

Thinking about it now, I suspect that's where the kernel of my life philosophy was formed—I must be a servant of people, to help people become what they can be, under God.

This is the reason for Pax.

Larry Eisenbeis—Tsakones

Pax is OK, apart from the fact that the former Pax-man is unhappy the rest of his life. Perhaps unhappy isn't the right word—restless might be better.

Pax changes a fellow: breaks up the old patterns, reshapes his dreams, cuts away the foundations of living for material gain, raises questions, opens up challenges.

To be in Pax is a shaking experience, unsettling. One finds himself in difficult situations making decisions and reaching conclusions he can never forget.

Larry looked up and repeated:

"It's OK but I've never been satisfied since. I simply can't settle down into the expected routine of just making money when I know that in many parts of the world there are people I could help by being with them and sharing a little know-how.

He really meant it. For, many months later, as these lines are being written, Larry and Anette, his slight but stalwart helpmeet, are settled on a farm in Brazil.

Larry is a farmer.

Born on the farm, raised on the farm, farm experience as a Pax man, a BS in Agriculture in college, director of a Pax farm program, South Dakota farmer following Pax service.

Larry is a farmer.

He was born May 31, 1934, in Marion, South Dakota. He grew up in an ordinary rural Mennonite community.

Zion congregation of the General Conference of Mennonites was his church home. The country school several miles from home took care of eight elementary grades. Then Larry went on to Freeman Junior Academy. He graduated from high school in 1952.

Track and basketball claimed his attention in sports. In the music world he also found a center for life—piano, choir, a school quartet, and later some barbershop singing.

Larry went on:

Father's hobby was carpentry. Later he became a cabinetmaker. I grew to enjoy it too, especially since he had a shop on the farm.

My interest in peace as a way of life probably began with our pastor, Rev. Russel Mast. My parents nurtured that interest and speakers visiting our church often made some contribution to my thinking on the peace position as well as on missions.

So Pax seemed a natural. When I applied for Pax service in February 1953 the program was still quite new.

There were 33 fellows in my orientation group. Out of this group, one went to Paraguay, two went to Africa, and thirty went to Europe. We sailed from New York on July 29. Initially, the group of thirty was divided up and located at Backnang, Enkenbach, and Wedel—ten men at each. The latter project was just beginning.

I was assigned to Wedel. But after a short time, Curt Janzen, European Pax director, asked for five additional volunteers to go to Greece.

Near the end of November Ralph Shelly and I left for Greece. The other three men waited until the new year.

Elbert Esau, the incoming director, met our train in Salonika late in the evening. He took us to a hotel room, gave us a sack of oranges for our late supper and arranged to meet us in the morning.

Breakfast consisted of yogurt, bread, butter, honey, and hot milk. Hardly typical for us. And none of it looked too good. But this was Greece.

That day we drove out to Panayitsa, where the first unit was located, in the old Chevy Carryall. Ralph and I slept in the loft of the tool shed—it was very cold.

My first assignment was to build furniture for the new unit at Tsakones—table, chairs, benches, beds. And to learn Greek. Alex was our teacher.

Alex Mavrides was the interpreter for the unit. He had come out to Panayitsa in April 1952 with the first Pax unit and served until Pax withdrew from Greece in 1966.

Early in 1954 the other three fellows came down from Germany. One of them, Dean Zehr, joined Ralph Shelly and me to start the new unit. From Panayitsa came two veterans, Howard Landis and Willard Stucky, to help during the crucial beginning months. Both made an excellent contribution in this orientation period. They knew the language well, could joke with the residents, and also were able to sense the lingering skepticism of the older people.

Tsakones is a village of 800 people located in the county of Almopia, Nomos Pellis. It is a two-hour drive from Panayitsa, about 35 miles, and about two miles from Aridea, the county seat, where a later unit was located.

The village suffered much the same fate as did Panayitsa during the fighting of previous decades—depletion of milk, stock, and draft animals, damage to houses, large-scale evacuation and consequently no cultivation of land. So here again agricultural rehabilitation became the pattern of work.

This was a good experience. It was up to us to lay a foundation. The first group of fellows could either make or break the success of our venture.

A second interpreter was hired for the new unit. It was at this point we probably became fully aware of the critical significance of an interpreter.

Gregory Schinas spoke good English and was a fine interpreter. He came to us from the U.S. Information Service. However, he happened to be a member of the Jehovah's Witnesses who were not respected by the Greek people, nor the government or the Greek Orthodox Church. These reactions developed into local problems of acceptance which plagued the unit for years. Fortunately, by April 1954 he and his family emigrated to Australia. This was the best thing that could have happened.

Moving the furniture I had made from Panayitsa to Tsakones was a major undertaking. The Chevy Carryall and the trailer pulled by a tractor were heavily loaded. From Panayitsa it was necessary to drive into Edessa, then back out to the Aridea Valley in which our small village of Tsakones was located.

Our home was the second story of a house owned by Apostolos Apostolides. The house was laid out on a Turkish floor plan with a large hall which led into the three large rooms. We always had a good relationship with the couple—called them Grandpa and Grandma— although there were adjustments necessary with American young men living so close to elderly Greeks.

On the first night we dragged my newly built table into the hall. Howard Landis had cooked spaghetti. Somehow spaghetti dropped to the floor and through the cracks onto Grandpa's bald head below. He was quite excited and upset by this development on our first night. But by the next day, after the story had made the rounds in the local coffeehouse, he began to see some humor in the situation.

Later on, Grandpa had another gripe, quite understandably. One of the Paxers owned a pair of wooden shoes which he used occasionally for house slippers. When this happened, Grandpa would come to me and ask if I could possibly arrange to keep Denzel Short from clumping around overhead.

Without a matron at that time our rooms were seldom models of order or cleanliness. Usually this didn't bother us. At least, not until the Governor of the area and the Director of Agricultural Services came to see us one evening. They didn't stay very long, just long enough for us to resolve to be better housekeepers so that they wouldn't regret having brought these Americans to the village.

Our first full season at Tsakones was not spectacular. Dean Zehr spent much of his time breaking land with a Ferguson tractor and plow. His days began at 5:00 a.m. and by 8:30 in the evening he still had a list of impatient farmers waiting for his help and wondering why he didn't put lights on the tractor so he could run all night.

Some of the land had not been cultivated for forty years and was covered with heavily rooted sagebrush. We seldom plowed land that the farmers could work with their oxen.

Occasionally the priest thought his land should be plowed without delay. But the land he had was put on the list along with the others.

One had to be a diplomat to handle requests like this. Or to accept the misunderstandings which came inevitably. One night a farmer came in and gave Dean a really rough time. He charged deliberate delays and favoritism. Dean listened to the harangue for a long time and finally, tired of it and tired after a 15-hour day on the tractor, he said to the Greek farmer, "Do you know, I think you'd complain if we hung you with a new rope." That broke him up; he went away in good spirits.

We helped restore an irrigation program, did some

garden crop work, and demonstrated the value of fertilizer. We experimented with local and hybrid corn and discovered fertilizer was the key to success with either. Local corn fertilized doubled normal yield. Hybrid corn fertilized tripled normal yield.

We raised some wheat, edible beans, and cow peas for livestock feed. A poultry project, including a small incubator facility, led to bird improvement in the area. This project began in 1955 with the purchase of eggs from the American Farm School near Salonika. Hatched from those Rhode Island Red eggs, about thirty laying hens in 1956 were producing eggs for the two kerosene incubators. At one time three Lancaster County, Pennsylvania, hatcheries donated more than a thousand White Rock eggs. Chicks were kept to three or four weeks, then sold at cost to villagers who agreed to meet certain housing requirements and feed balanced rations.

Each year the poultry program varied, depending in part on the interest and abilities of available Paxmen, in part on community response and market, and in part on the results of various experimental aspects relating to breed of bird, housing, and feed developments.

By 1960 the project had reached a point in growth and validity that marked a degree of permanence. Today, in the Aridea Valley, only a few kilometers from Tsakones, stands a new hatchery building, proudly owned and operated by one of the farmers involved in the early Pax work.

Kermit Yoder, in the May 18, 1960, issue of *World Pax News* offers an interesting peek behind the scenes:

"With four incubators ready for action and new batteries being assembled in Salonika, the poultry project began its 1960 program by swinging immediately to full hatching capacity on January 5.

"Since that date the four incubators, later assisted by an additional one which stepped up full hatching capacity from 1,600 eggs to 2,000 eggs per every 22-day hatch, have been pushing forward full steam. From their trays have come some 3,095 chicks. . . . After their first glimpse of light, the majority of them are moved to the adjacent room where the warm temperature and 'homely' atmosphere of the batteries and fellow sojourners in life await them.

"Between January 5 and April 20, 25 different villages and 108 individuals have been associated directly with the poultry project; most of the work has been in the Aridea Valley, but it also extends into the Panayitsa area from where Pax has recently moved. In addition to direct placement, chicks have been given by the Children's Home Program of Greece, by home economists who give ten chicks apiece to girls' club members, and agriculturists whose principal placement is with boys' clubs.

"The Leghorn layer type bird has been in greatest demand, claiming 43 percent of the total, the White Rock 35 percent, and the Rhode Island Red 22 percent. Orders remaining to be filled register for 1,600 Leghorns, 1,050 Rhode Island Reds, and 700 White Rocks. More orders are coming in. Demands exceed those of last year.

"Why the increase over last year? The answer lies almost entirely with the change of emphasis of the poultry program. In former years it was the large (100 birds or more) commercial flock that was most encouraged by the project. The emphasis has shifted to the replacement of the local native (Andopian) flocks with the improved breeds. Large flock placement has not been disbanded; quite to the contrary, as demonstrated by the four large flocks placed to date and the request for nine more. The largest flock this spring is about 200 birds.

"The procedure through which the individual villager acquires his new village flock is simple: An initial trip into the village is made and the vehicle is stopped in the 'square' of the village, where usually several of the main coffee shops are located. A short time there, or in the coffee shops, and there will be a curious, varied group crowding around.

"If it is the very first visit, a general introduction will be given of the program. Those who wish to receive poultry request the number and breed they want and if possible make down payment toward hatching.

"The date arrives, the proper number of chicks are put in their traveling boxes, loaded in the jeep or Land-Rover, and away go the poultrymen for another chick distribution. Unless the individual is not in the village, it is only a matter of minutes until the recipient is there and asking about his chicks.

"The scene that follows can be rather humorous. Men, women, and children crowd around the jeep, straining to catch a glimpse of these American chicks. While the average number of chicks for each villager comes to 20-25, the range varies considerably. A man who is to receive nine, steps up without a basket or any means of carrying them to his house, 'Never mind, just give me my chicks.' A moment later he walks proudly away with all his chicks tucked gently under his coat like an old mother hen puts them under her wings.

"Meanwhile several women are making a fuss that only a woman could make over 'such darling little things.' Kids climbing all over the place, owners trying to choose just the chick they want, questions being asked from all directions, chicks escaping their boxes.

"The eggs for hatching are obtained from the previous year's laying flocks at a price above the local market. These flocks are still under careful supervision of the poultrymen and when diseases or other complications arise it is always to him the villager goes. The owner of a large flock is required to feed a balanced ration which is not necessary in the case of small replacement flocks.

"The price the villager pays for the purebred chick is only the cost involved in hatching and raising the bird to its distribution age. This amounts to approximately ten cents for a one-day-old chick to 25 cents for a four-week-old one. To eliminate the problem of providing heat for the day-old chick, many of the villagers prefer that they are fed for several weeks in Pax batteries.

"Among the many other responsibilities required of the men who head this sizable project are such things as candling eggs, turning incubator eggs five or six times daily, and careful attention to temperature regulation in the hatchery. Bookwork requires much time and patience. Exact records are kept, feed rations must be ready for all occasions, and medicine available with the knowledge to use it properly. It is not uncommon to hear that the poultryman is in some village up to the north checking some mopey flock. . . ."

Another major program was that carried out in the canning of vegetables and fruits. A little work had been done in food preservation in Panayitsa. But it remained for the Paxmen at Tsakones to develop the potential of this technique in a way that has benefited all of rural Greece.

Canning at Panayitsa was done in glass jars. However, cost of the jars and shortage of supply inhibited aggressive development of the program.

When the canning began at Tsakones glass jars were still being used. CARE provided seven jars per family. Unfortunately, some used these jars for other purposes but many families cooperated fully. It was quite a sight to enter home after home and see seven jars of peaches or some other fruit occupying a place of honor on a narrow shelf along one wall. Preserved fruit or vegetables were considered so valuable at the time that they were even included in the dowry of girls.

The Paxmen did some work in a number of villages as well. This spread the advantages of food preservation over a much wider area.

In 1954 tin cans were introduced in Tsakones and from that point on the canning program blossomed into one of the more significant contributions Paxmen have made to the country.

The fellows did a lot of research trying to get this project off the ground. Both the inadequate diet of large numbers of people and the incredible waste of fruits and vegetables pointed to food preservation as an urgent need. Finally they found a canner manufactured in Germany that really worked. They bought ten canners and placed them in ten villages. The first year the fellows canned approximately 35,000 cans. The second year they canned more than 85,000 cans.

About this time CARE heard of the success of the Pax canning program. CARE administrators investigated and decided the project deserved a substantial boost.

For 12 years CARE had been importing glass jars and pressure cookers to teach home economics classes. They had worked with local factories toward the production of low-cost quality jars, but were unsuccessful. When they learned of the Pax work with cans they switched also and consider this technique to be three times more successful than the previous program.

Later both the Ministry of Agriculture and CARE arranged for canning seminars. Before Pax had fully played its role in this canning development Paxmen like Bill Nice and Roger Beck were teaching home economists and students from all over Greece the use of this German canner. One year CARE bought 25 canners and brought home ec teachers together in Athens for a seminar. Bill taught this group all he knew about food preservation using this sealer technique. Each girl had a canner to work with during the course of the seminar. At graduation, each teacher took her canner along to the community in which she was teaching.

CARE was elated with the potential of the program, not only because of the thousands of kilos of food being preserved but also because the Greek home economists were becoming so interested. The next year they bought another 24 canners and conducted seminars again, later distributing these canners strategically throughout the country. In 1966 CARE imported 200 canners and held a seminar for home economists in all of Greece. The idea snowballed and extended seasonal diet possibilities throughout the year.

In Tsakones the canning season began usually early in July and continued through September. Peaches, beans, eggplants, and green beans were only some of the fruits and vegetables preserved for winter use, as well as for winter sale at higher prices whenever there were surpluses. Later the program was extended to meats, particularly poultry.

In the first years Paxmen carried full responsibility. But as the idea gained acceptance, villagers became involved in the cannery operation. By 1959 the cannery equipment was turned over to the community of Tsakones and it is still functioning to serve village needs.

Each year the community rents the canner to an individual who administers the project. For his services he receives a small commission on the cans which are sold.

Eventually the Pax unit sold the original ten canners to interested villagers for around $100 each, complete with various-size replaceable discs for use on different-size cans. All of them were placed somewhere in the Aridea Valley, a certain percentage of each year's gross being charged to help pay for the sealers.

As a project, canning has shown its value. Proof of

this is the establishment of four other cannery projects on a private-enterprise basis. It is probably inevitable that the community canner will give way to commercial developments. But this in turn tends to raise the general economic level of the area still further because of the increasing demand for fruits and vegetables.

Larry said, "You know, we get a lot of satisfaction from knowing that the early efforts of a few Paxmen have constituted such a worthwhile gift to the country."

After Ivan Holdeman left, Elbert Esau came to take his place as director for a year. Mrs. Esau was a nurse and carried on quite an extensive nursing program. This was one of the few times any of our Greek units could offer competent medical assistance.

Another noteworthy part of the program was hog production. A new strain of hog was imported and a demonstration project set up in Tsakones as had been done in Panayitsa. The same pattern was carried out in various outlying villages. Demonstration consisted simply of showing what could be done in terms of rapid growth, good health, and marketability when good stock was well housed and well fed. There was also a program whereby a young gilt was placed with a Greek farmer to raise. From her first litter one gilt was returned to the Pax unit and in turn placed with another farmer.

This program worked out well. But some of the feeding experiments which were attempted in a comparison of imported and native hogs didn't succeed. There were some situations in which the Paxmen bit off more than they could chew—they simply didn't have sufficient technical background.

During the years when Paxmen were located at Tsakones, there were often one or two fellows working at Ioannina with the Inter-Church Service team.

Larry describes this program:

The team there was international, coed, and interdenominational, including fellows and girls from England, the U.S.A., Denmark, Greece, and the Netherlands. In addition to Church of the Brethren and Mennonite representatives, there were Lutheran, Dutch Reformed, Disciples of Christ, and Greek Orthodox personnel.

Their pattern of work was different from ours. Instead of a unit located at one place, they scattered singly or in teams of two to surrounding villages. The work itself was quite similar, including crop and garden demonstrations, poultry improvement, veterinary aid, canning demonstrations, improved cultivations, and seedbed preparation practices, as well as introduction of hotbeds for seeding. But instead of one person specializing in one area, each person or team served as director of all projects in the village to which he had been assigned.

The group was broken up during the week. Each Saturday was reserved for reports to the director at Ioannina and group interaction. Sundays the young people spent together in the only unit experience they could enjoy. Monday morning they all returned to their respective villages.

Of course, we did some of the same kind of village work. But in addition we carried on a substantial program at our home base of operations.

Our unit life was important to us. We had a good group. Of course, social life in a Greek community was not easy to fit into. Our Mennonite heritage had taught us against dancing. And while couple dancing was frowned on as sin by the Greek Orthodox Church, the Greek folk dances were encouraged.

Many of the fellows did not participate for conscience'

sake or because of general feeling in the unit. I suspect if some of the Paxmen went back now they would view this differently and probably see this as another opportunity to relate to the people.

Perhaps the most difficult times, with respect to the folk dancing, was at the winter weddings. We were invited to a great many of them. And the Greek girls felt they had to find a way to get the American boys to participate in the dances.

Naturally, these social occasions were important to more than the bride and groom. Not only the Greek girls but many mothers of Greek girls were delighted to have available such a constantly replenished supply of young Americans. It seemed every Greek mother was busy pairing off her daughter with a Paxman. The highest goal of a mother was to relieve her daughter of the drudgery of Greek wifehood—by marrying her off to an American. A mother would be willing never to see her daughter again just to marry her to an American Paxman. For the mothers there the Paxman carried an element of prestige and status.

Because of this, even though we encouraged the Paxers to enjoy some social contact, we had to be very sensitive to local practices. Any sign of specific interest in a girl could quickly be misinterpreted by her parents. So much so they'd be expecting to see him shortly at their home making formal inquiry about the kind of dowry available.

The Greek dowry system, especially away from the large population centers, is not necessarily guided by love or desire. Frequently it is simply a matter of economics—with which father can a young man make the best deal?

In the Greek culture, interest in a girl is never really shown until after the dowry arrangements have been completed. This meant we Paxmen had to be extremely careful in our relationships.

A highlight of our service was the visits to Panayitsa and Tsakones by King Paul and Queen Frederica of Greece. The queen met the Paxmen at these locations and was greatly impressed with their work. Her formal message of thanks to Mennonite Central Committee emphasized her gratefulness for two things—the villagers' enthusiastic appreciation of Pax work and the excellent relationships between the Paxmen and the Greek Orthodox State Church.

My last few months in Tsakones were lame-duck months. I became ill with hepatitis in July, so I didn't get much done before leaving in October 1955. Although I had decided I would like to spend more time in a similar type of work, I hardly dreamed that four years would find me returning to the Aridea Valley.

But I did. After a wedding and school.

Anette and I had become engaged in 1953, before I left for service. We were one engaged couple who made it through service—more than 75 percent don't. On December 29, 1955, we were married.

I spent a year at Freeman, then went to South Dakota State University and got a BS in Agriculture. Anette got her BA in elementary education.

During 1958 William Snyder of Mennonite Central Committee approached us and reported they were changing the unit leadership pattern in Pax to a longer-term arrangement. Although Anette and I had rather hoped some door in South America would open, we gladly considered his invitation to return to Greece and accepted it.

From Frankfurt, Germany, we drove a new 10-passenger LandRover to Greece. Took with us a matron, Kathy Miller, and two new Paxmen, Dale Linsenmeyer and Kermit Yoder. We arrived in Greece on July 2.

Tremendous change was evident everywhere—more

and better roads, self-propelled combines, twenty times more tractors—it seemed as if Greece had awakened.

We drove to Panayitsa. But it had changed also. Strange faces came out of the unit house. Tsakones was different. A new unit had taken the places filled by familiar Paxers.

Our instructions were to phase out Panayitsa and reestablish in a new area. For seven months we lived there and then, after extensive surveys, selected the entire Aridea Valley as our field of operations with a farm headquarters on the outskirts of the town of Aridea, just three kilometers from Tsakones, one of our old homes.

To help us in the construction of a house and farm buildings on the farm at Aridea, the five-man Builders Unit was sent down from Germany. All of us—Builders Unit and seven-man agricultural unit—lived at Aridea. During this time no Paxers remained at Panayitsa, although some follow-up work was being done. Also during this period we were searching for ways to phase out the work at Panayitsa, especially the dairy project.

Frankly, this was difficult, largely because the Greek farmers felt we should continue doing the work in the program and continue subsidizing feed deficiencies. We felt the time had come for the project to stand on its own feet, or fall. It fell, although not before it had brought a great many advantages to that community as well as many others.

As soon as the house on the farm at Aridea was completed we moved in and Aridea became headquarters for the Pax program in the entire valley, including Tsakones and more than 40 other villages.

Pax was good to me. During more than two years as a Paxer, I grew up. I learned to slow my pace, to be more concerned with people than with things. I think I became more tolerant both of myself, in the tension between idealism and reality, and of others.

During the four years I served as a director of Paxmen I found nothing to change my opinion about Pax. Pax is a valid idea. It provides a structure in which young men can discover and share their gifts and abilities. It offers a service that is down-to-earth and relevant.

I'd be forced to admit some times of discouragement. There were some days when I wondered whether we had made even the slightest impression on our Greek friends.

One of those days, Dean Zehr and I were walking down the road. In the field to our left an old man was struggling with a stubborn mule. A neighbor, not seeing the two of us walking, called to the old man and said, "Just use a little Pax patience on him."

Then I knew. And was encouraged again.

Raymond Dyck—Aridea

"Why should a peace church be in Greece doing research on hot peppers?" This was the opening question in Director John Wieler's address on the ceremonial occasion when the unique Pax farm at Aridea was turned over to the Ministry of Agriculture in Greece.

Pax and peppers may not appear to be compatible. However, the thirty persons who gathered that morning of January 21, 1966, did not need to be told that pepper research, agricultural demonstrations, stock improvement, and canning programs were simply channels through which words and deeds flowed from people to people in an effort to say, "We care. We want to help. Let us live with you for a while."

Although the form or time was then unknown, in

effect the ceremony had been planned almost 14 years before. In April 1952 five Paxmen came to Panayitsa because the Mennonite church they represented was concerned to meet and answer the needs of people, whatever they were or wherever they existed. Since Greece had suffered so grievously, what better place could be found to help carry a burden? And where could one find better emissaries of this way of love than those men who were saying, "We cannot be party to destructiveness—to ravage a land and wound a nation and kill its people. But we can and will come to you, to share your suffering, to bind your hurt and show you, as well as we can in everyday living, the way of Christ."

So they came—dozens of them came, and went—to be part of a chain of caring which drew discouragement and even despair from the heart of a people. And as they worked in Panayitsa, in Tsakones, in Aridea, and many other villages, this day was made. This day when the handing over of a key symbolized the gift of millions of hours of planning and travel and sweat. This day when the intangible gift of presence and concern and sharing took on tangible form. This day when one heard again the echo of the Paxman's motto—everything "in the name of Christ."

"I wasn't there for the ceremony," said Raymond Dyck. "But the major part of my work in Greece was pointed toward it."

Raymond Dyck came to Greece from Kansas. He was born at Newton on February 27, 1938. His parents, Mr. and Mrs. Peter Dyck, were farmers, so Raymond grew up on the farm. Grade school, then high school kept him occupied until 1956. From there he went to the University of Arkansas. In 1960 he was graduated with a BS degree and in 1962 with a Master's degree in horticulture.

Raymond picked up his story on the school track:

I ran my way through school. Received a track scholarship. Actually, track paid most of my college expenses. 4:16 was my best mile. That wasn't spectacular but it was fast enough to keep me in the running as a student.

During my two grad years I also had an assistantship in horticulture.

It's a little difficult to pinpoint my reasons for going into Pax. None of my thinking was rushed; I took quite a while finding my way through. Of one thing I was certain: I had to find some way to be more than an objector to war. I wanted to do something positive.

I'm sure my Mennonite heritage contributed something. And my pastor helped. But most of my conclusions grew out of personal thought, rather than discussions with someone else.

My interest in Greece developed through a Greek friend at the university. So when I decided to take a peace position and applied to MCC for Pax, I indicated Greece as a preference. My application was accepted.

When I had my Master's degree, I was ready to go.

There was a period of orientation at Akron, Pennsylvania, and another brief orientation at Frankfurt, Germany. I traveled to Greece in a VW Combi and a French Deux Chevaux with Klaus Froese and Dick Kauffman. The trip took three days and was a very special experience for me. I had been sympathetic to Europeans before. So Klaus and I found a commonness that developed into a close friendship.

We went straight to Aridea. It looked pretty bleak. There had been not a drop of rain since April. And in the blasting August heat the reception of an agriculturist looked questionable.

Larry Eisenbeis was director at the time I arrived.

He had hoped to place me in an educational program, related closely to the demonstration aspects of the farm and designed to give special help to local people. But the government wouldn't approve the school. So my first year was a bit difficult and uncertain.

Every Paxman hates to mark time. Ray Dyck was no exception, especially since his training and assignment led him to expect responsibility compatible with his interest.

The farm dates back to 1960 when the Greek Minister of Agriculture gave to the Paxmen, or rather to their parent body—Mennonite Central Committee—20 stremmas of land. Later a request for an additional 30 stremmas was granted. And still later 50 more stremmas were added, making a total of 100 stremmas or about 25 acres. Technically, the land still belonged to the government but it was made available for experimental and demonstration purposes.

Originally the land was useless and barren. Empty of buildings, the entire area was covered with sagebrush and ferns. The soil lacked humus and nitrogen. Even to the Greeks, who farmed some rather unproductive areas, it was only wasteland.

Where once lay almost total desolation, there now stands a farm. "The farm the Pax boys built," say the townspeople of Aridea. They are proud of it. While the barren soil was made to bring forth a harvest and the farm buildings were being built they would walk past it just to see the transformation. A paradise, they called it later.

It is a beautiful spot. Near the road stands the striking two-story house, large enough to include office space and a home for the Pax family. White stucco, the dwelling matches other farm buildings in color. An outside stairway leads to a spacious balcony and the director's apartment. The house is circled with a fine lawn. And around it all runs a well-trimmed hedge.

Just behind the house stands a stately row of poplars. Behind them loom the mountains with a covering of clouds hung low near the base and between the peaks. To the left of the farm buildings—cow barn, rabbit pens, hog barn, feed mill, implement shed, shop—and just beyond the silos are fallow fields in their winter rest. The farm is served by a well 31 meters deep (a little more than 100 feet), drilled to provide ample water for irrigation purposes. Everything testifies to the deep dedication and strenuous efforts of the Pax unit and similarly to the dogged persistence of the Ministry of Agriculture in maintaining the gift to which the government has attached such significance.

The Aridea Valley contains a total population of around 45,000 living in 45 villages. The largest, Aridea, has a population of near 5,000, and lies very near the center of the valley which is about 35 kilometers long and 20 kilometers wide (22 miles by 12 1/2 miles). Mountains run the circumference of this area—Almopia in Nomos Pellis, the birthplace of Alexander the Great. Beyond the mountains to the east, 120 kilometers distant, lies Salonika, better known to Bible readers as Thessalonica or to the modern Greek as Thessaloniki.

Part of the Aridea farm program involved extension programs in the villages throughout the valley. Generally, the elements of these extension programs matched what was being done at the farm for demonstration purposes. In some cases periodic visits were made to supervise village projects. In other cases, Paxmen or Pax girls lived in the villages.

One of the villages where significant work was done was Periclea, about 30 kilometers from Aridea and very near the Yugoslavian border. Population was about 450. Dale Linsenmeyer moved there in January of 1961 along with a second Paxman and an interpreter. The villagers gave them a straw shed for their home.

Their objectives were to find some channel for communication to ascertain if possible why previous projects there had been unsuccessful and to begin some form of community development program.

Their first assignment turned out to be home improvement (their own home). They built screens, plastered walls, and built a toilet. Because of the short growing season, they built a hotbed to start plants. They also rented land for a garden. Along with that Dale developed several hog projects in Periclea and neighboring villages. Here, as elsewhere, the men would try to select a more progressive farmer who would follow instructions carefully and institute a demonstration project with him.

With the vice-president and secretary of the village he succeeded in organizing a choir in the church.

Village life at Periclea was lived on the subsistence level. There was enough food but little variety—the morning meal at 10:00 a.m. consisted of bread and cheese made from goat or sheep's milk. The afternoon meal at 2:00 p.m. usually included beans and potatoes. The late evening meal at 9:30 p.m. featured more beans with garlic and olive oil. Seldom was there meat available except when lambs were slaughtered at Easter.

Houses were stone, plastered with mud and straw. They were roofed with shale. Clothes were made from the wool of sheep, spun into yarn, knitted and dyed.

Periclea was one of five villages in the Aridea Valley served by resident Pax persons. These villages, because of distance or inaccessibility, were beyond the reach of most government services. As a result of this off-the-beaten-track situation, as well as bombings during World War II and serious hardships during the years of guerrilla warfare, some of these villagers tended to be extremely suspicious of foreign strangers.

However, living in the village with the people changed this early suspicion to warm friendship, and made possible noteworthy contributions. This was especially true of some of the girls assisting Paxmen by this time. More than one matron, challenged by the opportunity, found time to do village work in addition to her other exacting duties. In a few instances, matrons were transferred for more than a year to village locations. In addition, girls from other European countries, such as Germany and Holland, served with teaching programs in sanitation, nutrition, personal hygiene, food preservation, cooking, sewing, and some demonstrations of first aid.

To have women on a Pax team was an innovation. Except for Paxmen who served with the interchurch unit at Ioannina, the pattern was completely new and at first quite unacceptable to the men. Rather strangely, they seemed to assume that the presence of women downgraded their manhood. The first matrons in both Greece and Germany carried the brunt of this reaction, but they were finally tolerated since this freed the men of "women's work" in the unit. Directors' wives, when they first came on the scene, faced a peculiar situation. Part of the time the fellows simply ignored them as an appendage to the director. And part of the time they seemed to require her to play the role of sister, sweetheart, and mother, all rolled into one delectable bundle.

However, adjustments were made in time and Paxmen began to rid themselves of their male provincialism. But when girls came to actually participate in teamwork and carry specific and continuing village responsibility, some of the less mature Paxmen again saw this move as a reflection against their masculinity.

Some of this was understandable. Pax had pioneered

in situations, particularly in Greece, where uncertainty, hardship, and sacrifice were common. Living conditions, at the beginning, were primitive and makeshift. Their willingness to do this in circumstances many women would have rejected became a special badge which was passed on abstractly but proudly to succeeding Paxmen.

But they forgot two things: First, the unit was now well established and living conditions were improving. And second, there is also a special breed of female volunteers for whom hardship is only a challenge, and whose willingness to sacrifice and ability to absorb great difficulties is matched only by the spirit of the most dedicated Paxmen.

"By the time I got there," said Raymond, "the girls were accepted. Oh, we fellows would get a bit cliquish at times and make our plans separately. But relationships were good and the girls, generally, were doing fine work.

"Care had to be taken with living arrangements in the villages to avoid misunderstandings. Some of the fellows wondered why there couldn't be more married couples serving, apart from those in directors' posts. There were a number of situations where a husband-wife team could have worked much more ideally."

Village work included a chain gilt program as well. Paxmen usually kept at least four or five sows and two boars on the farm. This purebred parent stock was used to provide gilts. The Paxman placed a gilt with a farmer and from the first litter took a gilt and placed that with another farmer.

At first villagers would be apprehensive. But one trial in a village was usually enough. And the Paxmen, instead of being overrun at the farm with unwanted gilts as they were at first, were forced to set up a waiting list of interested farmers.

Along with this program, 12 purebred boars were placed in 12 different villages to upgrade local stock and to maintain improvements gained in the chain gilt program. Before long this resulted in more than 70 percent of hogs marketed in the area being pure-bred or crossbred.

Swiss and Angus bulls were placed in villages also. And in an attempt to alleviate the feed problem seriously aggravated by more and better cattle, 70 Saamen goats, good milk producers, were placed in eight different villages. The farm also served as an artificial insemination center for sheep and goats in a combined program with the Royal National Foundation, the Artificial Insemination Program, and Pax.

The stock breeding and chain gilt programs terminated when the farm was turned over to the Ministry of Agriculture. But not before vast improvements in area stock had been made.

However, the poultry program continues. John Tsompanides, a local farmer, purchased both hatchery and feed mill. Paxmen gave him considerable assistance in bookkeeping procedures, the art of hatching, feed formulas, and development of rations. In fact, even after the unit was disbanded, several Paxmen from Crete maintained a close contact to insure success.

Considerable feeling attended the decision to turn over the poultry business to private enterprise. Some insisted that a co-op arrangement would have been much better. But after evaluating the problems co-ops in other areas were facing in becoming established or even in being maintained, it was decided to establish one man in the business.

John Tsompanides had long been a friend of the Paxmen. His home was open to incoming persons to help in their initial orientation. When a Paxman arrived, he was frequently force-fed the language for two or three weeks in classes with the interpreter.

Then he would be placed in a Greek home for a few weeks, to observe Greek family life, eat Greek food, practice the language, and generally learn those elementary lessons of acculturation so important to sensitive service.

Tsompanides had worked with the Paxmen in various demonstrations in the village of Zoforia—stock improvement, feed processing (he had the first silo in the area), and poultry. His progressiveness and interest had long been proved. So it was with confidence, even in face of normal new business problems, that the hatchery and feed business were sold to John.

The poultry program began, as at the other centers, with importation of eggs from quality hatching stock, the development of a demonstration flock on the farm and the placement of three- and four-week-old chicks with individual farmers in the villages. The earliest objective was the replacement of the local hen with a heavier bird and a better egg producer. The first eggs came from American Farm School stock at Salonika. Sussex and New Hampshire strains were introduced. Small chicks were distributed in the villages according to lists provided by the Ministry of Agriculture.

In light of the early beginning, it was fitting that the continuity in poultry should be centered in a hatchery.

However, this change did not take place until 1965. Long before, as early as 1962, the phase-out of the Aridea farm program was discussed. This was a difficult period for the Paxmen. Youthful, exuberant, filled with idealism, they had come to Greece to give themselves sacrificially, to make concrete contributions.

But the plan for phase-out hung over their heads. In fact, *phase-out* became a very bad word in the Aridea unit. It sapped initiative and destroyed morale.

For some reason, organizational plans for this pattern of contribution had not reached the rank-and-file Paxer until he arrived on the field. Compounding the problem was the fact that administrators were being sent to phase-out a program barely begun, in fact.

Various alternatives were considered. The church, the bank, the American Farm School, and other agencies declined the responsibility of continuing the farm program. Not until the prospect of expanding crop research projects was considered, did there seem to be a logical answer to the desire for continuity.

That is where I came in, said Raymond:

If we were going to turn over the farm to the Ministry of Agriculture for research purposes, then we would need a significant research program.

And that's where Dr. Bekiares also came in. He was director of the research station at Ptolemais. Interestingly, ten years before, he had spent a week with the fellows at Panayitsa, polishing his English, before going to America to study. Alex had been his teacher then.

Now Dr. Bekiares had a direction from the Ministry of Agriculture to study our farm program at Aridea. He met with John Wieler, the director, and me; did studies on economic, soil, and climate factors; then proposed to the Ministry certain research projects. His recommendations were accepted. By the fall of 1963 wheels were already turning on the transfer. And from the spring of 1964, all our research on the farm was programmed by Dr. Bekiares.

This included experiments to determine crop rotation feasibilities in wheat, barley, and peppers; experiments with alfalfa and experiments with strawberries; potato varieties; experiments with onion sets with special reference to weed control problems; and experiments with as many as 48 different varieties of hybrid corn, both American and Greek.

But the big push in my work was experimentation with peppers. It had been concluded that the main thrust of the farm program at turnover time would be agronomic. The poultry effort would be continued through the hatchery business, privately owned. And other stock improvement projects would be considered as having made their notable contributions and would be phased-out.

Hopefully, I was to have a Greek assistant in research who would then provide the bridge to later government administration. This was not to be; for, even though I extended my term from two to 3 1/2 years, this man did not arrive until after I left.

This did not seriously hamper my own work, although the uncertainty about whether there could be continuity and a satisfactory conclusion to my experiments was cause for frustration. One does not complete studies like this in a year; four or five years are usually necessary.

Simply stated, MCC Pax was in the country to meet needs. Already their work had accomplished much in a number of areas. But the essence of continuity and permanence had to be symbolized concretely somehow. The farm could be that symbol, providing its program highlighted some dramatic need. The Greek pepper problem concerned every alert research agronomist in the country. But nowhere had anything substantial been done. So it seemed that an additional lasting gift to the Greek people would come into being if the pepper problem could be resolved.

My assignment, therefore, was to find or develop a good variety of sweet pepper—local or imported, that would produce a sweet paprika powder, exportable to the world market, which could utilize a $300,000 pepper plant built before the country had found a marketable pepper, or even before research had been organized.

There were only two local peppers—the one was hot, and the other was hotter. The value of hot peppers on the market was only one third of the value of sweet peppers. Yet nothing had been done to expand the use of the sweet-pepper variety.

To find a good variety of peppers I wrote to universities in pepper-growing areas. In the U.S.A. these turned out to be located in the Southern states. Other countries responding included Spain, Yugoslavia, Bulgaria and, of course, Hungary, which is a primary pepper-growing country.

Through one means or another we obtained seeds from these countries. The director of a bank in Salonika helped us. The owner of a pepper factory gave us invaluable assistance. By the second year we had brought together more than 50 main varieties. Through crossing, we were working at one time with a total of around 500 strains.

In pepper-plant culture we were concerned with such elements as planting time, rate of planting, direct seeding (rather than transplanting), different fertilizers, and different methods of weed control. We uncovered some interesting results.

If we planted 18 days earlier than normal planting time on June 10, we had a 30 percent greater yield and a 30-day earlier maturity. Customarily, 10,000 plants per stremma (one quarter acre) had been used. We planted 7,500 plants per stremma with exactly the same harvest results. We found direct seeding was just as good as transplanting but with a somewhat greater problem in weed control. And that the use of the three basic fertilizers gave us better yields than the use of one or two or none.

In the peppers themselves we were working toward

three major objectives: satisfactory color, sweet taste, and good drying percentage. The overall objective was to find a sweet, non-hot pepper which would grind up satisfactorily into a visually attractive paprika powder for a world market.

Purity of strain, yield factors, variability in planting times for a longer pepper factory season, adaptability to various growing areas in Greece, and climate limitations were additional elements we needed to keep in mind.

Color was one of the tricky parts of the experiment. For a long time I could find no record of research on color quality. Finally, I discovered something the Hungarians had done back in 1910. This was just part of a total review of pepper literature I did in the course of my work: the listings were complete in English, although not all of the material was translated into English.

We had to establish criteria for the determination of good color. This was difficult because different evaluators tend to be quite subjective. No one could reach conclusions with finality, but it was clear we had to please both the field buyers and the market consumer. In the end, we set up visual tests carried out with persons representing these groups over the course of several years.

Several other factors made the final selection of color difficult. After grinding, the oil and the seeds pick up the pigment and gloss every particle. Seed percentage also dilutes color. It is one thing to look at peppers in the field and another to look at peppers after they are ground.

The grinding process was simple; drying not quite as easy. We needed a means to measure one of the quality determinations—through drying. To provide a drying percentage, water must be removed and weighing done before and after.

The first year we used an incubator. The next year I drew plans for a dryer which one of our Paxmen, a carpenter, built. I did the electrical hookup. The most important variety results came because of this little dryer. We'd cut up the peppers, weigh out one kilogram, then dry; weigh later and compute the percentage of weight lost in drying.

This helped us also on color determinations. We'd cut up peppers, dry, then grind. The samples were then laid out on a table for visual comparisons and selection. The person who helped us most in color was the Greek private pepper factory owner. I really enjoyed working with this man. Of course, we had a number of other people helping us in this, giving color preferences on 15 or 20 samples. We never got around to purchasing a color measurement machine.

In planting, we planted rows with the wind rather than across, so there would be little chance of cross-pollination. Also, the plots were not located close to each other. We saved enough seed from all the promising varieties so that we could move ahead on any one of them.

We dabbled also in the development of mechanical equipment to be used in pepper culture. This included demonstrations and testing of equipment from other countries. One of these was a pepper seeder or planter and another was a pepper cultivator.

During the course of the entire project, in addition to Dr. Bekiares and other agricultural men, we worked very closely with local businessmen: the director of the co-op government pepper factory, a private pepper factory owner, the banker from the agricultural bank, and the local extension service.

We also tried to stay in touch with pepper farmers. Some of what we were doing they could have done as well had they had certain information available. For example, they didn't realize the problems of cross-pollination—that through wind currents a sweet pepper field could be infected by a hot pepper field. But they were extremely helpful to us in taste and color selection.

Partly this was done by establishing pepper research projects in three other villages, in addition to Ptolemais and Aridea. The five basic varieties we decided on were tested further. This enabled us to get more seeds, to let farmers see them, and also help us decide which ones to develop.

When I finally left we were quite close to our objective. On the basis of our work in 1965 we selected five of the best varieties and cultivated them under controlled conditions. By 1966 two new varieties were selected—one fifteen days earlier than the local variety and one fifteen days later than the local variety. This will give the pepper factories a longer season. Hopefully, when the project is completed, there will be sufficient seed to share with pepper farmers and enough left over to continue work on purifying the seed.

Ray's work with peppers constituted a singular contribution to Greece.

"Mission Accomplished" is a term sometimes used too carelessly. But the acceptance of the farm by the Ministry of Agriculture indicated satisfaction and the reaching of a certain milestone. Actually two needs had been fulfilled in this project—an acute local, regional, and national need to establish a viable pepper industry requiring careful work in the breeding and culture of peppers. And also the need of MCC Pax to point the farm in a direction which would still be useful long after the Paxmen had gone on to serve elsewhere.

To leave the farm was difficult. Each success, as well as each failure, cast its peculiar spell on the unit. Paxmen came and Paxmen went. But always there was a feeling of belonging to a family that was dedicating itself to people.

The measure of the bond woven in those years between Paxmen and Aridea residents is not easy to take. Yet the comments erupting from a warm, lingering memory hinted at a strength of feeling that will long remain.

I listened to a lot of testimonies during the day I spent in Aridea. Testimonies from lawyers, store owners, a veterinarian, an agriculturist, a medical doctor, the mayor and his assistant, two countermen at the bus depot, the governor of Almopia—the entire region in which the Paxers carried out their work.

"Pax helped the area very much."

"The Mennonite boys did a wonderful job here. They took useless land and made it a paradise."

"Delighted to meet another representative of Mennonite Pax boys."

"We were a little hesitant at first. But the love the boys showed us won us over."

"They were like my brothers."

"They did fine work. The Pax boys weren't too good to be with us. They were willing to come to our own homes to help us—coming to us was the important thing."

Dr. Bekiares added. "The boys were good, excellent. I was very much impressed with their religious life— very much. It was a good example to others. I have never seen such young men who pray at the table and explain the Bible, and sing together, and who can work with each other as the Pax boys did."

Perhaps the most telling comment came from Father Georgis, the village priest. Although not unconcerned with the material plight of many of his people in the Aridea Valley, Father Georgis had another interest and saw another side of the Paxer.

Although near 80 years of age, he was an energetic man. He welcomed me warmly into his home. Almost immediately his housekeeper brought the typical spoonful of sweets and a glass of water. He settled back into the cushions of a settee and started to talk. Alex Mavrides, who had worked with the men for fifteen years and had come with me, interpreted.

"These were good boys, Christian boys. They helped me greatly in my work, even though they may not have known it. More people came to church, many more came to confession. They read the Bible more. The Pax boys were good examples.

"They helped me take the Word of God into the homes. Now, even now, when I go to the villages, the people remind me of the Bible distribution.

"At the first, I was hesitant. They called themselves Christians. After a while we could see that they were Christians. Then the people embraced them— the Mennonites embraced the people—they loved each other."

Father Georgis sat up straight abruptly. "I want you to know this is true. They loved each other. I am the spiritual head of the whole church in this area. I speak for the people. I know whereof I speak."

He settled back into the cushions again. And as he reclined, he went on, "I feel so happy; I have such great joy at the thought of the Paxmen I do not know how to express it. I have been so happy with the friendship and love they brought. And to you, I give my great love with joy for your presence.

"Our Lord Jesus Christ taught us to love each other and to work together. The church [Greek Orthodox] must learn to accept other followers of Christ. This the Mennonites have taught us to do."

I turned to Father Georgis, "The Mennonites have also learned from you. Until recently we have been quite isolated. But working with you here in Greece has also taught us a great many things."

Father Georgis replied, "War is bad. We should pray only for peace. But I thank my God for the wars which brought you to us."

106

I asked the priest how they could accept the Pax-men who were young and had many shortcomings.

He sat bolt upright and shook his finger at me with an energy that his earlier enthusiastic comments had not prepared me for. The tone of his voice was vehement. "That never happened! That is not so! They were Christians—good examples for my people. I would tell my congregations to live like Christ; the Pax boys would show them how."

As we walked to the door he shook my hand warmly. "They were Christians, different from us, perhaps, but Christians! My people accepted them with love because they always knew the Paxmen came with love."

I thought again of what Raymond Dyck had told me: "Living in Pax was unique. I don't know of a better place to learn tolerance and how to get along with people. Pax unit life was a tremendous experience in human relations. Of course, what we learned in unit life extended also to relations within the community.

"That was so important. It's a terribly ticklish thing to come from an affluent society and live in the midst of poverty.

"The Greeks are wonderful people, though. They put up with us during our periods of adjustment. And made us feel as if our small gifts to them were really worthwhile."

Perhaps Dr. Bekiares said this best in his acceptance speech on January 21, 1966: "What is the main meaning of [this] event? . . . that this farm is already getting changed into an institute of scientific research. Until now it was mainly the center of philanthropic activities. . . . From this hour it will be changed into a center of activities for the exploration of truth. The main objective of its work will be the revelation of the secrets of nature, the revelation of natural rhythms and rules, the revelation of truth in nature. . . .

"The withdrawal of our friends, the Mennonites, grieves me. We will miss wonderful friends and fellow workers. We believe they will grieve too. However, we are giving them one promise: the work that we started together will continue. The house which they built and shelters us at this hour will be maintained forever because it was built on strong stone, the Stone of the Bible. It will have the endurance and the duration of the Christian faith and the Christian love. It will remain beautiful and strong, like a lighthouse in the center of the area as an example of the most beautiful and the highest of man's actions, for imitation. Our friends the Mennonites have charmed us. They should be certain that we will never forget them."

Nor will Paxers forget Northern Greece. In Panayitsa and in Tsakones and in Aridea the confluence of streams of need was found. Men who came as resource found their own manhood. Resource reached out to need and in the giving found also a gift until giving and receiving were intermingled in mutual sharing.

And so a monument was built in Macedonia. For some it was a farm, buildings starkly white against the evening black of mountains rimming the valley of Aridea. For others it was demonstration and extension and improvement, laid stone on stone, on which has risen the glad thanks of healthier people. For others it was program and project continuity and some kind of permanence which institutions, in some strange manner, are expected to provide.

And for some—for some—it was people and relationships; deep friendships which warm memory keeps alive. This is the monument built in hearts that still stands in this day to mark a way of love and peace.

Perhaps after all, this is the greatest gift a man of Pax can bring.

PARAGUAY

Wilfred Unruh

September 10, 1952. I can remember a time when I heard some guys gripe about the meals at college. If I ever hear that again I'll give them "the word." I'm not griping now but . . . for the past two weeks we have eaten soup: soup with noodles, soup with rice, then noodles again. No other supplies are available. . . .

We'll have to ask MCC in Asuncion to send out some buns and sausages to add some variety to this liquid diet. And oranges. Oranges are cheap and quite plentiful. A few weeks ago we bought five hundred— two sacks full—at three cents a dozen, tree ripened and juicy as can be. When it rains again I'll make some more orange marmalade. I'm getting to be professional at it. Last batch lasted only four days—we six fellows were eating a pint a meal. That was following another soup kick we were on. . . . *There we have a quick peek into Wilfred Unruh's diary.*

That's what you'd call a balanced diet—noodle soup for two weeks, then orange marmalade for four days. Normally, workers (Mennonite Central Committee) have sufficient supplies for nourishing, although not always exciting meals. But sometimes in frontier situations they "make do." Of course, a little hardship or occasional sacrifices are a part of their commitment to service.

The men serving in Paraguay in the years before Pax existed as a program were called simply Voluntary Service workers. By 1953 Paxmen were officially at work in the country. But before that men of draft age and with I-W classification (by 1952) were serving as VS-ers.

July 12, 1952. VS means different things to different people, I guess. I'm sure a lot of people wouldn't expect what they would find here. We don't offer a direct service to people such as our relief, children's homes, and hospital units do. We're in plain old routine work, trying to show in the way we live, and especially through our attitudes, what we believe. *Another entry.*

Wilfred Unruh was born on March 3, 1932, on a farm near Goessel, Kansas. His father, John, was a dairy and grain farmer. The family were members at the General Conference Mennonite Church near Newton.

The Russian Mennonite community, speaking low German, settled here mostly in the decade following 1870. The original settlers, as well as most who followed, immigrated from Russia where they had gone years before from Germany. Within the memory of the most recent arrivals in the community the relief work of Mennonite Central Committee was a vivid recollection.

So during grade school and high school years, Wilfred heard from his parents much about MCC and its concern for refugees and other unfortunate people. This seed bore fruit.

In 1950, after high school graduation, Wilfred enrolled as a freshman at Bethel College. At that point he was planning a pre-agricultural course of study.

In the spring of 1951, the Korean conflict was going on. Several men had already left these Kansas communities to work with the first Pax Builders Unit in Europe. In Kansas, as in other areas, a deep concern was growing regarding this war and its effect on them and their young people.

Wilfred tells about that period:

The impending draft of young men was a real issue that spring. In fact, a number of pastors set up a meeting to ask themselves and their people about the Korean War, the needs it was creating, how

110

Hanging up Pax T-shirts, Algeria.

*John V. Driedger
and John Arn, Jr.,
Austria, 1960.*

Pax Chorus, European MCC Workers' Conference, Germany, 1954.
Opposite page: Vienna, Austria, 1960.

ALTERNATIVE SERVICE

OF THE
UNITED STATES
OF AMERICA

This service has been set up by the American
Gov't for those young men who are
conscientiously opposed to Military Service.
It is our belief that we accomplish more by
working with the people of the world in Peace
and Friendship. As members of the Church of
the Brethren and the Mennonite Churches,
we are rebuilding this war damaged Protestant
school in the Spirit of Reconciliation.

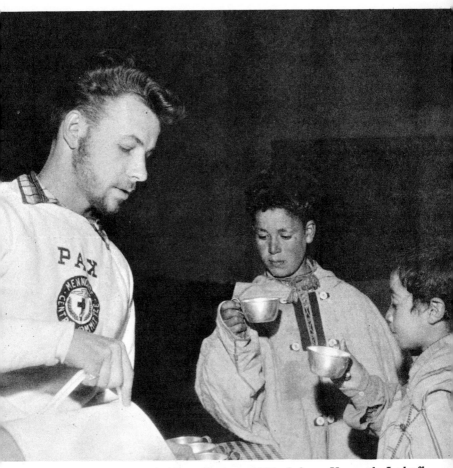

Opposite page, above: Aridea, Greece, 1961; below: Kenneth Imhoff, Egypt, 1955. Above: Peter W. Neufeldt, Algeria, 1963.

Below: Austria, 1957. Opposite page, top: Kermit Yoder *Greece, 1957; below: John Epp, Hong Kong, 1961.*

Opposite page, above: Jacob W. Thiessen, India, 1963; below: Joseph T. Hartzler, Algeria, 1965. Above: J. Lester Groff, Jordan, 1960.

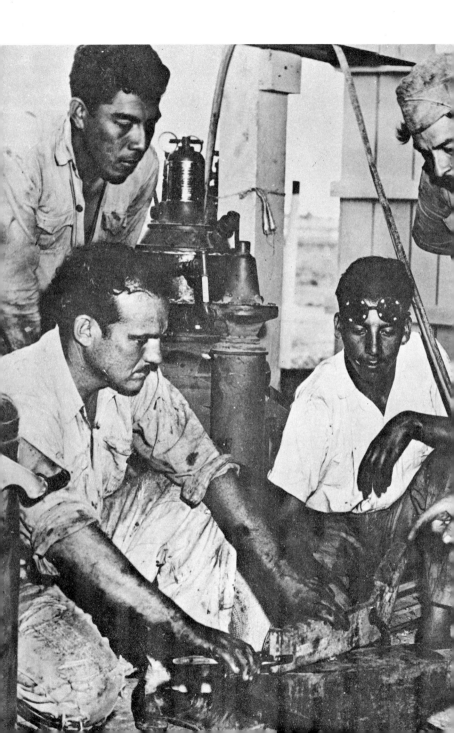

Leland Stalter,
Paraguay,
1959.

Gerald Dyck, Thailand, 1961.

Valentine Yutzy, Woodrow Ramseyer, and Howard Burkholder, Korea,
1955.

Dale Weaver, Greece, 1960.

Joe Haines, Jordan, 1960.

Opposite page, above: Doug Hostetter, Vietnam, 1967; below: Randall Ratslaff, Haiti, 1966. Above: David Nisely, Bolivia, 1966.

*Left: Larry Regier, Liberia, 1961.
Above: Harold Kauffman, Haiti,
1962.*

Earl S. Martin, Vietnam, 1967.

Larry Landis (right) with former MCC Congo Director Elmer Neufeld, Congo, 1963.

Jon Snyder (right), Dr. Carlson (middle), Congo, 1964.

Richard Fulmer, Bolivia, 1967.

James Garboden, Morocco, 1967.

Carl Kauffman, Vietnam, 1966. Killed in a motorcycle accident, Singapore, September 16, 1967.

to meet these needs and how to prepare for a possible draft.

Finally a pastor suggested, "Perhaps we shouldn't wait until the government is breathing down our neck; let's do something before we are obligated to."

That got through to me. The thought of giving before obligation forced me to was intriguing. That, along with my father's deep appreciation for MCC assistance in the past, brought about a decision to do some kind of voluntary service work.

Later that spring of 1951, MCC set up a two-week regional orientation school at Goshen, Indiana. I attended, expecting to go on to work in a mental hospital. However, during orientation I was asked to consider Paraguay. Although I hadn't thought of or planned for overseas service, I called my parents. To my surprise, their enthusiasm matched mine.

Wilfred Unruh was fortunate. Parents of Paxmen serving overseas are not always supportive of a Pax work stint.

Prior to the road-building project, which began in 1953, several volunteers worked in Paraguay under Servicio Tecnico Inter-Americana Cooperacion Agricola, the Paraguayan counterpart of the U.S. Point Four program. Here they were engaged in a strong program of agriculture education and medicine. The first two volunteers from MCC worked in agricultural extension and farm development.

At that time also, Point Four was working heavily in a wheat program. Administrators were interested in having farm boys from North American wheat areas to help develop a commercial or mechanized wheat program in Paraguay.

Wilfred goes on to describe his work:

Three of us went down on September 1, 1951. For several months we worked at an experimental wheat

135

farm and learned some of the language and a bit about the culture.

Then in February 1952 we moved to a farm in Southern Paraguay. This was beautiful prairie country —unbroken sodland. The organization wanted to see what we could do in developing wheat production in this virgin territory.

The nearest town was San Patricio. The countryside was open grassland spotted with palm trees and some scrub trees. Scattered across the five hundred acres given to us for the wheatland development experiment were termite hills which became one of our chief hazards. They were simply clay mud dug up by ants or termites, heaped into mounds a foot or two in height, and sun-baked.

One of the men, working at night, hit a termite hill with a front wheel of the tractor and knocked some of his teeth out. These hardened mounds were solid and not easily broken down.

Housing was provided in a private home about ten miles from our project. Later, though, we built an A-frame at the project and hired a cook.

February 3, 1952. We were in the house-building business yesterday. It was still too wet to plow, so we built a shelter, using 12-foot sections of tin to make an inverted V type of structure. We ran a pole between two trees, laid the tin against the pole, and weighted it down. While we were building, it began to rain. We found it necessary very quickly to dig a trench around our tin tent to keep the water out. Seems we built it in a low spot where the rain usually washed down the hill. But it was the only site with good shade available. Once we get some beds I imagine we'll shack up here for workdays and go back to town on Sunday. Our house does need ends on it, though, to keep out the wind.

This was a good move. By this time four of us

were at work. At first we had one Farmall H. tractor, then later a second, both with two-bottom plows. If we were to meet our schedule, it became clear we'd have to work around the clock breaking ground and cultivating. Being nearby made this possible.

In addition, three Paraguayans and a technician responsible for them came to help us. We also had the use of a bulldozer for about a month to help uproot the larger trees.

Our first day was fascinating. The agricultural engineer with us took us to a certain point among the sagebrush in the great prairie and said, "Start off here, go over the hill and as far as the swamp." So we sighted along the peak of a mountain ridge in the distance, dropped the plow, and started off.

February 1, 1953. We had a busy week, strange to say. During the first days we plowed for wheat ground. We work in 6-7-hour shifts and get a lot done without anyone having to overwork himself. Then on Wednesday Lupe comes through and a surveyor comes out with him to fix the contour lines of our terraces. Being an exemplary outfit we try to do everything according to the books. So in this work here we will build terraces as a soil conservation technique showing what a typical farmer should try to do.

We first had all the surveying instruments brought out to us on one of Lupe's trips on the theory we could probably lay out the contour lines ourselves. We found out we were asking for more than we could take care of. In theory it seems easy to fix a level line along the side of a hill with the use of a transit, as a surveyor's telescope is called. However, one must drop this line several inches every 100 feet so as to provide some grade but not so much it washes or erodes the soil.

We got out in the field working with these instruments and setting a line along one hill when we began to realize that if we continued as we were we would end up way out at the other end of the field where we didn't want to go. The next day the same thing happened again in another field, so we just quit and told Lupe we didn't want to fool with it and that he had better have a surveyor do the job. This he did.

One of our biggest problems was supplies. There was some gas rationing but more serious than this were the gas drums coming to us half full of water. In addition to this, repair parts were not easily accessible. So when breakdowns occurred, we sometimes endured long waits.

We planted four varieties of wheat. Rainfall was fair. In spite of frost our first crop was quite good.

A high point in this experience was the harvest festival we had on the project in November. The government arranged an *asado* (outdoor barbecue) for the community. The Agricola agency and other government officials were present. The Minister of Agriculture came as well.

Since this was the first commercial wheat production in the country, everyone was elated. The officials were anxious also to show off this accomplishment of inter-country cooperation.

I remember we VS-ers felt a bit left out of some of the celebrations, especially after having done practically all the work. Nevertheless, the occasion marked a milestone of satisfaction in the success of the project and a foundational contribution to the country, *Wilfred wrote in his diary.*

February 1, 1953. This week my ego received a good boost when a colonist came to sell watermelons to us. I was the only *gringo* there at the time so I bought some. While making the sale he called me *el patron,* which means the owner or big boss.

February 8, 1953. There is a local superstition that one should never eat watermelon and then drink yerba tea cold. Such a combination would kill you by evening. Being boys we had to test it, so yesterday when everyone was around, we ate watermelon and drank plenty of cold yerba tea. Some were quite scared for us; to others, it didn't seem to matter. Anyway, we're still around today without even a stomachache.

I spent 18 months working at the wheat project. Then Servicio Tecnico Inter-Americana Cooperacion Agricola transferred me to their office in Asuncion to write reports on the total program. I lived at the Mennonite Central Committee center.

Living in the capital of Paraguay was interesting. There I became involved in the High German culture of the Mennonites in the city. After working hard to fit into the Spanish folk culture of a rural farm area, the adjustment was great. But I liked it.

August 10, 1953. I wish you could hear the sounds of town here on a summer night like tonight. It's like a circus of sounds. First of all, there is an old screeching narrow-gauge train leaving town. It sounds like those old wood-burners you see in a 1905 movie, which squeak instead of whistle and puff more than pull. Of course at nearly every corner there are several dogs fighting and barking; meanwhile auto horns blow incessantly. Driving in this town is *multi* different from driving at home. Here the law says that you are to honk at every corner, once when you're about 30 meters away, and again when you are about three meters from the corner. Luckily, that isn't observed very well or it would be nerve-racking. But they honk at every corner at least once. These new cars are mostly equipped with country horns that blast like a factory whistle and scare you out of two hours' growth. When the traffic slows down around 9:00 p.m., the roosters begin their early evening serenade which is repeated at any hour after midnight.

November 1, 1952. The roast coffee smell . . . was

139

one of my first memories of Asuncion. That and the special fragrance of orange blossoms, tropical wood smoke, and black tobacco cigarettes. . . . Each is memorable in itself; the combination is never to be forgotten, its memory like a nostalgic reminder of the city.

One of my last jobs before leaving was to operate the radio for an air-taxi service. This involved arranging passenger and baggage loads—incoming and outgoing—for a Beech Bonanza aircraft. Much of this work was with people who hadn't been in to "civilization" for ten or fifteen years or even longer. It was a fascinating way to end my service, *Wilfred writes in his last entry.*

In this year of 1953 also, Mennonite Central Committee began participation on a road-building project. A private North American construction firm was engaged to build part of the road and the Paraguayan government through U.S. Technical Assistance built the remainder of this Trans-Chaco Road stretching from the capital city of Asuncion to Filadelfia, one of the Mennonite colonies settled by refugees from Europe.

Paxmen operated heavy road-building machinery in the initial stages of the program. Later they spent most of their time instructing Paraguayan counterparts in both operation and repair. Most of this instruction had to be given in Guarani, so interpreters were on the scene constantly.

The Pax day started at 5:00 a.m., with one shift working until noon. Second shift worked until 7:00 p.m. Government surveyors staked the road and marked grades. Paxmen took over from there and were fully responsible for much of the remaining work, including the supervision of Paraguayan workers.

The completion of the road marked the beginning of a new era in transportation and trade for the Mennonite colonies, as well as other villages along the route. Transportation costs dropped from 9 centesimos per kilo air freight and 5 centesimos per kilo riverboat to 2 centesimos per kilo by truck. Although at completion the road was not yet all-weather, constant improvements are being made.

Wilfred summarizes his experience:

I came home in 1953, after two and one half years of service. It was clear that Pax service had changed my earlier plans to farm. Instead I went back to school.

Coming back to the American scene was rough. I had a lot of hostilities. So much in the country and even at college seemed to be irrelevant to the needs of the world. I graduated from college in 1957.

Pax changed my life. Even though I had one year of college before leaving, I was a pretty naive, provincial guy. Although I rebelled against some elements in it, I was still very much a part of the Goessel community. When I left and started service, I suddenly became aware that world culture did not find its center in Goessel. And more, that many world needs were much more urgent than the needs we felt in Goessel.

I'm not sure I accomplished overseas what I left to do. My hope had been to work in peace, to be part of a reconciling ministry. Whether we did this, except in a limited way in personal relationships, I don't know. Of course, we did help in food production; this was significant.

We faced one conflict on the job that was difficult to resolve. Our monthly allowance was $10 and we received full maintenance. To us this represented sacrifice, although not necessarily hardship. However, to the Paraguayan worker who received no more or even less and was forced to cover his and his family's living needs, this seemed like pretty good pay with no sacrifice.

I'm really biased about Pax. It's a tremendous program, one of the few, perhaps, in which the Mennonite Church has been truly creative. I know we were pushed by the draft. Even so, it represents a very significant approach.

Many Pax boys came from Mennonite homes where they were taught to work hard. Then overseas we were given responsibilities that made tough demands on us. Pax matured us. And I suspect we 19- and 20-year-old fellows did as good a job representing our faith as more experienced adults might have done.

Pax taught me the importance of people as opposed to things. What happens to people in a situation is a primary concern—how they can discover themselves, as well as useful purpose in life.

Pax started a whole train of questions. In fact, it has helped to produce a questioning attitude. For example, I wonder now about this idea of sacrifice. Sacrificial service is probably a misnomer. The person who serves isn't sacrificing. He is having an exhilarating experience, giving himself, learning, looking, relating to people, being challenged, growing. He becomes rich through his experiences. We shouldn't speak about sacrifice in the context of service.

Another thing I'm puzzled about. Pax and the idea of helping to reconcile introduced the puzzle. Does reconciling mean only being some kind of a benevolent referee. Or does the church choose sides—like Christ? Didn't He choose sides—the side of the afflicted and the poor?

I wonder, as people of Pax, don't we also choose sides, find ways to use the resources or power at our disposal to help the afflicted, to change the reasons for their affliction as much as we can?

Pax service put me on a long road. But interesting. A road on which I see unselfish sharing as the essential element. One on which I see Christ as having already walked.

I am more than ever convinced that at the heart of the Christian faith is the *self-giving* process. In this pattern you don't always look for a tangible result or return.

We talk to each other in different languages. Some are verbal and others are action-oriented. But whichever language we use and are adept in, our job is to share our faith.

This Pax enabled us to do.

WEST PAKISTAN

Arnold Harder

"Look, they're working!" was a familiar cry from the crowd that gathered to watch Marcus Lauver and me unload the land-leveling machinery from a railroad car. It was quickly apparent that the people in this locality had never seen Westerners engaged in physical labor.

There was plenty of that for the two men before their equipment was on the ground ready for use.

Two reconditioned John Deere tractors (Model A 45), two dozer blades fabricated to mount on the tractors, one tumblebug (a slip-scraper dirt mover pulled back of a tractor), one four-wheel wagon chassis, and one four-wheel drive jeep station wagon comprised the moving equipment list. There was also one set of mechanic's tools.

The machinery had been shipped in large crates, and loaded from the ship hold on to a semi-boxcar with sides six feet high. No large motor crane was available to lift the boxes out.

"We really worked," said Arnold. "A local government agency lent us a hand-cranked crane. We pulled the boxes apart and disassembled the machinery into smaller pieces to get it out of the boxcar; then put it back together on the ground."

Chak 36 was a long way from Waverly, Iowa, where the men had spent a week in equipment orientation. The equipment they used was purchased by Church World Service. It was acquired by a businessman from Waverly whose project known as "Self-Help" provides reconditioned machinery to destitute areas overseas.

A week in Akron and 36 days on board ship brought them to the capital of West Pakistan.

144

The men arrived in Karachi on March 9 "without loss from pocket or mouth," as one of the men put it. The trip by jeep from Karachi to Quaidabad was uneventful except for one flat tire.

That trip was made after a week in port clearing customs and completing police registrations.

Arnold started talking about the beginning of their service:

Quaidabad was our post office, but we were actually stationed at Chak 36, 16 miles away—13 miles of hard-surface road and three miles of sand.

Our jeep was converted on the 900-mile trip from Karachi to Lahore. It started out as a six-cylinder vehicle but along the way a rod went out so we just pulled the corresponding spark plug wire. From then on we drove a five-cylinder jeep.

The father of our land-leveling project, Friedrick Peter, lived in Lahore. He was connected with TSA, Technical Service Association, a Swiss-Canadian organization which carried out soil reclamation projects, provided a well-drilling service, assisted in poultry development with a line of Hy-line hybrid chicks, and also administered a needlework program with items being exported for sale in England, Canada, and other countries.

Actually, however, we worked directly under the land-leveling Sub-Committee of the Economic Development Committee which was responsible to the West Parkistan Christian Council. This council, working with Church World Service, was geared to help in the economic uplift of the Christian community, although this particular project was not limited to Christians in the area where we served. I was pleased about that, *Arnold said.*

The year and a half Arnold spent working with his

father on the farm was valuable experience. Yet not very much in Mountain Lake, Minnesota, prepared him for life with Pakistanis.

Mountain Lake had been home for Arnold. Except for one year at Freeman College, Freeman, South Dakota, his world was bounded largely by the limits of the Mennonite community where he was born on September 22, 1937, and where he attended school. Yet his vision for service and his commitment to principles which dictated that service grew from the provincial soil of his childhood and his church.

Arnold went on:

I had fully decided to go into the Army to serve my country. Then Pax captured my attention. I saw in the Pax program something that went beyond a draft escape. Its objectives matched mine. Its program provided a structure within which I could respond to my motivations to sacrifice and worthwhile service.

So, instead of enlisting in the Army, I applied for Pax.

And my Pax assignment took me to Quaidabad and Chak 36.

We arrived at our post on April 1, 1960. But because of foreign-exchange problems the government did not release the machinery until late summer. From April to June we did construction work and some surveying. In July we traveled to Muree, the hill station where missionaries spend the hot season, and enrolled in a course of language study.

I picked up the basics of Urdu, a camp language somewhere between Hindi and Persian. Punjabi was a regional dialect but Urdu was the national language so my 400-word vocabulary got me around.

By mid-September the equipment had arrived and was ready to be unloaded.

Our work locations were at Chak 36, 37, and 38.

These were simply numbered designations related to the elaborate and excellent canal system the British had laid out. The numbers identified nearby villages.

Water from the canals was usable for irrigation but a great deal of land was not level enough to make irrigation practicable.

In short, this was our job.

The region was semiarid. However, with irrigation crops were possible.

In sandy areas we insisted on grass crops to hold the soil in place. Elsewhere, cotton and sugar were raised on irrigable land. Also there were some vegetables and a high-protein legume which looked like a cross between a pea and a soybean. Wheat and other grains were raised on nonirrigable land.

The main canal was 125 miles long, with many different intricately arranged branches. It represented a tremendous engineering accomplishment. Irrigation was carried out with a gravity-flow system using inundation techniques.

Apart from grain crops which were planted after the heavy October rain and harvested the next April, the area could not have been productive. Annual rainfall totaled 1 1/2 inches.

The soil itself was sandy with some silt in it; quite productive after a few years of cultivation.

The three villages in the Tahl Desert in which we began our project were being served by three different Protestant groups: Anglican, United Presbyterian, and Salvation Army. We worked with these groups to help the farmers who had moved into these areas to settle the land after partition. Each plot of land totaled about 15 acres, a figure somewhat above the national average.

At the beginning of the project we charged for our work by the acre, then shifted to an eight annah per hour rate. Still later, when bigger equipment was used, the charge went to six rupees per hour.

The money was always paid in advance. The men worked up to the limit of hours paid for. Farmers trusted the Paxers implicitly—they never asked for receipts.

In fact, the reception from villagers was excellent. We were received graciously and there were no signs of hostility. The project was popular and widely known. On the basis of the Pax reputation for good work honestly done, landlords from villages more than 100 miles away came to invite them to level land in their areas. Other land-leveling facilities were available but the Pax program was marked by freedom from corruption and bribes. Consequently, the demand for their services was great.

Generally, villagers understood our program to be Christian rather than American. The acceptance of work by Christians in a Muslim country was significant, we felt.

Diet in the area is simple. Wheat is ground to make a flat unleavened bread called *chappati*. A highly spiced curry sauce made with lentils is eaten with rice. Sometimes vegetables or potatoes are used and occasionally mutton.

Pulao, another tasty Pakistani dish, contains rice, a little meat, and the ever-present spices.

We ate American- and Pakistani-style, especially after our palates became accustomed to the "hot" food.

One morning, after moving to a new project location, we sat down to breakfast. It was a cold morning— about 40 degrees Fahrenheit—and very damp. An all-night drizzle had chilled us through and we sat shivering. But not for long.

The breakfast was standard—curry and *chappati*. But the spicing was extraordinary, in spite of the fact that we thought we were accustomed to "hot" foods. After the first few bites little beads of perspiration began to

148

appear on our foreheads. By the time our meal was finished we were both sweating profusely.

Our work at Chak 36 continued until May. By that time 125 degrees Fahrenheit in the shade was common so we left for Gujranwala, to help in a technical school run by the United Presbyterians. Classes were held and practice provided in shoemaking, carpentry, locksmithing, forging, diecasting, motor mechanics, and machine shop.

There our main responsibility was maintenance of the motor vehicles. We were in charge of the motor shop, did some instructing and some supervision of about 50 students.

Our workday at the Christian technical school began at 6:00 a.m. and ran to noon. Then we had a long siesta and went back to work again at 4:30 until dusk.

Early in September 1961 we went back to the desert. Also that month we purchased an English Fordson Major diesel with blade. This 50-horsepower tractor was twice as large as the other tractors, so our work was speeded up considerably.

The next eight months were filled with more of the same—land-leveling. The summer of 1962 Marcus and I comanaged a summer camp program for Christian and Muslim boys between the ages of 8 and 16. Then in August our Sub-Committee decided we should move to Chak 75 A & B and 85.

So we loaded up the jeep and our flat-bed wagon and moved.

At the new location we started from scratch again. Our home was a tent. Our diet was limited. And our community relations had to be built from the ground up.

Of course, that was our job—leveling the ground so irrigation could be carried out.

Our reception here was excellent, even better than in the first location.

After our replacement by other Paxmen, the work

pattern was changed somewhat. The unit became mobile. A house trailer, fuel trailer, and tool trailer made it possible to move quickly and more frequently, serving a wider area and maintaining base closer to the work area. Two new larger John Deere tractors also came into use.

The Pax presence in these desert Pakistani communities involved a mutual learning experience. Perhaps the point at which our cultures clashed most directly was the concept of time. The American hurry-up-and-get-things-done attitude didn't mesh very well with the Pakistani there's-all-the-time-in-the-world-so-let's-take-our-time attitude.

It was good to learn from the Pakistanis. The experience changed me in many ways. Essentially, I grew up.

My Christian faith was strengthened also. Coming into contact with Islam and Buddhism made me appreciate my own spiritual heritage a great deal more.

Pax was good for me. It can be good for anyone who meets the requirements of adaptability, physical health, conviction (that what you're doing is valid), and a strong and growing involvement in the Christian way of life.

It could be very difficult, though, if these elements are missing.

Pax has given my life direction. The overseas experience has clarified my philosophy; I know now that I must give myself to help individuals in some way. And it provided for me an intensely fulfilling experience which has blueprinted a pattern for living and relationship with people I shall never forget, *Arnold concluded*.

Total acreage leveled in the Pakistan land-leveling project has not been phenomenal. In the first location, almost 150 acres were brought into production. Later locations have varied in number of acres, some more and others less. Of course, it is difficult to measure the physical well-being of people whose food supply, perhaps for the first time, has approached a level of adequacy.

However, as great or small as may have been the direct benefit resulting from the land-leveling project, the real benefit in the words of one Paxman was setting up and proving the idea "that the Christian's faith includes a practical concern for the everyday needs of man." In this the project has been and is eminently successful.

ALGERIA

Emory Yoder

In an Amish farm home near Hutchinson, Kansas, Emory Yoder was born on February 26, 1938. Less than 17 years later a people, struggling into nationhood, began to do battle with their colonial benefactors. In November 1954 the war in Algeria erupted and quickly shredded the uneasy truce which had existed between the French and the Arabs fighting for their right to self-rule. For seven years, deceit and treachery and flowing blood marked the land and its people with scars which still remain.

The Amish community was as far removed from the NLF drive for Algerian independence as the seventeenth century is from the twentieth. But in the scheme of things, out of this peace-loving background came a young man to serve his country by working toward peace, part of a task force which saw its mission in the needs of a wounded population.

Actually the Mennonite Church first moved into Algeria shortly after the devastating earthquake which struck in August 1954 destroying hundreds of homes in west central Algeria.

Early emergency relief was provided first. In May 1955 a small construction unit was established, sponsored jointly by French and United States Mennonites. MCC Pax supplied personnel initially from its European program. Late in 1955 the unit settled at Flatters where it worked until early 1959 when military pressure in the neighborhood forced its discontinuance.

The earthquakes brought into being the initial motivation to attempt meeting needs in Algeria. But very soon war was adding its victims to the earlier desolation and from that year to this the Mennonite Central

Committee has found in Algeria needs of every description and has tried to serve "in the name of Christ."

Paxmen have been part of the team from the beginning—a team composed of missionaries, teachers, nurses, doctors, agricultural experts, technicians, and others.

A conscientious objector to war, Emory came as a Paxman to add his contribution to the struggle for peace. His father was a farmer. During and following eight years of elementary school, Emory worked on the farm helping his father. Typically, he also enjoyed construction work.

Emory talked briefly of his lack of training:

My educational background was scant when I went into service. No high school or college. I probably could have contributed more had I received more education. And likely I'd have gotten more out of the experience. But frankly, this didn't seem to hamper me too much. My background was intensely practical and the situations I found myself in called for more practical background than theory. So I'd have to say I didn't really feel cheated then, even though I have gone back to school since.

Emory's academic trail following Pax service has led him from colleges in Kansas and Virginia to Strasbourg University in France, as well as on to graduate work. But by his own admission he might not have found this trail had it not been for the challenge to service he discovered in Pax.

I'm not altogether certain why I chose Pax. Of course, I had no question about entering alternative service of some kind. But about Pax; I'm not sure. I think, at the time I reacted a bit against doing what every other I-W did, fitting into the same pattern.

Another thing. I seemed to be meeting a number of

153

CO's who were taking care of their two years in rather plush circumstances; you know, close to home, cars, good salary. I reacted against that.

So I chose Pax and was finally accepted for service in Algeria. My family and congregation had a good attitude. They supported my decision.

I went in January 1960, stayed in until March 1962, a little over two years. It was a good period in my life, *Emory says.*

Before Emory arrived Paxmen had worked in a variety of situations—milk distribution, general relief, house construction, roofing projects. They were well liked. Many mission agencies asked for Pax assistance. One missionary said, "These Paxmen in one or two years have been able to get closer to the people than we have in twenty."

The earliest major construction project was carried out at Flatters. Thirty small block houses were built.

By 1957 the political atmosphere was extremely tense. Paxmen were caught in the middle and some felt they were being compromised. Since the army was in charge of the country, technically, the Paxmen built houses under army direction and protection. At the same time, they tried to relate to the Arab nationals. Out of these friendly relations grew the suspicion that Paxmen were supporting rebels with medical supplies. Consequently, there were pressures to disband the program and expel the Paxmen from the country. This pressure did force the withdrawal of a Swiss nurse working with needy Arabs but the Paxers were able to continue their rebuilding efforts.

Building was often sporadic. Materials were hard to find. Planning new projects was difficult. At one point the men thought they would be building houses near El-Biar. But this developed too slowly. So Sanford Kauffman and Emory went to Constantine where they worked in a boys' home. The work there was worthwhile but led to some frustration since they had come for construction. They stayed at the boys' home for almost a year—building became practically impossible.

Later Emory and Sanford went to Medea where the main project involved working in a regroupment village. (During the Algerian war, people were often forcibly removed from their communities and brought to regroupment centers in order to clear land for military purposes.) There the men helped to insulate the roofs of houses for the more needy in the village.

For a while they worked in an agricultural project. They helped provide water for irrigation purposes. In the same village they helped at a kindergarten center for children with tuberculosis or children of parents with tuberculosis. They also did some construction and landscaping. Of course, there were often pressing relief needs so they helped in distribution projects as well.

Emory says it was here he really got thrown into the French context and had to use the language. Getting next to the people, learning to know them, was good. In retrospect, he feels that this was certainly the richest part of his experience.

Emory was involved also in moving several volunteers to Belkitane, a village in eastern Algeria. The experience of moving is hardly worth noting. And the size of the unit could barely justify putting Belkitane on the map. But the Paxmen working here during the early 1960's made such significant contributions in their small agricultural projects that Algerian authorities encouraged the establishment of a major effort.

Out of this grew the community development and agricultural extension program later established at Henchir Toumghani.

Emory told me of his visit to Belkitane:

The end of light came quickly. It had been a tiring but satisfying day for the four of us gathered around the low, typically Arab table. There was Dick, a Paxer who had spent a good deal of time in the village facing the frustration of trying to communicate with people whose language he was just beginning to learn. Annette and Yta were Europeans who had arrived just that afternoon. I had come with them to help them move in.

Supper was over. We were having evening devotions.

Just as we were thanking God for having kept Dick in a very uncertain situation and for bringing us there safely, the clatter of submachine-gun fire shattered the quiet. Someone quickly blew out the kerosene lamp. We sat in the dark and waited until the shooting stopped and our own fears subsided.

Then we continued our prayer of thanksgiving. Devotions turned out to be very meaningful that evening. God seemed to be near. But pressing just as near were the needs of this village and the country we were praying for.

We were never allowed to forget that the country was at war. Of course, that fact didn't matter—we Paxmen had a job to do. This didn't eliminate, though, the clammy fear that crawled into the pit of our stomachs when we faced danger or realized we had just escaped death.

The last three months in Algeria I spent in a little village called Yasshir, located in west central Algeria. Widows of war victims lived there. Our job was to build houses.

Several other Pax fellows had been there before. They reported the situation in this pro-French nest was anything but ideal. The day we traveled out was no exception.

The old jeep was loaded down with supplies and with five Paxmen anxious to get to work. The last lap of the trip was through a mountainous area. No "law-abiding citizen" was permitted to pass without the protection of a military convoy. The area was "infested" with NLF troops.

The trip through the lovely Algerian *djebel* made one almost forget the imminent danger of a skirmish with the rebels.

About an hour before arrival at our destination, the Pax jeep and one other were given permission to take a shortcut which had not been used for some time. Both jeeps soon arrived at the village. We were invited to eat at the army camp the first night and were just ready to sit down at the table when the convoy pulled in. The grim look on the fellows' faces as they walked up to the barracks told part of the story. The terrorists had ambushed the convoy and five men were missing.

It's hard to put one's feelings into words at a time like that. Most of them are unexpressed. But one thing I remember—an overwhelming sense of God's direction and help.

In a wartime economy the CO is caught; he finds it very difficult to be objective or better yet, neutral. He tends to identify with one side or the other. Should I have suspended my feelings when my friends Mahoud and Mohammed, who ran a body shop, showed me their burns inflicted in torture after being rounded up as rebel suspects? Should I have hardened myself against sympathy when Mohammed, his eyes glistening with tears, told of how he was forced to watch his brother's execution? Is there a way to steel oneself against reaction when one hears the Moslem view of Christians? The only ones they have known have been representatives of tyranny and brutality!

I don't know. . . . I do know this. These experiences helped me to face reality better. I had gone into service with a flush of high idealism. I left service, not cynical, but with realistic views and convinced I must someday go back to this country and help work through the problems. It was hard not to become involved, especially when it was so obvious that even our inadequate efforts were of tremendous help.

The important thing was not the houses we built or the things we gave to people. Rather, it was our attempt to see things through their eyes, living with them, identifying with them.

My experience in Pax has revolutionized my theories about the way missionaries should work. I don't think there is a way to help people very much, short of total involvement.

The person who really wants to help must become involved in the struggles of the country searching for national identity, *Emory said thoughtfully.*

Emory extended his term three months, to March of 1962. Shortly after he left, in July 1962, the country gained its independence. But not without great cost. That cost is still being reckoned with.

The Mennonite Central Committee still works in Algeria, although no longer as an independent agency. During the course of the war, a number of relief and humanitarian agencies working in the country met in Geneva to lay the groundwork and make plans for a united postwar effort in Algeria. Out of this the Christian Committee for Service in Algeria was formed. CCSA, with headquarters in Geneva, is composed of 17 member organizations which work together in meeting needs in the country.

It is under CCSA that the farm project at Henchir Toumghani developed.

Emory concluded with deep feeling:

Algeria has been good to me. The country has given me a lot. I'm grateful. The experiences I had there have sharpened my philosophy of life. I no longer feel my life is my own. From a Christian point of view I owe my life to someone else. My aim is to do what I

158

can to give to other people what has been valuable to me, especially my Christian faith.

I can do this most graphically, I think, where the problems are greatest and the needs most pressing.

Camus wrote, "Man must make a real effort to reunite." I'd like to say that we must make neighbors. We won't accomplish that with things or by doing. It will be by dialogue—being with people.

One more thing. I'm still a CO. But in the situations I went through I really had to put my belief in the nonresistant position on the scales. Could I really love while I was being tortured, or if I saw a relative being murdered before my eyes? I don't know. That's a bridge I haven't crossed yet.

I do know this, however. Killing the other fellow wouldn't solve anything for me. And more than that, to really love in the face of all kinds of provocation requires a kind of commitment which goes beyond, far beyond, the blind unthinking reaction of force against force.

That's the kind of love I'd like to have.

Gary Mullet—Henchir Toumghani

Now, ladies and gentlemen, you've heard the story on the mare. She's a five-year-old daughter of "Society Rex" and heavy in foal to the great "Colonel Boyle."

All right, sir, what you gonna give me for her? Start'er right along here at two thousand, one thousand, five hundred dollars, will you do it?

A three-hundred-dollar bill I got, now four, who'll make it four? Four, four, wanta make it four? Four hundred dollar, sir?

Four-hundred-dollar bill, I got. Now five, five, five hundred dollar, at five hundred dollar, do you want her, sir? Five hundred dollar, wanta billy boma six, six hundred dollar, and here we go.

Six hundred dollar, bid her now. I've got my six and wanta seven hundred dollar, sir.

You're out, sir, got six over here, want seven from you, do you want her now at seven hundred?

And I've got your seven, who'll make it eight, pen her in at night and shut the gate. I got my eight and wanta make it nine. Do you want her, sir, billy boma nine, nine hundred dollar, give me nine. And here we go.

One thousand dollars, that's the way to do it, that's the way to buy her, at one thousand dollars; you'll want her in a week. Give me one thousand dollars and knock her in the creek.

Got it! Now eleven hundred and a wanta billy boma eleven, a one and one, eleven hundred dollar, sir. Eleven hundred dollar, are you done? Eleven hundred dollar, do you want her, do you like her, and here we go.

Now isn't she gonna look cheap in a few weeks with a Colonel Boyle foal by her side. We're not kidding anyone but ourselves. Here is a good going mare that has already produced. She's bred in the blue, and carrying her own guarantee.

Eleven hundred dollars. Got it now. Eleven-hundred-dollar bill and twelve, do you want her, sir? Billy boma twelve, twelve, twelve, twelve hundred dollar, sir.

At twelve hundred, now at the twelve. And thirteen hundred, do you want her? Do you like her? And here we go. I'm going to sell her now, right now, if you're done at twelve.

Thirteen hundred dollars. Do you want her? At thirteen? Twelve hundred, I have, twelve hundred, I will.

Twelve hundred I have and I will and here we go, yes or no, do you want her, sir? At thirteen hundred or no, and I . . . have . . . SOLD the horse at twelve hundred dollars.

Gary came early to his love of horses. With his father, a livestock dealer in Kalona, Iowa, and brother, he lived in a world of Hackney ponies. Raising and showing them grew into a way of life. Neither books nor teachers at Iowa Mennonite School changed his mind. After high school graduation in 1962 he found a door that opened still wider opportunities to work in his chosen field. He enrolled and was graduated from the Iowa School of Auctioneering in Ames, Iowa. Later he was asked by his alma mater to teach in the four two-week auctioneering courses held each year.

His goal—to become a national horse auctioneer—began rapidly to come into closer view. Gary sold horses in auctions in Kansas, Missouri, Ohio, Illinois, and Iowa. Although only 23 he was asked to manage the Hackney horse sale in Illinois. The childhood and adolescent interest, his love for Hackney ponies, opened up a whole horizon of possibilities. He was on the way.

Of course, his Selective Service obligation shadowed future plans. That he would serve his country through some form of alternative service did not seem to be a question. But where and how was not so easily answered. During his freshman and sophomore years in high school he met returning Paxmen and listened to their reports. The challenge intrigued him. From several opportunities—Algeria, Congo, Vietnam—he selected Algeria.

"It wasn't easy to leave for orientation at Akron— to leave the ponies and auctioneering. But I knew that service was a part of life and I wanted to go."

Gary went on. "Europe was rough. I wasn't happy about studying French. My assignment in Algeria was unclear. I was homesick for ponies and for my parents. Even when I first arrived at Henchir Toumghani things weren't much better."

Algeria is divided into departments. The administrative center of each department is called a prefecture.

161

Each department or region is divided up into arrondissements, each with its own center—a subprefecture. Each is divided into communes with the administrative center called Mairie (city hall). Even the communes (like townships) are broken up into ententes or subcommunes. Henchir Toumghani, formerly a commune, is now only a subsection or entente, part of the commune called Ain Fakroun, in the arrondissement of Ain M'Lila, in the prefecture of Constantine.

"The farm," formerly an old French military establishment, complete with tower, sentry posts, heavy stone and concrete walls, lies in beautiful country. But the homesick auctioneer from Iowa missed much of this in his first weeks.

Flat and level, the excellent though narrow road from Ain Fakroun passes large fields of potatoes: girls, boys, sometimes whole families, are digging and picking up potatoes. Scattered herds of sheep and goats graze on scant weeds along the roadside. Little clusters of huts—straw-roofed, mud-brick walls, some opening into courtyards—dot the open fields here and there. Elsewhere, ruins of French farms stand as mute evidence of a disastrous war that ravaged the countryside—roofs all gone, lonely walls thrust upward through piles of farmyard rubble.

In the distance, the horizon reflects the gaping uncertainties of a country left broken by war. Uneven black outline with rough humps peaked upward reach into the wispy clouds against an amber pink haze merging softly into timid lavender. Flat, flat, flat, broken humps.

Gary looked off into the late day as he approached the farm in a French Trois Chevaux, one of De Gaulle's "luxury specials" known more familiarly by Paxmen as the "ugly duckling" or simply "puddle hopper." Starkly etched against the jagged background he saw "the farm" come into view—water tower straight ahead, cluster of trees to the left, a wall broken at spots, large buildings within the wall, and off to the right a clutch of buildings that represented the postwar resettlement or regroupment village called Henchir Toumghani.

This was to be his home and place of service—chosen, yet thrust upon him.

Pax came to Henchir Toumghani in the fall of 1962. Since then, "the farm" has been home to Paxmen and matrons, nurses and teachers. Jean Carbonare, a CIMADE worker who later became a senior CCSA worker especially in connection with the reforestation program, visited the area and thought the old military site would have some value for a school or agricultural project at Henchir Toumghani.

Originally it was hoped the program could serve the neighbors, private farmers who were poor, especially in the fields of mechanics and literacy. This has changed somewhat and even though the farmers here are still being served, the Paxmen have been paying more attention to a higher level of literate persons spread over a wider area.

Henchir Toumghani—about 22 acres of land and buildings—was turned over by regional Algerian authorities to Mennonite Central Committee and CCSA, the Christian Committee for Service in Algeria. MCC works closely with CCSA as a participating group. The purpose envisioned for this farm was a training center for Algerian young men.

Vern Preheim, who served in Algeria as MCC director from September 1960 to November 1962, writes: "During the war MCC cooperated with CIMADE, a French relief organization. In addition to massive relief work we established a small community development team in a village called Belkitane located about 70 miles southeast of Henchir Toumghani. This team included two Paxmen working on limited agricultural projects. The Algerian authorities were so impressed with this project, even though its accomplishments were very small, that they began talking to us (MCC-CIMADE), even before independence, about the possibility of forming a larger training center where Algerian young men could work side by side with Paxmen from North America and thereby learn from them the basic skills and knowledge which they have about agriculture. This dream then was conceived early in the spring of 1962 when the independence of Algeria seemed imminent."

From that first dream there has flowered a program which calls for much of Gary's time in the farm office.

"What is your work, Gary? Do you have a title of some kind?" I asked.

He smiled that slow smile. "That's hard to say. I'm not sure what I am, whether my title would fit. I do the purchasing—market items and project needs. I take care of the office and do the accounting. Every Monday and Thursday I have an English class with the boys in the mechanics' school; that's so they can read parts manuals. Hodgepodge, isn't it?"

I nodded. Then he went on. "And I've been doing some veterinarian work. This spring [June 1966] I did a vaccination program on horses against an African horse disease carried by a fly. The Algerian government provided the serum."

"Do you like that work?"

"I enjoy working around horses. But I wasn't trained for this. It's hard when you have just bits and pieces of knowledge. But that's more than is available if we wouldn't be here; so I try."

Gary's work in the office keeps him close to every phase of the operation. Along with that he serves as one member of a four-person administrative committee. The agricultural director, John Rohrer, is chairman and functions practically as the executive officer of the total program.

The original intent was agriculture. This purpose developed into various projects: cattle, poultry, rabbits, field crops, gardens. Very early, a mechanics' school grew to prominence. And to meet other community needs, both a medical service and elementary school came into being.

Cattle—Five cows and one bull were imported from Holland. These were intended as foundation stock to aid in the improvement of local cattle and to provide a practical context in which to carry out a training experience for local farmers.

Two men are selected to work with the cattle on the farm. They work eight hours a day and a 5 1/2-day week. For wages they receive one third of the normal level in that area plus two meals a day. They are taught cow care, how to make trench silos, proper feeding, and crop management. They are helped to plant alfalfa and corn on their own land.

At the end of the six-month period each man is given one cow with the understanding he must fulfill certain requirements. The original application for participation presupposes a well—ample water supply. Before the cow is taken home a cow shed must be built. Some guarantees must be given that forage and silage are available. And the first female calf is returned to the farm.

In spite of the fact that one cow can make enough money to support ten people, even after the feed is paid for, the program has had uneven success. Water supply has been a problem and year-round feed management has also caused difficulties. Theoretically, a cow may be repossessed if she is not being treated or fed properly, but in practice this has never been done. Of the men who have had cows placed with them, about 40 percent are doing an excellent job, about 25 percent are "passing," and the remainder leave some doubt.

Artificial insemination has played a large part in herd improvement, as well. Two bulls were kept on the farm. As many as five cows were being bred each week.

Poultry—The poultry project has developed similarly within self-help and demonstration patterns. From a waiting list of interested local farmers, one is selected for a three-month training period. Under supervision he works in the farm's poultry program, earning 100 dinars per month. At the end of the period he also receives 100 four-week-old chicks, as well as sufficient feed for an additional ten weeks, provided that he has adequate housing available.

Farm poultry stock consists of pure Cornish, pure Sussex, and pure Leghorn, plus a Sussex hen cross with a Cornish cock. These flocks provide eggs for the hatchery and in turn stock for the demonstration and self-help programs. Chicks are also sold at about half of normal retail value, or roughly at cost.

One of the significant aspects of the work with poultry has been the six-day short courses. Principles of poultry management were taught, diseases discussed, feed medication demonstrated, and equipment shown and built. The short course offers a situation in which interest and skills can be evaluated and to those who show exceptional promise, special assistance can be given.

The overt success of this program is reflected simply but tellingly in the fact that "graduates" are selling hatching eggs to the hatchery. In addition, of course, there is a contribution to the economic welfare of families and an improvement in diet.

Out of the work to date it is hoped that a poultry serviceman contact plan can develop with careful and regular follow-up provided for those who have worked on the farm or have been enrolled in a poultry short course.

Rabbits—The rabbit chain program aims its benefits at boys. After careful screening boys are selected who can care adequately for the stock. Each boy receives a bred doe of Flemish Giant variety and later returns two of the offspring. Foundation stock is kept at the farm in demonstration cement hutches.

Field crops—Field crops relate closely to the work with livestock. Their importance for farm feed and demonstration purposes is primary. Secondarily, they offer a context for experimental efforts with irrigation, fertilizer, and grains or legumes of varieties not known in the area. The soil is a fertile silt-loam which grows small grains well without irrigation or fertilizer, but responds rewardingly to both for vegetables, corn, potatoes, and other crops.

Alfalfa is ideally suited to this area. With irrigation there can be six or seven annual cuttings. Wheat, barley, and corn can be grown successfully. Potatoes are a main cash crop with two crops possible each year—the first in April and the second in July.

Gardens—This project centered around children 12-14, with a few older. Twenty girls and fifty boys participated in the program from April through September. Tools are provided and twice-weekly classes are held at which times each student cares for his own plot. Perhaps one of the greatest benefits has been the cooperation learned waiting for irrigation water.

Carrots, turnips, squash, tomatoes, and hot peppers are local staples. Peas, beans, and lettuce are being added.

Medical—"You shouldn't overlook the medical program here," said Gary. "There are no Paxmen in it but we're really all part of the same team. Mary Leatherman is doing a fine job as nurse."

Daily patient load in the dispensary runs close to 100. Rounds of immunization for tetanus, diphtheria and whooping cough; prenatal care, postnatal in-

167

structions; common and not-so-common ailments—all of these the nurse handles alone except Fridays when a doctor visits, diagnoses, and prescribes. The adjustment to service beyond the bounds of professional nursing, such as shifting into patterns of diagnosis, was difficult. But the doctor's weekly availability lightens the load somewhat.

Mary understands the importance of the team approach. "All of us are spokes in a big wheel—none very important—yet all together extremely important."

Perhaps this illustrates most graphically one of the good reasons for "losing" Paxmen, distinctive as their contribution may be, in the total effort of service and reconciliation wherever there is need.

School—From the beginning of work at Henchir Toumghani, the classroom has constituted an important tool in service to people in the area. Although the initial seed idea dealt with some form of agricultural service, the need for a mechanics' school rooted itself early and firmly in the developing program and has been making a consistent contribution ever since.

Before classes opened, school leaders visited the mayors of three areas to arrange for tests to be given to prospective students. These were aptitude and interest tests administered alike to young men from poor and rich families. They come from an area within 70 kilometers of Henchir Toumghani.

Tuition is free. Dormitory space and meals are provided. Free transportation to school on Monday and home on Friday is made available where necessary.

Discipline is very strict. Any person not applying himself is replaced from a long waiting list. Free-time activities are their own responsibility since the fellows range in age from 18-26.

The curriculum is divided into a three-year program. Year one covers metalworking. Year two deals with principles of motor operation—diesel and gas, with both theory and extensive shop experience. Year three expands and refines the theory offered in the previous year and allows more time for practical work and problem solving. The senior year offers a full morning for shop. Afternoons are scheduled to cover English classes, driver education, and advanced theory.

One remaining problem is placement of graduates. Government agencies, farm garages, and city garages will absorb some. A few will go back to their farms again. But others will suffer because even though the need for trained mechanics in the country is great, there are not sufficient structures through which these needs can be channeled.

Nevertheless, the general school experience, the organized patterns of group living, the academic discipline, the exposure to another religious view—all add up to a contribution to persons that can help each graduate regardless of where or how he may serve.

"Working with these people hasn't always been easy," said Gary. "Their value systems are different, their culture is so far removed from ours. And part of our problem is communication. Some of us stopped in Belgium for language study—others studied when they arrived. But for our work here with an Arab population, French is not too useful."

John Rohrer writes in a summary report, "There are 8,900 people registered in the commune office at Henchir Toumghani. The people located here are Berbers and speak the Chaouia dialect among themselves. Many men know some Arabic, but the women seldom do. Some men can communicate well in French, especially those who worked on former French farms or have worked in France. But the majority know . . . little or no French."

This is a man's world. Rarely do women leave their houses, and then only veiled. Even on Wednesday, the busy market day, Ain Fakroun streets and shops and

169

market square were empty of women. Men stood and walked everywhere, dressed in the familiar *cashebihs* (hooded woolen garments with sleeves and arm slits) and turbaned heads. Coffeehouses were overflowing with raucous laughter and trading banter.

The market square—a large field at the edge of town—was filled with hurrying men. They crowded the muddy grass corridors formed by mounds of clothing piled on burlap, large displays of shoes, stands with mountains of oranges, tangerines, carrots, potatoes, red hot peppers in from the coast, stocks of water kegs and containers, whole grocery stores under tent or awning and hucksters hawking refreshments—sheep and goat intestines freshly roasted. Others, older men, stood with dignity observing the scene.

To the left noisy voices bargain for a dozen sheep. And beyond, in the area reserved for slaughter, newly purchased animals are led for killing. Here stands a goat, an Algerian Berber at its head. There is a flash of metal in the sun, and a quick slit in the throat. The man steadies the trembling goat a bit, then stretches out the body as it collapses.

When the bleeding has stopped, there is another quick slit in the right hind leg. The long reach of knife slips between hide and flesh on the leg—up toward the abdominal area. Then he puts his pursed lips to the tiny slit and blows—a tiny air bubble following up the leg, expanding, moving across the abdomen, enlarging, around the back and down the other three legs. Then he lifts the carcass and blows in more air until hide and carcass are free from each other, though the one is still enclosed in the other. He drops his large balloon in the shape of a bloated goat to the ground—the skinning process practically complete—and goes to the next.

Gary spoke reflectively:

Life here takes a bit of getting used to. But I don't know of any place I'd rather serve. This has been a great unit. A unit of fifteen seems just right for me; I'm glad I didn't end up some place alone.

I enjoy just being in the office, guys coming in; we talk about our work, how to improve, how to solve problems; I like this.

We work here pretty much as a team, more than as individuals. We pitch in and help each other. Tease each other too. You should see us at mealtime. *So I watched.*

The comradeship and banter is obvious. Small talk and important issues. Material matters and spiritual probings. Silence, sometimes, and hilarious laughter. Reports of work are shared. Plans are laid out for reactions. Concerns are passed around. Frustrations are expressed. Feelings are vented. And the teasing—in good humor—always the teasing.

The dining area is like home base within the large rambling structure. The complex of rooms seems to wander around the courtyard. But always the three tables stand at the center waiting for the "family" to gather around. Three meals or coffee and hot milk in midafternoon. *Hey, whose turn in the kitchen? And don't leave the table until matron Kay excuses you.* Scripture reading, a hymn, and prayer in the morning. Mail call once a week. *Did Kenneth George Beachy get any mail? Wow! I'll say he did!*

Behind these scenes of unit life is a dedicated matron. Laundry and ironing—square miles of it—baking and cooking—enough to fill 16,425 empty stomachs during the year—and always cleaning—acres of cleaning. Just being big sister or mother or aunt or friend to someone in the unit. Or providing the touch of home away from home—music in the background, special desserts, a timely smile, or an interested question. Or offering the wisdom of maturity to balance the enthusiasm of youth.

Gary went on:

Our unit is ideal. Of course, we have problems and differences, but each person seems to fit in well. This has been a tremendous experience in group life.

But I did have one disappointment. Too many returning Paxmen leave the impression there are only beds of roses in. Pax service. That isn't true. Sometimes I was discouraged by all the things that hit me. Of course, the discouragements taught me a great deal —learning to handle them has helped me. But I want to be realistic when I return home and tell the Pax story.

"Were these problems of adjustment partly culture shock, Gary?" I asked.

He answered:

I suppose so. Man, things were really different. Strange foods. A language barrier. Unfamiliar surroundings. Different patterns of living. Attitudes toward things and people I was unaccustomed to. Children out in the cold with hardly any clothes, runny noses, watery eyes, bodies shaking with cold. This was followed by frustration—how in the world can we help? —so much to do and seemingly so much apathy toward help.

Part of the problem also was adjusting to unit life; I had never lived in this kind of group before. And perhaps most difficult was not knowing what I would do. Now I realize it was better to let me find my own way through—but then it was rough.

I'm not at all upset by the fact that I had disappointments. They have been valuable. In fact, all the frustration of adjustment and the discouragements were not too high a price to pay for the fulfillment I experience now.

Since I'm here in service, I've often wondered what we are trying to do at home—raising ponies, being an auctioneer, running a sale barn. Why do we want to expand? I'm not sure all the reasons are good. If I'm an auctioneer to get a lot of sales to make a lot of money for its own sake—that's one thing. If I'm an auctioneer to get a lot of sales to meet a lot of people to help them as persons, to be a witness for Christ to them—that's another thing. Coming to that conclusion, I guess you'd call that spiritual growth.

Here I've learned to take time for people—to relate to them. This is important to me now. This can make any kind of legitimate work become important. Do you know, I suspect that's the biggest thing that's happened to me at Henchir Toumghani, beginning to understand that I serve Christ best by serving people.

That's what I want to do at home. I'll still be an auctioneer. Same kind of work, but I'll be doing it in a different way.

Dennis Bontrager—Camel's Neck

If the farm at Henchir Toumghani is located at "the end of the world," then Camel's Neck was pushed off the edge.

This is where, for two years, Dennis Bontrager served his country. And in that service gave himself to hinterland Berbers in an Arabic-French culture. Buffeted by a senseless war, embittered by the needless dying and family losses, despondent in the daily fearful struggle to patch together again a life worth living, these Al-

173

gerians constitute an almost forgotten residue of hapless persons bereft of purpose. In some cases, even their remaining self-respect has been plundered by witless giveaways—political or humanitarian—which agencies and organizations have squandered in a first fitful surge of misplaced sympathy.

"I wonder about this," said Dennis. "What is it that really counts? When do we serve?"

Dennis grew up near Buffalo, New York. Born July 23, 1945, he spent his elementary and high school years in both parochial and public schools. A year of college topped off his academic experience. During summers and following college he learned the trade of block-laying and worked at his trade briefly before entering service.

Pax service had been long in his mind. As early as 14 he began to consider it, although at that time Paxmen were still paying some or all of their expenses; this looked impossible.

Dennis tells it in his own words:

Later I noticed one thing. I had had a year of college but still could not decide on a major. No sense of direction. However, Pax fellows coming back from service did have purpose. Something seemed to have happened to them. They knew where they were going.

I thought of alternative service at home. But nothing appealed to me. I wondered if there was any sacrifice required if one just stayed around home or at least in familiar surroundings, with a job, reasonably good pay, a car and all that.

I decided I really wanted to help people—somebody needy. I wanted to sacrifice something.

After I decided on Pax and completed my application I went to a winter-term Bible school in Ohio. Three weeks later I got a call from Akron inviting me to

174

consider Algeria. At first I said no—it sounded too hard. But then I prayed about it and changed my mind.

A few weeks later, following orientation, I woke up in a French-speaking home in Wavre, Belgium. The first month was extremely rough; I had never studied French before. No one in the home spoke English. Of course, each day I attended school, as well.

Belgium was a good bridge to Algeria. But the real orientation took place between June 15 and 27. I drove a car from Frankfurt, Germany, to Algeria, traveling through France, Spain, and Morocco. I arrived at the Algerian border at the time of Ben Bella's coup d'etat. For three days and two nights I waited for the border to open so I could enter. With little gas and no Algerian money it was good to see the IVS fellows (International Voluntary Service) in the first town 30 kilometers from the border-crossing point.

Dennis looked at me and said simply, "I grew up on that trip."

And that matches what Tony Enns, the Algerian MCC administrator, said: "I saw Dennis come to Brussels, a shy young man, perhaps a little scared. Now he has matured to the point where he is running an entire project himself. You must visit Camel's Neck and see for yourself what he is doing. Bontrager is lifting thirty kids from illiteracy to literacy."

Construction was the one word given to Dennis as job description. Construction at Camel's Neck. For a few weeks he helped in small construction projects around the farm at Henchir Toumghani. Then he went out to Camel's Neck.

Camel's Neck isn't far from Henchir Toumghani— only a short vulture flight. And by jeep, only 17 kilometers (about 10 1/2 miles). Directions are simple. A few minutes from "the farm" you turn off the road and follow a single rutted trail across a potato field, past a

175

small cluster of mud-walled, straw-roofed homes, out toward the faintly visible craggy horizon black in the sudden dusk.

"See that cleft in the horizon," said Russell Yost, my jeep driver and Dennis's partner in isolation. "That's the pass. Camel's Neck is just on the other side."

We drove—for almost two hours—following eroded hillside contours, picking our way past boulders scattered across the dry bed of a stream, pushing upward to and through the mountain pass, down again, losing our way in a plowed field, finding a trail again in the starlight, past *mechtas* (tiny clusters of Berber houses) which Russ recognized and then finally, finally, coughing to a stop at the spot he and Dennis called home.

A small courtyard encased with a high stone wall. One building—one-room dwelling in the center, dispensary and schoolroom at opposite ends.

The night sky drew our eyes. The light of the stars filled the great semicircle above us. At the foot of the sloping hillside below the house-school-dispensary lay a dry flat salt bed. Turning we saw the crag-strewn horizon reaching almost from our feet to the first star.

The first assignment given Dennis here was to plaster the house and finish the courtyard we had just walked through. Then he built a house for someone nearby, gathering the rock from the fields. Later he worked on a reroofing project in one of the *mechtas.*

Dennis didn't wait many minutes before he began to share:

Each roof cost us $200. Six roofs—$1,200. That's when I started asking questions about how we could serve best.

I wasn't here long before I discovered many of these people are not impoverished—not by their standards.

Some of them own a hundred sheep—or more. At $25 per animal this represents quite a bit of wealth. They can go out and buy a wife and pay $1,000—in cash.

It's very bad to give. Perhaps when people are destitute through no fault of their own, one may give a few things, carefully. But ideas, education, understanding, spiritual insights—these are the best things you can give.

A good illustration of my point is the very first Pax building project in Algeria. A small village was built and given to the people. I think I would have left the people in their tents and just started teaching the children. Some for whom houses were built are again living in tents. Some of the richest people in the valley are living in tents. But houses make good, solid statistics. Directors of organizations like statistics. People at home who give money like statistics. So sometimes we Paxmen get a little confused and spend our time making statistics—so many cows providing milk, so many chicks peeping, so many houses built.

Sometimes I get the feeling Paxmen are judged by the statistics they report. Don't misunderstand me. Sometimes these things we work at and give away are important and necessary. But other times they cloud or hide completely the real contribution fellows make.

Let me tell you about one Paxman—Leroy Penner—who didn't succeed very well in making statistics. In fact, some judged he was just putting in time. He spent a lot of time building a well—now it's caving in. But if that "failure" hadn't worked the way he did, I wouldn't be here. There wouldn't be a school here. These kids would still be completely illiterate.

He just lived with people, spent his time getting to know them. Took an Arabic name. Ate their food. Sat with them by the hour. Gained their confidence. Saw

177

the need for a school and dropped the seed. He shared his dream with the next Paxman who came out. That was Gary Unruh.

Gary lived with the people too. He spent a great deal of time in their homes. He didn't say, *You need a school.* Rather, *What do you think of the idea of a school?*

After a while they asked if he could help them get a school. So he and an Algerian collected money from the families in the nearby *mechtas.* Then the men and boys collected rocks, helped carry rocks, carried water, and mixed mortar. Together they built the school. Only one thing was given—CCSA provided the roof.

These people are proud of their school. But the Pax guys had to have a lot of patience to wait until the people decided to build a school.

Now I'm teaching here—because a couple of Paxers were willing to forget statistics for a while, were willing to look like "failures" for a while. See what I mean? *Dennis asked.*

Gary Unruh served as the first teacher—in the building he and the Algerians built together. When Gary terminated, and a replacement was not immediately available, Dennis, the blocklayer from Buffalo, was asked to teach. He agreed, on condition that he could spend another two months in Belgium for language study. This request was approved. Dennis began his first experience as a teacher on September 5, 1966.

His classes total 36—all boys between the ages of 9 and 16. Twenty-one meet from 8:00 a.m. to 11:00 a.m. and fifteen meet from 12:30 p.m. to 3:30 p.m. School days are Monday, Tuesday, Wednesday, Friday, and Saturday a.m. Curriculum includes French, mathematics, geography, and hygiene.

During the 1966-1967 school year, half the student group had no knowledge of French. Classes are conducted in Chaouia, the Berber dialect, which both

Dennis and Russell have learned during their stay at Camel's Neck.

The students enjoy being in school and are interested in learning, although not all are strongly enough motivated to come without "help" from fathers. The Berber fathers are proud to have their sons in school and offered Dennis "carte blanche" to provide beatings whenever they were necessary to keep the boys in line.

But teaching is not the only assignment Dennis has found for himself:

The dispensary work is another big chore. I don't enjoy it. Really, I have no business treating anyone. All the background I have is a Red Cross course in high school. But with this limited knowledge, I know more than anyone else here. So the people come— and I do what I can.

Actually the dispensary work is important. The people are glad it's here. They all want an injection. You've got to know when they are sick—how am I to know? I'm so far out of my field, there's nothing but frustration. I may send someone away who is really sick. The next person fools me into thinking he's sick, so I give him a couple of aspirin.

The frustration and the solitude, they're with me a lot of the time.

Gets a bit lonesome out here—just the two of us all week. And Russ is gone all day in his work. *Russ is the other Paxman living at Camel's Neck.*

Russell Yost, a Coldwater, Kansas, native has more than two years of college with a major in chemistry. His farm background has given him a love for the outdoors which is useful in his work on wells and springs, crop assistance, and other technical helps he provides to improve the lot of the farmer.

Where springs are present Russell helps villagers

and farmers to make water more accessible through tiles placed in trenches. Where wells exist he offers know-how to line them with concrete casings. Where no water supply is available new wells are dug. While the results of Russell's work may be less measurable, his people-contact is extremely important. In fact, he says, "For the most part my work could be called social work—the things that are going to last are my successes as a social worker."

Both men have fitted in well. They make a fine team—and are appreciated in the community. Of this they have not always been certain.

Dennis recounted an experience which really tested this appreciation:

Weekends we try to get back to the farm for mail, good meals, and just plain fellowship. One Sunday night, when we returned home after two days at Henchir Toumghani, we discovered the house, school, and dispensary had been broken into. We itemized the missing things and found their value totaled $160.

Some of the men in the neighborhood had gathered while we were checking the missing items. We called them around us and I spoke to them in Chaouia:

"All right; this is it; we're finished. This is your school. You built it. We're here only to serve you. If you don't want us, just say the word. But don't stoop to stealing to get rid of us."

Of course we knew these men knew who had done the job and perhaps even where the stolen goods were hidden. So we talked pretty straight.

"Now either you give us $160 to cover costs or see that the stolen items are all returned. Otherwise, we're finished here; we're not staying where we're not wanted.

"We're going back to the farm. If you want us to

180

come back you will have to come down there and tell us."

We left right away. That was Sunday evening. No one came on Monday. No one came on Tuesday. No one came on Wednesday. I really sweated it out—began to be afraid everything had gone down the drain.

Wednesday night, just before Bible study, three men knocked at the gate and said all the items had been returned. They wanted us to come back right away. But we waited until Thursday morning. When we got there, everything had been returned—clothes, tape recorder, radio, everything. Not a thing was missing.

That was a bit rough, knowing we had to be firm, yet fearful that our firmness could close the door to further work there. But we also knew that respect for the program was at stake.

For Dennis and Russell, respect and appreciation are no longer in question. Both program and Paxmen have won their way into the community.

Life at Camel's Neck is simple—and incongruous. For Dennis and Russ, two men alone in a single room on the edge of a dried-up salt lake, their work is their life. Living is reduced to the bare essentials of sleep and food and daily sweat. No frills, few amenities; each hour and each tomorrow is stripped to its stark minimum. And in each soul stripped naked of false coverings, essence and true worth are revealed. Each being stands—without the crutches society and man's own dishonesty often provides—or falls. And in the falling he learns how to get up again—to stand more certainly.

In every cultural and social desert the smallest breaks in routine bring response.

"Do you know," Dennis said to me with deep feeling, "you're the first person who ever came to see us and stayed overnight."

181

Overnight began with supper—MCC beef and gravy, a few potatoes, canned vegetables, and chunks of bread. Russ did the honors as cook, creditably. We ate at a small table half full of the staples which hardly deserve a trip to the cupboard three times a day—large tin of crackers, crock of jam, butter, sugar, canned butter, extra bread.

Dennis erupted, "Hey, man, tomorrow there's football, at 17:45, three games. Buffalo is playing one."

One of the incongruities, shortwave radio, brings into the room the flavor of another world. Even the books—philosophy, science, fiction—seem almost out of place. But they're staunch friends, and needed.

There was a reading from the Bible, 1 Thessalonians 2:17-21, in French. (Dennis and Russ try to keep up their French even though Chaouia and Arabic are the coin of the local linguistic currency.) Then, at 9:30, with conversation lagging and languid responses, I said, "You fellows probably want to get to bed before long. We can talk again in the morning."

"I suppose we should hit it. It's past our bedtime now—an hour and a half."

"Seriously?" I looked at the two.

"Seriously. Eight o'clock every night. It's warmer in bed. Summers we get up at four and start work. Now we sleep in until six."

Next morning we slept in until six. The new day started in a cold room, with cold water for the waker-upper splashed generously on the upper torso, face, and neck. Then a colder sprint up the hill. (This house boasted a detached bathroom—most Algerian houses in the interior have none.) Later, as the sun rose higher and crossed the courtyard wall, we stood pressed against the warm stones and felt the chill dribble away.

We looked out to the morning peaks touched with early color, over the valleys—salt bed, plowed expanses, mechtas, a horseman in the distance, and nearby on foot an adult in hooded cashebih with a small child shivering along beside.

We were silent for a time. Then Russ broke the quiet with an almost reverent word. "Man, I like it here."

And Dennis, "I too. It's interesting. But I am looking forward to going home."

Dennis went on:

I expected cultural differences—perhaps not this great, though. I had to keep telling myself—you wanted something like this with sacrifice and hardship. I really did. And I'm glad my service has been here.

It seems like a long time. In reality, though, it's not. In Pax you just live day by day—do whatever you find to do. Living that way, time takes on a different perspective.

Then too, I'm different; I've changed a lot, learned so many things. I'm learning all the time. Just leave New York and a guy begins to learn. I didn't realize I was so stupid before I came.

I've learned something about faith too. I think I have come into closer contact with God than ever before. That's not very easy to talk about or describe. But the first weeks of school Russ was on vacation; I was here alone in a strange and new situation. One day I opened the Bible and read God's Word in Joshua: "Be strong and of a good courage." That helped.

You know, I didn't choose to be here, in Algeria, but I wouldn't trade this place for any other I've ever heard of. I'd never trade any part of the experience.

It wasn't always pleasant. You do without things, a lot of things. But actually now I feel I got what I wanted—sacrifice, hardship, a chance to do something worthwhile, to help people.

It's funny, how I've changed. When I left the U.S. this looked like an interruption. I wanted only one thing, to get ahead and make money. Now I want to do the very thing I considered an interruption. I want to be sensitive to people and their needs, to help them.

You know, being needy makes you grateful. I never knew what that meant. Now I know what it means to be grateful for a glass of cold water, green grass, trees, my parents.

Another thing. Being needy also makes you sensitive.

I've discovered two things here: what it's like to really need and how wonderful it is to have someone else come and help when I was the most needy.

That's what I want to do and be. You could say that's my philosophy of life. *And that's the story of Dennis Bontrager, Paxman.*

From college student to blocklayer to teacher of Berber children in the Algerian hinterland. From purposeless studies to meaningful daily work. From a Selective Service obligation to a gift of one's self to the world's needy.

If he can take it, if he's ready to grow—this is the path a Paxman walks.

CONGO

Jon Snyder

I was standing in front of Dr. Paul Carlson. Suddenly I felt an object being slipped into my hip pocket. Dr. Carlson whispered, "Here's my New Testament. Give it to my wife."

We were in front of the presidential palace from which Rebel President Christophe Gbenye was directing the rebel movement of Simbas against the incumbent government. He was speaking; had just finished identifying Carlson as a major (allegedly in the mercenary army) and promising his blood to the crowd. Dr. Carlson thought this was the end.

That morning, November 18, began in an air of fear. A little seven-year-old boy rebel came into our cell and said, "Get up, my dad's coming in."

An officer came and said he wanted all the Americans. Gene asked, "Missionaries too?" The answer was a quick yes.

I asked, "Professors too?" Same answer. *Jon Snyder could do nothing but go along with the group.*

There were eight Americans who left that cell in the morning hour—the U.S. Consul Michael Hoyt, Vice-Consul David Grinwis, three other consular staff members, Dr. Paul Carlson, medical missionary serving with Covenant World Missions, as well as Gene Bergman and Jon Snyder, MCC Paxmen working in the Congo.

A large mob filled the street outside the prison. Their chanting cries had reached through the prison walls even before the men were herded out of the building.

Four of them were put in the rear of a Volkswagen and four in a jeep. Slowly the vehicles forced their way through the pressing, hostile crowd.

185

Jon tells the story that is still etched deeply in his mind:

Before long we arrived in a large parklike area around the monument erected to honor Patrice Lumumba. The monument had been the scene of other executions. A crowd of well over five thousand people crowded around and, it seemed clear to us by now, they were here to witness more death today. We learned later the crowd had been told to gather for the execution of the Americans. The Belgians with us in prison had heard the news but hadn't told us.

The four of us in the Volkswagen were ordered into the back of the jeep along with the others. There was little conversation.

During the 45 minutes we sat and waited many in the crowd nearest the jeep poked and prodded us. Some of them were boys no older than 12 or 14. They would gesture with their knives to parts of our bodies and pantomime carving and eating.

Finally we were taken out of the jeep and ordered to walk down the sidewalk leading to the Lumumba monument.

I really thought this was the end of the road—a sidewalk forty feet long.

Mr. Hoyt, the U.S. Consul, led the way. I was near the end of the line. Suddenly, there was the sound of a car skidding to a stop. A man spoke. We all looked back to see who had come.

It was General Nicholas Olenga, the commander of the rebel army. He looked us over, each of us. Then he gave orders for us to get back in the jeep.

A rebel major objected; he demanded the death sentence immediately. General Olenga grabbed the coat lapels of the major and threw him back into the crowd.

We crowded back into the jeep again leaving behind a crowd clamoring for our death. A driver took us to the villa occupied by Rebel President Gbenye. There

186

also a crowd had gathered—perhaps half the size of the one at the Lumumba monument. They were in a vicious mood.

We were lined up before Gbenye. Our pictures were taken. Using several microphones he addressed the people first in French, then in Lingola. It was clear the mob was intent on our death. And clear also that Gbenye was having some trouble controlling them.

Then he spoke of Major Carlson. That's when the doctor slipped his New Testament into my pocket.

When Gbenye mentioned Lumumba's name the crowd started chanting and quieted a bit. That's when he ordered the guards to return us to prison.

After having had our emotions stretched and wrung out waiting for a death which didn't come, the comfort and relaxation of prison seemed like home.

Strange to see how experiences change perspective.

Oregon was home to Jon. He was born in Portland and grew up in Canby. Eight years of grade school and two in the local high school laid the foundation of his education. Then came two years at Western Mennonite School and college at Hesston, Kansas, and Goshen, Indiana.

Jon did a lot of thinking, even as a high school student:

During Western days I began to think of my service. My first decision was to accept nonviolence as the way I wanted to go. Later it became clear to me that I couldn't be truly nonviolent in any part of the military, so I decided on alternative service.

The two years at Hesston College sort of settled my thinking in this direction. Then during the two years at Goshen College I took a lot of philosophy courses along with my math major. Some of those courses in Ethics, Christianity and Modern Thought, as well as others, forced me to reexamine my ideas. But I came through that period of searching and thinking still more certain that I could not participate in the destruction of life—even at the cost of my own.

Pax appealed to me for several reasons. Probably most significant was that the program matched my demand for a positive and constructive alternative to violence. I had talked to former Paxmen and their description of opportunities attracted me and confirmed my desire to help somewhere in an underdeveloped country. Pax also seemed to provide a context in which one could be an individual and not become trampled by the herd. Of course, along with all of this, I was intrigued by the fact that MCC Pax represented a coming together of all Mennonite groups. I'm sure I don't understand, even now, all of the wonderful implications of this kind of brotherhood, this working with each other, but back then as a student I knew that I wanted to become a part of this whole experience.

June 1963 marked graduation. In October I went to Akron, Pennsylvania, for orientation. My application for service had indicated Europe as a preference. But MCC asked me to consider the Congo. I was happy to go.

Jon arrived in Kinshasa (Leopoldville) on the evening of November 13. His assignment was to work as accountant at the Universite Libre (Free University), a fledgling Protestant institution located at Kisangani (Stanleyville). He came to Kisangani on November 22, the day President Kennedy was assassinated.

Opening exercises for the university took place the following day:

My work as accountant included purchasing and serving as general assistant to the business manager. I enjoyed my work and especially the university atmosphere.

During this first year there were thirty students, all Congolese. Actually, they were all taking a preparatory course prior to university entrance, since they were not quite ready for college. Most had come from Protestant mission stations.

The existence of the university was a major miracle. On June 30, those who had dreamed of this school were told it could operate. All they had then was a president and a few secondary school buildings.

Within three months a faculty was recruited—a Congolese vice-president and professors—one Greek, one German, one Italian, one Lebanese, and one English.

To be a part of this new international and partly indigenous venture was quite exciting.

French was the language of the academic world. It was sort of a prestige thing to speak French. But Swahili was also spoken as a trade language; and the official language, adopted by the army, was Lingala.

My job put me in an administrative position with relation to certain staff members. I learned quickly that whites tend to assume a stance of authority over others. This bothered me. The problem wasn't easy to work at when one carried certain responsibilities. But I did have good relations with our bookstore manager.

Until the first of February I lived in the dorm with the fellows, as sort of a dorm supervisor.

But my days were spent in the business office.

I ate meals with the students. Noon meal was usually rice and fish or beef; once in a while, potatoes. The evening meal had a bit more variety.

Evenings were my own for soccer, writing letters, and reading. I did a lot of reading.

In March 1964 Gene Bergman and Irvin Goessen came to repair apartments. Three months later when the students went home and the dorm closed we three moved into one of these apartments and hired a cook to prepare our meals.

There were in Stanleyville nine large three-story

apartment buildings which were to be used for university professors. When the additional Paxmen arrived, some were vacant and others were occupied by squatters. All, at one time, had been used as barracks by the military and required total renovation.

Windows had to be replaced. Doors had to be rehung. Locks had to be fixed. The water system needed major repairs. And, where former tenants had built fires on kitchen floors, flooring had to be torn up, replaced, and tiles laid.

Gene and Irvin had a number of Congolese helpers working with them. Their conversation one day reflected the disparity in our incomes even though we Paxmen thought our level of living was sacrificial.

The workers asked what income the Paxmen received. Gene replied, "Fifteen dollars a month."

Since this was roughly equivalent to a Congolese laborer's monthly income, it appeared as if the Paxmen were truly adapting to the local economy and standard of living. That is, until one worker reminded them, "Yes, but all your food and lodging are paid for otherwise. With the same amount of money I must pay for food, lodging, and clothing. And that is not only for myself but for my wife, as well, and all our children."

On June 30 Dr. Melvin Loewen arrived to serve as academic dean of the university. During July we became aware that something was brewing. The northeast was estranged from the rest of the Congo. Political turmoil seemed to mark our area. Public services like schools and roads were deteriorating. Since there was a strong Moslem population belt running through Stanleyville there were Moslem-Christian tensions. Half the people in the city spoke Swahili and the other half spoke Lingala, so there were language tensions and subsequent breakdowns in communication.

In all, there was a lot of uneasiness.

On August 3, just two days after Irvin Goessen completed his Pax term, the rebels attacked Stanleyville. After a couple of days of fighting they took the city.

During this period we stayed in our apartment.

One night, at 3:00 a.m., the rebels came to search the apartments. Since these apartment buildings had been army barracks, the rebel army wanted to appropriate them for housing. They went first to the apartment of the German professor and his wife. Then they came to ours, wanting to know why we were there.

Through the early morning fog the rebels took us about a mile to their headquarters for further questioning—the German professor, Gene, and me, along with three of the men who had been helping Gene renovate the apartments.

While we were there, other rebels searched our apartment and found a voltmeter which they thought was a secret radio. During the questioning our workers sat in front of us. Frequently the Simbas clubbed them on the head with rifle butts.

Finally they released us. Probably, had we been living in a private home we would have had no problem at that time. But occupying former army barracks seemed to implicate us.

A short time later we moved in with the Melvin Loewen family.

On August 23 an order was given that all American consular personnel were to be executed. As Americans, we expected to be included. But the Belgian consul interceded and the plan was not carried out.

More than two months later, near dusk on October 28, we were outside enjoying the evening breeze. As Congolese strolled by, several of them said to us, innocently, rather than maliciously, "Tomorrow all of you will be executed."

The next morning at ten o'clock a jeep came to the

mission compound and picked us up. Of course, authorities had made a survey of the town earlier and knew where all the Americans, Canadians, and Europeans were. We were taken to the courthouse porch for a "trial."

Our documents were checked. Gene and I were U.S. citizens. We were asked to step aside.

Dr. Melvin Loewen was also present. The rebels checked his Canadian passport, then asked to see the passports of his wife and children who had U.S. passports.

He replied, "You have already seen mine. Why is it necessary to see theirs?" So they let him and his family go.

Gene and I were taken to prison and put in a cell with the five U.S. consular officers and Dr. Paul Carlson.

The cell measured fifteen feet by twenty. There were concrete slabs on the floor. Planks rested on these slabs to form our beds. Central Prison had an aluminum roof. During the day the building became very hot. At night, if it rained, the incessant clatter kept us awake.

Food was brought in for the eight of us by the missionaries at the LECO bookstore across the street. On our first day in jail we printed 2 *Pax* on an empty matchbox to let them know we were there.

A little later two Belgians were brought to our cell. One was the Belgian consul and the other a businessman. Although the President of the rebellion, Christophe Gbenye, had given orders no one should see us, one day a colonel badgered his way into our cell. He lined us up and went down the line slapping our faces. I turned a bit with the slap so the officer hit me a second time. The Belgian at the end of the line ducked and the colonel missed him completely.

This so infuriated the officer that he knocked the man to the floor, pummeling him and kicking him.

Then came November 18 and our trip to the Lumumba monument with its last-minute reprieve from execution.

On November 20 all Americans and Europeans were taken to the Victoria Hotel. Rumor had it that Jomo Kenyatta was to arrive, inspect the condition of the hostages, and arrange for their release. However, nothing further happened that day.

The morning of November 21 started off well. Although nine of us were staying in one room, it was the first time in three weeks we were able to bathe and shave. But later in the day all of us were ordered outside. Many of the hostages were herded into a bus and truck. There was not room for all so about forty were left behind.

No one really knew where the two vehicles were going. Some believed the mercenaries and the national army were near Stanleyville and the hostages were being removed to some hideout in the jungle where they could still be used by the rebels as pawns in the bargain they were trying to strike. Others surmised they were being taken out to their death.

However, late that night all were returned. The bus had broken down.

During that day I did a strange thing—strange since I was a hostage and a prisoner. I called Dr. Melvin Loewen from the Victoria Hotel to tell him what had happened.

The twenty-second and twenty-third of November were reasonably quiet. But the twenty-fourth was different—much different.

We were on the fourth floor of the hotel. Early that morning, about 6:15, we heard the sound of planes. Looking out in the direction of the airport we saw a number of parachutes in the air. Apparently Belgian paratroopers were coming in to try and rescue the hostages.

We had breakfast. Then Gene, Dr. Carlson, and I had a period of prayer. We expected this would be a long day.

Shortly after seven the Simbas came to our floor and ordered everyone out. There were almost three hundred of us there, mostly Belgians. Except for forty or fifty who managed to hide on the roof and in closets we were all assembled in front of the hotel. Then we were formed into a column three abreast and told to march toward the airport.

I don't think at first any of us were sure why we were there—to serve as a shield for the rebels when they met the paratroopers or to be released. Later the colonel who was in charge told us we were going to die.

As we walked we could hear the machine-gun fire getting closer. It sounded as if the paratroopers were well on their way into town.

After the column had moved about two blocks we were ordered to sit down on the street. There were fifteen or twenty Simbas guarding us. A machine gun was set up to the one side of the street. Other Simbas came up insisting we should be killed before the paratroopers arrived. The colonel seemed to be stalling for time.

I'm not certain what happened next. Perhaps one of the younger Simbas lost control and started firing. But in a few seconds twenty or more of them were spraying the group with bullets and the machine gun slowly moved its chattering death along the line.

When there was a momentary pause for reloading, I ran and jumped across the wall in front of a house. Eight of us hid in a small storeroom. A rebel came into the house but overlooked us.

The firing continued sporadically. It was during this time that Dr. Carlson was killed.

Shortly after, Gene, who had huddled in the street during the ghastly minutes of the massacre, led two Belgian paratroopers into the house where we were.

We helped carry the dead and wounded, then walked the rest of the way to the airport. Once we had to take cover from sniper fire.

Planes evacuated the seriously wounded first; then the living hostages were airlifted to Leopoldville. The two Paxmen were met by Dr. Decker, the president of the university; Elmer Neufeld, MCC director; and Dr. Kenton Brubaker.

I embraced Dr. Decker, lifted him right off his feet. All the pent-up emotion of the past months, particularly the past week, seemed to let go in that one moment at noon of November 24 when we touched down at Leopoldville.

We spent two weeks in vacation on the coast. Then both Gene and I returned to Leopoldville where a university in exile was being formed. I went back to my bookkeeping and accounting chores and completed my term of service.

I think for the last weeks of captivity I had felt like one of a number of chess pawns. The fact that we were human beings didn't seem to count for much. We were part of a political game that was being played. Death seemed a certain end for many of us. The real questions seemed to be when and how.

When I felt certain death was coming at the Lumumba monument I believe I felt more relaxed than during the days of uncertainty when we couldn't be sure what would happen next.

The whole period of Pax service forces a fellow to grow up, to stand on his own two feet. Meaning in life begins to emerge from one's involvement with people and their problems.

In Pax, helping in a place of need seems to be the pattern. But at home, the paycheck is a prime motivation. I was bothered by the materialism I found when I returned; and I was sure it wouldn't get to me. It's rather overwhelming though. One sort of settles into the eight-to-five routine and forgets the sordid conditions in which many people live.

Things aren't enough. In service, to give things is a mistake; rather, one must give himself to help people themselves acquire what they need. Here at home, things become something like a god, but they don't provide meaning in life.

I'd like to go back to the university in the Congo; perhaps there, for a while at least, I can fulfill my desire to serve in a place of great need, without reward.

That's what Pax taught me.

Wilbur Bontrager

"Roasted caterpillars took a little getting used to. But really, they're not bad."

For Wilbur Bontrager, living with a Congolese pastor and his family at Kenge in the Congo, food was one area where adjustment was necessary. Rice and "luku," an almost tasteless manioc dish with the consistency of dough, were the local staples. Sometimes there was chicken to dress up the meal. More often there were fried or roasted caterpillars, monkey or rat meat, even flying ants eaten raw and live.

"Rat meat has a strong flavor. I prefer monkey."

Wilbur truly "sat where they sat." Home during this period was a small mud hut with a thatched grass roof and mud floor. His "family" was honored by his presence with them. And his willingness to share native life made its mark in the community, as well as on his hosts.

In fact, a final plaintive request from the pastor, his host, illustrates better than anything else the importance of his contribution. "Why couldn't 'Bontrag' stay for always?"

But "always" hadn't been in Wilbur's planning when he left home near Buffalo, New York. Born October 30, 1942, on a farm at Alden, New York, "Bontrag" was raised in a Conservative Mennonite home.

Since his father was an auctioneer, as well as a farmer, Wilbur had opportunity for exposure to a substantial cross-section of community life. But his home influences were strong and these were laced with spiritual concern and direction.

Wilbur emphasized this:

My parents influenced me greatly. My Aunt Bonnie, coming back from service in Ethiopia, also got through to me. At college—Hesston and Goshen—I met foreign students. Along with these factors were the missionary visits to our church and the church periodicals, describing worldwide service, which came to our home.

I couldn't help but think about some kind of service. When the draft board got around to me, Pax seemed the natural thing to do.

Of course, earlier I had done a lot of thinking about the conscientious objector position. I'd rather call it Christian pacifism. I know it sounds simplistic and a bit ridiculous, but it seemed clear to me that I could help people more by being in Pax than by being in the Army and shooting them.

Originally I was assigned to Korea. But this was changed. I expressed a preference for agricultural work and for a "primitive" culture. I wanted to be where needs were obvious and where cultural differences would be a challenge to maturity.

November 1, 1964, I left for Congo by ship. At that time language study was not yet a part of our orientation. So, unfortunately, I arrived in the country without any acquaintance with French. Studying language after I arrived during the period I was adjusting to other aspects of the culture was very difficult.

Since Wilbur completed his service, policies have been changed and all Congo Paxmen spend time in language study.

Pax work in the Congo was not new. Although MCC Pax entered the country formally in autumn of 1960, young men completing their I-W alternative service had been working there as early as 1955. One of the earliest Missions-Paxmen was Larry Kauffman, who later drowned in the Kisai River. Another, Fremont Regier, completed his term in Congo, finished his Master's degree work, and served a term in Mexico under General Conference Board of Christian Services. Then he returned to head up the CIM-MCC agricultural program in Nyanga.

The first Paxmen assisted missionaries of the Congo Inland Mission in station and vehicle maintenance, carpentry, and the building of a large primary school.

Those who arrived in 1960, a few months after the nation gained its independence, located in Leopoldville and several other scattered stations. They assisted in food and clothing distribution, refugee resettlement, hospital maintenance, construction, and agricultural projects. Some served as clerks and others taught English to Congolese teachers.

MCC Pax worked closely with the Congo Protestant Relief Agency. CPRA had developed a highly flexible program to meet the changing needs of a country so recently come into nationhood. And on their teams Pax provided some of the personnel which met both relief and rehabilitation needs. Along with CPRA, Paxmen also helped inter-Protestant institutions at Kimpese— Ecole de Pasteurs et d'Instituteurs and Institut Medical Evangelique. Several others worked with a Swedish mission organization.

By 1964 Paxmen were deployed at a number of locations: instructing at a CPRA-related vocational school and refugee training center in Thysville; transporting supplies to a German-Swiss mission working in the Kwango; church and school construction with the Presbyterians in Leopoldville; printshop work with LECO (La Librairie Evangelique Au Congo), to name only some.

There seemed never to be enough Paxmen to go around. From many areas and agencies requests came for Paxmen that had to be denied.

Of course, one of the constant problems was to find assignments sufficiently challenging to the Paxmen. Sometimes missionaries were less than thoughtful and Paxmen concluded they had become glorified errand boys. However, generally there were excellent relationships, their work was deeply appreciated, and Paxmen served well in their specific assignments, as well as in the building of intercultural bridges.

Wilbur was candid as he talked about his work:

I had asked for a "different" culture and I got what I asked for.

The first four months were spent in Kinshasa (Leopoldville). There I was foreman of an eight-man construction crew building houses in a new mission complex. Two were skilled masons, the rest semi-skilled or helpers. Along with some bookkeeping and hauling supplies, I had my hands full.

Of course, my job must have been a picnic compared to the one Fremont Regier had handled almost ten years before for the CIM mission. He supervised a construction crew of sixty men, hauled some supplies, and did vehicle maintenance. Or compared to the job of Lonnie Gering, who supervised as many as 90 men in some stages of building churches and schools for Presbyterians at nine different locations.

The houses we built were of masonry construction using homemade blocks and plastered. Roofs were asbestos.

The big problem on this first job was language. In addition to French which I was just learning I had a sustained contact with four tribal languages: Lingala, Kituba, Kiganga, and Gpendi. I got along best in French; Gpendi was next.

Our workday started at 7:00 a.m., with two hours off at noon. We'd work until 5:00 or 6:00 p.m. In addition to language I faced the problem of no experience in construction.

Of course I knew how to handle tools. Working around the farm summers and during the full year I helped Dad gave me some background. But I had never planned buildings, nor had I ever supervised workers.

However, one learns fast. Perhaps the fastest lesson I learned was the delegation of responsibility. Very quickly I discovered that too much aggressiveness on my part and failure to delegate work assignments resulted in the workers sitting around and letting me do the work.

Labor relations were also somewhat difficult. It seemed friendliness with the crew led them to expect favors. So I had to learn to be an administrator on the job rather than a friend primarily.

Then I was transferred to Kenge where I lived with the family of a Congolese pastor. This constituted another big cultural jump and a massive learning experience after only 16 weeks in the country.

When I found the Congolese culture a bit too burdensome I'd slip over to the Catholic mission for an evening or a day. To be with the folks there, eat a meal, and share with each other always boosted my spirits again.

It was a good experience for me. But I believe it resulted in better relations between Catholics and Protestants as well.

My work in Kenge was done for a Baptist mission. Here I was general supervisor of the construction project working with a Congolese foreman who spent all of his time on the job. Part of my job also was the transportation of building supplies from Kinshasa, a distance of 280 kilometers (175 miles). The trip took from seven to nine hours with a number of ferry crossings.

I drove a four-ton 1964 Chevrolet stake truck. Four tons was our normal load limit. I also hauled some sand and rock locally.

Wilbur's travel experiences were not without their difficulties. But they were limited compared to another Paxman, William Janzen, who was located at another station. William also hauled supplies from Leopoldville.

Normally he took two Congolese workmen with him to build or rebuild or repair bridges before it was safe to cross. Within a space of fifty miles there were eighteen bridges. During certain seasons it took as long as two weeks or more to traverse this distance. And there were times he took along as many as 25 laborers to help in the work on bridges.

This meant going to the nearest village to find the chief, get permission to rebuild, then looking for materials. Sometimes Janzen hired ten or fifteen local men to assist.

From Kenge Wilbur transferred to Nyanga to help in the fledgling agricultural development being established on Congo Inland Mission land. Fremont Regier, who had spent one term in the Congo, was given responsibility for this project.

Regier came to the Congo late in 1964 and settled temporarily in Tshikapa. During the first six months of 1965 he visited with government officials and observed agricultural stations, demonstration plots, and extension programs in the Congo and other countries such as Nigeria and the Cameroons. Finally COMAS, the Congo Mennonite Agricultural Services Committee, settled on Nyanga as the location for the new program.

It was agreed that the farm—100 acres given to CIM in 1930 as an agricultural concession—should serve as the base for an extension program.

Regier set up a number of goals for the farm: (1) to work toward alleviation of protein and general dietary deficiency; (2) to improve the economic standard of the Congolese; (3) to help in Christian stewardship of natural resources and possessions; (4) to teach healthy attitudes toward honest labor and conservation of resources; (5) to give positive witness to personal faith in Christ reflected by living, working, and serving in a Christlike way among the Congolese.

Among the agricultural problems Regier will have to solve are soil leaching, low nitrogen content in the soil, high soil acidity, erosion, and tropical diseases. Along with these will be other factors: present farming patterns, certain cultural practices, and limited marketing possibilities.

One of the first needs in this area, near to rebel territory, was to build up the animal population. All the animals had been killed by soldiers in need of food. Buildings were built—cow barn, rabbit pens, chicken house, duck shelter—as much as possible from native materials readily available to the jungle.

Stock was brought in and the farm became a supply center where breeding stock was developed. About the time I left, after 14 months of service, the foundation of the farm program was quite well laid and the farm was becoming a true extension center.

In the next stage European stock was brought in for crossbreeding with native stock. Also a store was developed where farm supplies are available: small-equipment items, nails, seeds, and other necessary materials. A vegetable crop improvement program was set up, as well.

Wilbur spent his last months of Pax service helping Regier get the farm program started:

Much of the land was covered with brush when we came. That job was still far from finished when I left.

Pax was good for me. But at times it seemed I couldn't pull through the periods of loneliness. To be out there all alone was rough; I think a unit of two or three should be minimum, especially where there are no other Europeans around to whom one can relate.

Loneliness cuts morale. I suspect I could have been twice as efficient and useful had this problem been taken care of.

It wasn't helped by the attitude of some missionaries that Paxmen can do anything, can put up with anything. At times it seemed we got caught with the dirty work; in fact, one man said Paxers are here to be told what to do.

However, that's only one side of the coin. Many wonderful experiences linger on in my memory, especially those enjoyed during the time I was living with the Congolese family at Kenge: a communion service, tom-toms in the village, my first real contact with Congolese family life and village customs, literature distribution to the military along the road, sitting on a five-inch log ten inches off the ground through a three-hour church service.

I had a unique relationship with the local Roman

Catholic priest at Kenge. He was an open-minded Dutchman. We had many good times together in serious discussion.

My two years in the Congo in alternative service forced me to ask a lot of questions. For a period of time I doubted the Christian pacifist viewpoint. But after some of the experiences I had I'm more than ever convinced of its validity.

Of course, I don't have all the answers. And perhaps I'm not as rigid or dogmatic in my position as I was when I left home. Yet I am certain I couldn't go into battle and take life.

Congo gave me perspective, a broader point of view.

It has also made me critical of the North American way of life. People at home aren't really living. Most people are so busy grubbing for money they don't even notice that life is passing them by.

Personally, I have become more reflective. I think I've learned to know something about myself, my potential, and my limitations. I've come to some conclusions about values—the transiency of things and the meaning of relationships. I'm taking a deeper interest in world affairs. Issues of international importance touch me now. I'm more aware so that everything seems to mean more than it used to.

And I've been struck with the worth and the potential of the individual; masses seem less important and persons more so.

Perhaps this was because I was accepted. The people in the village accepted me fully. This made my Pax service seem worthwhile. I suppose the biggest compliment I received, after I had lived in the village awhile and become better known, was "If the white man 'Bontrag' is your friend, then you are our friend too."

And that is the heart of Pax.

CRETE

Louise Friesen Claasen

"Who ever heard of Spanish rice without green peppers in it?" asked a Paxman.

So the next time we had Spanish rice I put in green peppers. And then, from across the table I heard, "Louise, this Spanish rice would have been good but the peppers spoiled it." Said with a big, good-natured grin, I couldn't take offense, especially not when, from another quarter came a loud ejaculation, "Oh boy! This is just the way my mother makes Spanish rice."

Louise went on:

Cooking for Pax fellows can be an exhausting, sometimes exasperating, experience. When there are five, you are trying to imitate the good home cooking of no less than five mothers—not to mention Virgil's mother, or mine. Each fellow has his own likes and dislikes, and usually these are not deep, dark secrets.

I learned early that several of the fellows didn't like the tiny sprigs of bright green that can dress up a dish so nicely; certainly not in soup where floating "grass" was out of place. So I didn't put celery in the potato soup. You guessed it! After the soup was ladled and the first few tentative sips were taken—"This soup is delicious, but a spot or two of celery would have made it just perfect."

Foolishly, I thought desserts would be easier. Then I hear: "Boy, this is great apple pie. Wouldn't some ice cream taste good with it?" or "Get a load of this chocolate pudding, but wouldn't some whipped cream make it even better?"

So it goes when you cook for boys from Mennonite homes in America who have been spoiled by all the good things that are available there, and usually

205

taken for granted. When they enter Pax service where there is a limited food budget and serve in a country where most extras are unavailable, a matron-cook may often feel as if she has drawn the thankless job.

But then comes the day, quite unexpectedly, when faces around the table light up and one of the Paxmen exclaims, 'Hey, fellows, this stuff isn't half bad!'' Their enthusiastic agreement means you've hit the jackpot and you finish the meal sitting on Cloud Nine secretly planning how to ring the bell again.

Being a Pax director's wife has been interesting. Every day you're the cook and the housekeeper. Every week you're the laundry lady. Once in a while you're the mender. Sometimes you're a substitute mother and other times sister. When the wrong kind of letter comes, or there aren't any letters at all, you may be the mother confessor. And some days you feel as if you're nothing—a necessary but unnoticed part of the landscape whose worth could be proved only by its absence.

But I'm glad we're here. Crete is an interesting place to be. Getting to know the bishop has been a fascinating experience. I wouldn't trade it for a lot of things we could have back in America. As a matter of fact, I don't think I'd want to give up any part of my life.

That, against the background of her refugee childhood, is a singular comment.

Life, for Louise, began in West Prussia. She was born in a little village called Elbing on August 18, 1939. Her daddy was a baker; as oldest son in his family he carried on the family business. However, by the time Louise came into the family, her father was already fighting in the Second World War. She remembers only two of his occasional visits home.

Then in January of 1945 they were told the Russians

206

were coming. They would have to leave home. Louise looked back in her memory:

We loaded our bare necessities on a wagon and started our journey. There was my aunt with two children and mother with four plus a bicycle and a baby buggy. My little brother was only two. Planes flew overhead.

The night was cold. But hurrying through the forest I warmed up. So I pulled off my new blue winter coat. Somehow I lost it. I was just five but I remember feeling bad. It was the only coat I had.

Their flight took them to Danzig in time to see the city bombed into ruins. Then to Denmark for four years of life in refugee camps. Louise remembers. The first camp in Denmark was a four-story building normally used for car storage. Each family was given an allotment of straw to sleep on. There was food but sometimes we could hardly eat it.

The next camp was better—an old army barracks. Each small room had three or four families in it. Although crowded, each family kept their own corner clean. Here I started to school. On the first day we were told to bring a blanket and a roll of toilet tissue (the European kind is hard and slick on one side). Benches were lined up as desks, the blanket was to kneel on, and the toilet tissue was our writing tablet.

Then we went to Oxbol. We stayed at this *lager,* or camp, the longest time. It was on the shore of the North Sea and I remember many wonderful times there —playing in white sand, swimming in the cold water, playing hide and seek in fog so thick you couldn't see your hand in front of your eyes, bending down where the fog had lifted so we could find our way to school. Much of my remembered childhood took place at Oxbol.

Before we left for another camp and our return to

Germany, I remember walking around inside the barbed-wire fence arm in arm with a new friend I had just found and singing:

> *Heut noch sind wir hier zu Haus,*
> *Morgen geht's zum Tor hinaus,*
> *Und wir mussen wandern, wandern,*
> *Keiner weiss vom andern.*

When we went back to Germany in 1949, families were divided among farmers in the Pfalz. Since mother had four small children, no one was very eager to have us. We lived in two rooms on the Heidelbinger Hof near Zweibruken. While here I attended school in a small town called Contwig.

Then, in July 1950 we traveled to Rotterdam to take ship for America. There an "uncle" had arranged a home for us in Kansas. We had a whole house to ourselves, and a cow, and there was no barbed wire. We lived frugally, but there was enough. In a sense, we had found home.

I had a very wonderful mother. Her hard work was matched only by her great faith. Even when nothing seemed right she never complained. She was 32 when we crossed the ocean and went to Whitewater, Kansas.

I never missed things until I got to high school. There, as a teenager, I felt out of place. Others had many things I didn't have. And I was shaken also during my two years at this Christian academy, by the superficial level of friendships and lack of honesty. The last two years at a public high school were good—there was a good economic spread of students so I felt more at home. I graduated in 1957.

Then came four years of college—at Bethel. This was my very best school experience. I graduated there in 1961.

Between my sophomore and junior years in college I did a summer of Voluntary Service in California, working in a camp for crippled children.

That summer I'll never forget. I learned to be free. A good friend there opened the door to my freedom. She showed me I didn't need to feel inferior. When I stopped worrying, selfishly, about everyone watching me, and started looking for others to whom I could give a little of myself, a whole new world opened up. I was free to think of others because I had been freed from thinking only of myself.

It was all so wonderful.

When I found myself, I discovered I wasn't at the bottom of the ladder. I did have some capabilities. And with that consciousness came the willingness to accept myself as I was.

Then the old worries about self and appearance and opinions of others dropped away; it was the inner self that really counted.

I'm sure out of all this grew my desire for service to others, my willingness to give myself to people in some way. I wasn't ready to settle down and have babies right away. In fact, I decided then I couldn't ever just be an ordinary housekeeper in an ordinary suburban area and live my life away. I decided then I would have to be somewhere where I could help some-one—do something to make their life happier.

The first years in college were years of doubt. I faced a kind of crisis with reference to Christianity. There seemed to be so few persons really following Christ. I got a bit cynical; once tried to throw God out of the picture entirely.

But that left me floundering more than ever. A prof helped me to see that others were searching too and that one's search, if it was honest, in itself didn't destroy faith.

209

By graduation in 1961, I had discovered a meaningful basis for life—simply living each minute as it came, trying to follow the way of Christ.

I met Virgil in church. We went Christmas caroling a few times. This was before he went to Pax Service in Paraguay. When he returned we dated and discovered our common desire to serve people. That drew us together and into marriage.

Now we're in Crete. Virgil and I planned to do this kind of thing together. I'm not here just because I'm his wife and I felt my place was with him. I came, without reservations, because I personally want to serve. Having been a person in need I cannot ignore those in the world who have needs.

Of course, being director of a Pax unit is a big job; and I want to help him in that in every way I can. *She was obviously happy.*

An interesting chain of events led MCC to establish a Pax unit on the island of Crete.

From the Greek Orthodox Diocese of Kissamou and Selinon at the western tip of Crete, came Alexander Papaderos to Germany for advanced studies. While he was there he met Peter Dyck, director of MCC services in Europe and North Africa. From this grew an invitation to provide a team to give technical instruction in the schools Bishop Irineos was planning—specifically in the areas of metalwork and electricity.

Later Bishop Irineos visited the farm in Aridea, Greece, and invited MCC to help him set up an agricultural program as well in his diocese. He felt such a project could also be used for training purposes in livestock husbandry, crop management, and agricultural theory. In addition the farm produce could help to feed the boys in his hostels.

The hostel development lay at the center of the bishop's planning. The 350 villages in his diocese represent home to shepherds and farmers who watch their meager flocks and till small orchards of olive trees and some vineyards. Many of these villages have limited academic opportunities.

So the bishop dreamed. He dreamed of hostels located at and near Kastelli, his own residence, to which boys could be brought from the villages, housed, and taught in schools he would build.

But Bishop Irineos is more than a dreamer. Through intense dedication to a single-minded purpose—the welfare of his people—and endless hard work, he has found ways to bring his dreams to life.

Originally he spoke of a technical school for 25 boys. A few short years later, at Kastelli alone the technical school enrolled ten times that number. Today the bishop's hostels provide housing and his schools education for 800 boys and girls who otherwise would have grown up into ignorance.

The first school was begun in 1961 with 18 boys and two MCC representatives—a young man from Germany and a Paxman from America—as teachers. Six years later 23 faculty members were teaching mechanics, metalworking, and electricity. The government now pays the teachers and the bishop provides food and lodging. The first class was graduated from a four-year course in 1965.

Also in 1961 Orpha Zimmerly, a Pax matron in Germany and MCC village worker in Greece, came to the island to assist in the girls' home economics school started by the Bishop Irineos. Begun with one teacher and 12 girls, this school has grown to nearly 80 students.

The coming of Pax to Crete and its developing program has been tied closely to the work and vision of the bishop. At times this has been a limiting factor which has seemed to slow growth and perhaps inhibit the initiative of the Pax team.

On the other hand, this pattern of work fulfills precisely the basic principle emphasized so strongly by

Professor Agorides of the School of Theology at the University of Salonika. As he observed the work in Macedonia with both its strengths and its weaknesses, he said with great force, "If your church wants to work anywhere in Greece or Crete, find yourself an energetic, progressive bishop and ask how you can help him. Work done in this setting will endure long after you are gone."

Bishop Irineos fits this description. Although over 50, his eyes sparkle with enthusiasm. One senses quickly a barely controlled exuberance for life, a deeply sensitive spirit and a dynamic in planning and execution that could be misunderstood by less aggressive persons.

He has a great love for the people in his diocese, based on two factors, he told me.

As a boy on the farm he saw the great poverty of Cretans and determined some day to change this. Later, with his dedication to service for God, he placed himself in God's hand to be an instrument to help his people. He recounted briefly some of the things he was doing and, then seemingly to be sure I got the point, he said emphatically, "Whatever I do to help is possible only because of God's help."

The 40,000 people in his diocese respond in kind. They love their bishop because they know every drachma or dollar he can lay his hands on is spent on their welfare, not on himself or to elevate the prestige of his bishopric. This fact is known all over the island and throughout Greece. Far and wide he is spoken of as a good man and a deeply committed Christian.

The key to the acceptance of the Pax efforts in Crete is constituted simply in the fact that Bishop Irineos invited the team. Although many of the peasants were puzzled by the existence of non-Greek Orthodox Christians, they trusted the bishop's judgment and accepted the Paxmen as an integral part of the bishopric.

The bishop is grateful for the Pax presence. He said, "This is an excellent example of collaboration between Christians. I would like to show that Christians from the Mennonite Church and Christians from the Greek Orthodox Church can work together as Christians should. This is for the glory of God."

Of course, where human beings are involved, the glory of God sometimes gets bumped around a bit. With every plan subject to the bishop's approval and every monetary detail in the program dependent on the funds he has available, the occasional restiveness of idealistic and aggressive American Paxers may be understood.

Yet, even though the bishop is penniless most of the time, and there is no certainty on program, and a benevolent despotism is difficult to appreciate against the background of American democracy and experiences of consensus, the Paxmen seemed unanimous in their satisfaction at working so closely with the Greek Orthodox Church and specifically with Bishop Irineos. Their praise of him and his love for the people was unstinting.

"He is an unusual man. At first we were overawed. But we found he could talk to a new Paxman or a peasant in the field as easily as to the pope or high government officials. Now we just accept him—as he accepts us.

"Sometimes Virgil gets discouraged," said Louise. "Things move so slowly. Then we remember that the farm has really only started. We can't see results in one year."

The agricultural phase began at Kolymbari, 15 miles from the port of Chania, February 1965, with the arrival of Bill Nice and Roger Beck on the island.

Program proposals had been written up but little had been done in terms of groundwork. So the first two men waited out the daily rains in considerable discouragement while they sought to discover some bridge between the bishop and MCC in their respective understanding of the draft proposals.

Generally, the plan was for MCC to provide personnel, equipment, animals, and some financing. The bishop would provide land, tractor, buildings for livestock, helpers on the farm, and living quarters.

The biggest problem was land. The first Paxmen thought there was going to be well over 100 acres of the church's land available. But the first year they "farmed" a total of 1 1/2 acres. All of this was put into vegetables—potatoes, spinach, vines, cauliflower, among others. Boys from the nearby newly built hostel helped in the planting.

But it was obvious 1 1/2 acres of vegetables wouldn't support the livestock the Pax unit had hoped to bring during that first summer. And since there were no buildings to house cattle, this part of the program was delayed. When no work had been done on the buildings by fall it was pointed out that livestock could not be brought until housing was completed.

At that point, Bishop Irineos provided sand, cement, and one or two laborers. Several Paxmen came down from Greece to help and by November 15, the cow barn was finished and work begun on a hog barn.

John Wieler had drawn the plans for the buildings. For foundations, stone from an old Turkish castle was used. A local contractor helped to stake the areas.

The fellows also brought in a cement mixer and a block machine. The bishop provided cement and sand so they could begin making blocks.

Since then the building program has developed fairly well with the hog barn completed, a poultry barn built, a feed mill structure finished, and milk house and brooder house on the way. Land area available has been increased to seven acres, still not nearly enough to maintain the cattle which finally arrived in June 1966.

Louise remembers that occasion, as does every Paxman there at the time:

This was a big event, especially after the numerous delays. At the outset people had been skeptical. Then their amazement at the building skills of the Paxmen overshadowed the skepticism. But when the cow barn was finally finished and still month passed month without the arrival of cows, the doubters seemed to triumph.

At last came a letter from MCC headquarters saying that the cattle would leave about June 22. Virgil spent a whole day at the telegraph office waiting for the final wire.

The shipment came by air, landing first at Heraklion, then coming on to Chania. All of us waited anxiously for the DC-4 to touch down. The town looked festive that Saturday night. Many who had given up hope were out on the streets to welcome the cattle. Finally, the cows had come to the farm.

We tied them up, watered them, and had them settled a little after midnight. They were all in excellent shape. Eight of the heifers and the one cow were bred.

United States AID paid the $16,000 transportation ticket. Two Beachy Amish men came along to care for the shipment.

That was a big weekend. It seemed now that our work was beginning to shape up. Although livestock were only a part of the total plan, the arrival of the cattle—one cow, eleven heifers, and one bull—symbolized movement of the program into a future. Included in the shipment were fifteen gilts and five boars along with some equipment: shallow well pump, milk cans, pails, and milkers.

Initially, the food grown found ready use in the hostels. But the present purposes have grown far beyond that part of the dream.

Virgil outlines our farm goals as follows:

1. To improve agriculture on the island of Crete through both a farm school and extension program when the boys leave school.

2. To be a demonstration farm.

3. To provide a source for improved livestock. It is hoped farmers will buy stock and upgrade the local stock.

4. To produce food for the educational hostels—vegetables, milk, eggs, and meat.

The feed mill is designed to serve the entire community. And the poultry project, we hope, can be useful in upgrading poultry stock in the villages.

When the cows from America first came whole families stopped in to see them. And there is still a steady stream of visitors who have heard of the farm and want to see for themselves the comparisons between Greek farm stock and ours. During 1967 an estimated 3,000 people visited the farm to see our work.

We're glad for this and for the confidence represented in their increasing acceptance of ideas which we are finding helpful.

Our experiences during the last part of 1967 and early 1968 have been most heartening. The farm has become known as an Agricultural Development Center. We have received excellent commendations from Mr. Iliakis, Director of Agriculture in Chania County where the ADC is located. The manager of a local 50-cow dairy operation has visited us many times to secure information helpful to him. Purchases of dairy stock, especially calves for breeding purposes, have been so heavy we have been forced to stop taking orders because requests far outdistance current supply.

The swine project too has developed a long waiting list of farmers anxious to purchase stock. More than a third are sold for breeding purposes. Some hogs are fattened in order to supply meat to the student hostels. Hogs which are sold to farmers are normally delivered by the Paxmen. This gives them an excellent opportunity to get out into the villages, meet the villagers, and discuss with them their problems and concerns.

Nearly every village family has chickens running around the yard. So the work in poultry has had great demonstrational value as well. Placement of breeding stock, sale of hatching eggs, development of a broiler program, and use of poultry and eggs in the student hostel dining rooms justify all the work the fellows have done in this area.

The field program includes the use of herbicides, greenhouse management, and development of a vegetable- and fruit-canning project. The feed mill has carved a significant place for itself in the effort to provide balanced feed for stock we are selling. The demonstration and extension features in the ADC outreach are increasingly basic. A swine-breeding service is offered for native sows and gilts, as well as for stock we have sold.

In all, the current growth and increasing acceptance of our work makes this an exciting time to be related to the ADC. Every project on the farm is listed in the 1965-1975 development plan for Crete. We think this work is beginning to play an important role in the development of agriculture throughout the island.

Like a flower that stays in bud a while, the Pax contribution in Crete has begun to bloom. The early frustrations and growth pains look less important now as we see the present response to our work.

Of course, there are still problems—and unanswered

questions. Where do we find a farm manager? What type of relationship should we develop with the agricultural department? With a small acreage how shall we solve our feed problems? Where can the bishop find money so that we can function as planned? What about markets and the social aspects of production—for example, the fact that people refuse to eat cheese unless it is made in part at least of goats' milk?

But this is why we're here. To find the questions hidden in the problems of the island and then look for the answers.

However, there's something deeper than that. Both Virgil and I feel strongly that the core of our contribution is found in how we as a unit function, live together, and get along. And then how each of us relates to the people we meet.

These are two areas where I feel I can help. And there are opportunities, in and out of the unit. Outside of the unit, one is always learning to adjust to Greek ways.

When we first came to Greece, we were shocked again and again by the frank curiosity and unabashed questions of the Greek people. Of course, this is most true of villagers, with whom we have the most contact. As I'd walk to Kolymbari to do the grocery shopping, I would meet many women on the road. In the first meeting with most women the line of conversation seldom varied: "Good morning. How are you? Where do you live? How long will you stay here? Are you married? How long have you been married? Do you have any children? Why not?" Then we'd walk on.

How we lived was also a matter of curiosity. One morning, just before lunch, an unexpected visitor called my name outside the door. (The Greeks seldom knock. They stand outside, calling out the name of the person they wish to see, expecting that person to answer the door.)

My visitor was a middle-aged lady from the little village nearby. I had never met her before but she seemed to know me very well.

I ushered her into the house expecting to learn the purpose of her visit. She asked me how I was and other similar questions, meanwhile thoroughly examining every detail in the kitchen. Before I had time to answer her questions and return the polite questions about her health and her family, she was already in the living room, opening the door to the bedroom. Then I understood the purpose of her visit and let her continue inspecting our living quarters. She also had a peek through the office door.

Finally she came back to the kitchen where I was turning some fried liver. She commented on our wonderful house and added that she must be on her way again. And was gone.

This has happened many times, as women from the village have come to see me for the first time. We have discovered these brief contacts to be bridges across which we travel to meet each other.

The same has been true of other contacts. Village festivities, social occasions, family feast days, marriages —all become opportunities for relationship and ultimately service. The sharing of ourselves is the essence of that service. Without such sharing the things we give or the activities we promote or the projects we develop are quite empty.

That's a big job.

A second area Virgil and I have talked of is the liaison we maintain between our unit and the supporting church. Here too we want to make a contribution.

One matter which has disturbed us a little, along with our unit as well as other units elsewhere, we've heard, is the apparent preoccupation with things. For example, here in Crete we are told by MCC that the program's relationship with the Greek Orthodox Church is important. Yet in our reports we're never asked about our relationship to the church, just about buildings, livestock, and material things. The intangible elements of our work are seldom probed.

Another thing. We'd like to see our administrators stop in oftener to sense, and help with, this non-material progress.

We think a real gift to the life of the Cretans as people would be for a theology professor or student to spend several years here just having dialogue with our Greek Orthodox friends. Nowhere could there be a more congenial atmosphere for such sharing. Who knows what the results could be?

As I said before, the big job though is in unit life—just to be the kind of people living together whose witness will make an impact. That's not real easy. A group of single fellows living with a married couple. But if Pax means anything, it means peace.

We've had a good group. Yet there has to be a lot of give and take—in many ways.

For example, our toilet is the detached, garden path model. With seven or eight in our family there's usually a morning lineup. One of the fellows said, "If you go early, you hurry because people are waiting to get in. If you go late, you hurry because people are waiting to eat breakfast."

Then there's the question of roles we play. Sometimes Virgil and I feel like Mom and Dad. Other times like big brother or big sister. And sometimes we're not sure.

Paxmen are interesting. Most of the time they're men, incredibly mature, skilled, and able. But sometimes they're little boys far from home with a touch of homesickness or discouragement. Perhaps one of our heaviest burdens is trying to find ways to help each fellow see the worthwhileness of his work. And then to fill in the gaps caused by distance from their loved ones, or personal problems or frustrations which come during adjustment to a strange culture.

Of course, I have the same kind of problem occasionally. There are times I feel I'm not doing anything worthwhile as a cook. I'd like to be out with people more and be a friend to many.

I'd like to be a neighbor. A helping hand. A listening ear. To communicate. To share.

I guess that's my philosophy of life. To be aware of people and to be aware of the world. To make others happy. To live every minute. To be truly alive. Somehow to reflect the lessons I learned as a child during our times of need.

Crete has taught me much. The Paxmen have taught me. Working with Bishop Irineos has helped me learn some necessary lessons. Virgil and I have been learning together.

This is life. In the final analysis it doesn't matter much where we are—in Crete or Kansas. But how we relate to people, communicate with them, love them— this is where meaning is found.

It's strange, isn't it? We had to come to Crete to see this more clearly.

VIETNAM

Earl Martin

Caught in the matrix of an unholy crusade, the people called Vietnamese strain to give birth to a nation. Nor are they being helped by the foreign mid-wives who, in decades and centuries past, have added to the agonizing travail by their own selfish arrogance. In this day, the corpse of the not-yet-born nation chokes the future with death. And the past, alive once in tomorrow's womb, now clogs the gasping breath of hope with the crud of despair.

"He motioned toward the adjacent building. The four other Vietnamese privates dressed in their green uniforms nodded. As we approached the building the stench put us on guard. He pulled open the slatted door . . . there they lay. Pale and yellow. Still in death. Stinking, mangled bodies. The six stretchers sticking to the floor in pools of coagulated blood—a feast for the overfed flies buzzing in the blazing afternoon heat. Dirty, bloody torn uniforms still clinging to the six corpses.

"We broke our gaze and stepped aside; a middle-aged Vietnamese lady approached the door in a state of semishock. On sight of the bodies she lost control of her emotions. Were her husband or son here? She tried to look again but turned away sobbing. The soldier led her around the side of the building and opened another door. Twelve more corpses. Again she turned away, great dry sobs racking her body.

"Suddenly it is difficult to think of war in terms of politics or economics or ideologies. Right now it doesn't seem to matter who should rule the country—President Diem, General Ky, President Thieu, Ho Chi Minh."

What does it matter whether it is VC snipers who cut

down some American mother's son? Or a terrorist duo from North Vietnam that kills the wife and children of a South Vietnamese army colonel? Or a company of Marines who slaughter an unsuspecting VC platoon? Or bombs made in U.S.A. which reduce a corner of Hue to smoking rubble and crush a thousand bodies?

What does it matter?

Death always smells the same.

Into this desolation where peace is slivered daily into a million bloody shards come the men of Pax. Not many. But enough to say, "There are also men who love. Men who do not need to kill to serve their country."

Earl Sauder Martin was one of these—a man of Pax. With others of the Mennonite Central Committee team working under Vietnam Christian Service, Earl took his place as a messenger of peace, as one who labors to reconcile instead of to destroy.

Lancaster County, Pennsylvania, was home to Earl. The town: New Holland. He was born April 28, 1944, and lived his growing years on the 35-acre farm marked by Box 12, Route 2.

Earl's growing years were marked by parental interest:

Pop and Mom's primary concern was to bring up their children "in the nurture and admonition of the Lord." They were not outspoken about discipline, but somehow we always knew what they expected of us, and I felt pretty rotten when I didn't live up to their expectations.

Pop was creatively spiritual. Every morning, usually long before getting up had ever occurred to us, Pop was on his knees at the parlor sofa. I suspect it was this consistent and deeply personal relationship Pop had with his God that shaped his convictions and principles for rearing his seven children. Mom loved us all intensely, and that love embraced a yearning for her children to know the best in life. To Mom, the "best" meant being in the Lord's will.

Six years I walked to Maple Grove. That little red schoolhouse symbolized practically everything I have ever learned or felt, in school and around people— the insatiable urge to know, a striving for mastery, the joy of relationship, the exhilaration of play, the satisfactions of work, the reward of honesty.

Honesty was a big thing with me. Truth was pretty important. But I learned my lesson the hard way— after putting up with the pain of falsehood for a long time.

I had just received a new penknife as a gift. The morning after, I was showing it off by whittling at a maple twig. But in the unaccustomed scraping I carved a cut into a finger. I ran to the teacher for a bandage. Too late I saw my mistake. She would ask for the knife. So, when she finished the bandage and asked where I had hurt my finger, I said, "I stumbled on the path and a sharp cinder scratched it open."

To my nine-year-old mind sin was clearly defined. I knew I had sinned. That sin had to be confessed or there would be no forgiveness. And it was not Miss Brendle's forgiveness that worried me; it was God's forgiveness. He had heard the lie and should I die He would have no mercy. I would have to confess to escape judgment. But the penknife was fully two years old before I forced my way up that oiled wood floor to Miss Brendle's desk. Through tears I stammered my confession. *Then I could face God again.*

Earl attended public high school where he was active in Youth for Christ.

His work experience began on the parental farm. But he reports his mother's comment, "Earl, you often work harder getting out of work than you would have to if you just got on with the job."

Earl changed, though. Working away from home was good for him—and for his parents. He was able to prove to himself, and to them, that he could work, even at jobs he didn't like. He spent two summers at a poultry-processing plant—one summer pulling backs off chickens on a "dis-assembly line" and the other summer washing trucks in the plant's garage.

Then he got a job at Sauder Chevrolet in the Parts Department, afternoons after school and full time for three summers. There he learned a lot about the need for accuracy, as well as how to get along with people.

While Earl was a junior high student the Mennonite Central Committee was calling for Pax assistance in Vietnam. Late in 1956 two Paxmen were transferred from Germany to work in Saigon, one in the MCC office and one to help in mobile clinic work. By 1958 four Paxmen were on the roll working at Banmethuot in the medical clinic and material aid distribution.

Until Daniel Gerber's abduction from the leprosarium by the Vietcong in 1962, Banmethuot figured most largely in Pax work in the country, although in 1960 some assistance was given also at both Nhatrang and Saigon.

A leprosarium operated by the Christian and Missionary Alliance was located south of Banmethuot in the central highlands of South Vietnam. Three Paxmen, Don Voth, Leland Good, and Alan Hochstetler, began work early in 1959 on a patient facility to house 30 additional persons. Voth served as unit leader and general administrator; Hochstetler as construction foreman.

Wood for the construction was cut by hand by Vietnamese woodcutters from a termite-proof jungle hardwood right where the tree was felled. The tree from which almost all of the wood came was two meters (about eighty inches) through at the base and a good twenty meters to the first branch. This was cut up by hand.

Four Raday workers were hired to do manual labor, dig trenches, make 6,000 cement blocks, mix cement and mortar, and haul fill dirt with the Power Wagon. One Vietnamese carpenter did nearly all the woodwork for the two wings, including finishing out the interior, making cabinets, beds, and other items.

Some building at the Nhatrang clinic hospital was also carried out during 1960. And in Saigon, during the same year, there were various kinds of relief distributions.

For several years, although MCC continued work in Vietnam, the only Paxman in the country was Daniel Gerber, a free man until May of 1962, then held in captivity by the Vietcong. Several reports say he is alive and well, but these cannot be confirmed.

During this time Earl found his way to Hesston College and began a liberal arts program.

Earl studied hard but, as he says:

I rarely let studies interfere with my extracurriculars. I felt education was in no way restricted to books and perhaps some of one's best learning took place on the tennis court, at the bird sanctuary, or in the chapel.

In many ways Hesston was a shaking of the foundations for me, a secularizing two years. The study of history and religion, with a more liberal interpretation than New Holland had given me, opened exciting new vistas of discovery. I found the courage to ask questions I had feared before to ask. *This process continued in Earl's further studies.*

Before leaving for service Earl spent one term also at Penn State University. The distance between Hesston and the university campus was great. While struggling to span it, he discovered a new awakening and a growing hunger to expand experience. His interest in international affairs was sharpened; so the response to an invitation for service in Vietnam was natural.

Of course, prior to this, other motivating factors entered the picture.

Earl describes these:

Perhaps it was the missionaries in our home telling exciting stories of their work. Or maybe it was those current events classes at Maple Grove when we talked about Australia and the Suez. Maybe it was the letters from my brother Luke in Germany or Raymond in Somalia. It could have been the foreign exchange students in high school and college. Or perhaps it was just that big world map hanging on our living-room wall.

Whatever it was, I had known for a long time that someday I would go. Go and learn. Go and discover. Living "abroad" was nothing less than a mandate from myself to me. How else could one really know and understand? How else could one shake that shackling feeling of being provincial, of being small? So the desire to know and the uncertainty about a college major or profession and the discontent in Penn State's depersonalized atmosphere brought the seed of thought to germination and into full flower burst the latent desire for adventure, for travel, for experience, for the new.

For Earl, desire and dreams merged into one and pushed him toward fulfillment.

Earl is not an unusual young man, except for the fact he may be more honest than most. To crave experience is a concomitant of youth. And Pax, many times, provides the opportunity for wider experience set in the context of service, both to country and fellowman.

But no one should be fooled. Factors impelling into

overseas service are not simple. Few twenty-year-olds find their service motivations full of unalloyed altruism. Selective Service regulations exercise a certain organized pressure on young men whether they join the military or perform alternative service. Public opinion adds to the pressure. Childhood teaching on love and service carries more or less weight. The appetite for new sights, new smells, new people is present. And, for the men of Pax, there is almost always the hope of finding during their years of service work that is constructively useful. Earl was no exception.

He recounts:

When I boarded that Boeing 707 in Philadelphia, my step was light. Surely I would miss Mom and Pop and "my girl." But the time had come to take my place more surely in the adult world of service and responsibility. I had little anxiety about what lay ahead. I was never very articulate in my expectations of three years in Vietnam. Enough to know I would be sharing life in a new culture. This satisfied me.

I was especially excited about coming to a war zone. Since war has been the experience of so many peoples of the world, I prized the opportunity to experience with them, to try to understand the forces and feelings that comprise a war, to be where people faced its horrors, and to carry some of their burdens.

If there were any messianic visions surrounding my coming to Vietnam, they were not of converting the multitudes to Christianity or even to a new way of life. I first wanted to understand and appreciate their way of life. But I think I liked entertaining the prospect that I would be an ambassador for peace in Vietnam, a minister of reconciliation within some small pocket of the conflict.

Vietnam is at war; perhaps more correctly, there is war in Vietnam. Many Vietnamese question seriously whether this is their war at all.

It seems a little silly to ask whose war this is. And sad. Because this war which no one wants and no one claims as his own is tearing a land apart and ruining a culture and debasing a people.

Take, for example, the little town of Pleiku. You make me tired, Pleiku. Damn you. You are the prostitution of everything good in Vietnam. Dung. Offal. Your streets are dirty. Your prices are uncouth. Your little boys laugh rudely at foreigners. Your little girls cling like so many lampreys sucking attention and money.

His whiskered face was kindly. He looked at me as if he knew me—probably another GI in town for a ride. He overheard me talking to several high school boys about being in Pleiku for a few days and butted in *"Ong o Quang Ngai, phai khong. . . ."* (You're of Quang Ngai, aren't you? And you came to Pleiku for a break, didn't you? You like to play, don't you? You like to play with girls, don't you? I'll get you a girl to play with you.)

Down the street, I stopped for a cooling drink. The loose-bloused waitress leaned over me, "What is your name?" She snuggled closer, "Oh really, are you working in Quang Ngai? . . . That's my hometown." Her friendliness was becoming too obvious. But apparently I didn't respond quickly enough; she hurried off to snag some Marines who had just walked in.

Pleiku, your soul is damned. Where is the restraint you once knew? Where have your polite and gracious children gone? Where are your peaceful streets? Where are your honest shopkeepers? Where is your respect for foreigners? Where are your men and boys who work in the fields and small industries? Where are your virgin girls who once epitomized beauty and poise?

(The shopkeeper said he remembers the time when none of these 20,000 American GI's were in the Pleiku area.)

Earl, like other men of Pax, is appalled at the horrors involved in the rape of a nation.

It isn't just the bombs. Or the search and destroy missions. Or the napalm drops. Or the defoliation. Or the deserted villages. Or the plundered fields.

If the damage were done to things alone, atonement could be made more simply. But the damage is being done to people.

Nor is it just the gut torn open. Or the third-degree burns. Or the sightless eyes. Or the limbs chopped off to stumps.

If the damage were done to bodies alone, healing and therapy and artificial limbs could lighten the problems. But the damage is being done to their spirits.

And it isn't just the soldiers who are killed. Or the women who die because they were in the wrong place at the wrong time. Or the children who peer closely at a strange plaything on the jungle path and have their heads blown off. Or the old people who just can't make it anymore and give up and die.

If the damage were done only to those who die, one perhaps could add up the cost and rationalize an answer. But the real damage is being done to the next generation and the next and possibly the next. The moral fiber of millions is being marked and scarred with a nameless and frightening malady.

This is why a Paxman must come, in the name of Christ, to be a presence. A presence which speaks caring. Caring enough to be with those who suffer while they are suffering.

Earl lives and works at Quang Ngai, located close enough to the South China Sea to be graced with cool afternoon breezes which rustle the ever-present bamboo trees. It is the commercial center of the province bearing the same name. No large industries are established here but there are many small businesses. Depending on VC activity in the area there is freedom to travel as much as twenty kilometers from the city. Beyond that, travel is limited to aircraft.

Quang Ngai is a delightful place even though the war is all around. The hues of the evening sunset tinge leaves and flowers with a touch of liquid twilight. The gathering dusk brings forth the chirp of a contented sparrow, the graceful kowtowing of the rice seedlings, the whisper of evening air through the stately bamboos, the shout of a child's delight as he plays in the street. And as the twilight slips away, lanterns appear, low-turned and bobbing.

Or the new sounds of morning bring freshness to the spirit. A school girl reciting her lesson. A young lad practicing a new song on his guitar. The bread boy calling out his wares on the street. The common sounds of living.

There are also the sounds of death.

The insane clatter of Army tanks clanking their way out of town. The incessant din of Army trucks and jeeps getting about their business of making war. The lacerating scream of Phantom jet fighters as they dive to rain fiery hell on terrified villagers. The earth literally vibrating with the saturation bombing of midmorning B-52 raids.

And the sounds of appreciation. Earl expressed these as he recalled visits with friends:

Being foreigners we have always been treated most graciously. And there seems to be genuine appreciation for our presence in Quang Ngai.

Mr. Quang is the government service chief of agricultural cooperatives. We accepted his invitation to dinner one evening as he commented on our presence in Vietnam: "First of all we like someone who can speak to us in our language. We want to make friends with you and come to understand you as a person

and as a Westerner." And in his Vietnamese gracious-
ness which a foreigner may consider to be flattery,
he continued, "We like what you are doing in Quang
Ngai. We appreciate the sacrifice you are making in
order to help our people, especially the refugees. We
love to see you riding bicycles when most of the other
Americans are driving cars and trucks."

Then there is the sound of honesty—the questions
shaped to probe deeply.

From the moment we climbed the ladder into their
second-story cubicle, we knew an exciting evening
lay ahead. As we squatted around a raincoat spread
on the floor as a tablecloth, his wife was setting the
dinner before us—traditional North Vietnamese rice
meat roll with fish sauce, and beside each place,
Coca-Cola. While Pat Hostetter asked the blessing
on the food we felt a spirit that superseded national
and cultural differences.

Perhaps Quang and his wife could live more ex-
travagantly than they do. But then Quang's life is
centered around people more than things. The sim-
plicity of the one room which was home to them reflected their general attitudes toward life. We knew
that the tasty meal Mrs. Quang had prepared for her
four guests was quite special. And we were reminded
again that many of our friends in this country eat
more modestly than we.

An evening breeze flickered the candlelight as Quang
cleared his throat to speak: "Our people appreciate
when you come to our country to help. . . . But I want
to ask you one question. In what way will you help
us?" The query came simply and sincerely. Yet it uncovered a world of feeling and understanding—both in
ourselves and in the people we had come to serve.

"Many of your people come to our country with the
honest intention of helping us, but many times they do
not help us but hurt us." I thought at once of the

mistaken bombing of innocent villages or the fact that American soldiers had obliterated all that there had once been of his rice farm, his fruit orchard, and his old farmhouse. But he brought me back to earth with "I don't mean the war people although that is bad, very bad. I am thinking of the people who come in peace to help us; instead we are hurt."

Quang's question to us was pertinent. Our group has been involved in distributing food, clothing, and other commodities to our Vietnamese neighbors. Now he was asking us, "How can you give?"

As a Paxman, I wondered. Our lives had never been blessed with physical need. We had known only the unhappy fortune of possessing. Now we had come to a land which had learned the hard lessons of suffering and deprivation and desperate need.

Why had we come? What did we have to give? Had we come to serve our brother? Or were we here to give our consciences rest—our wealth-laden consciences. Never was our giving out of painful sacrifice; rather, out of unending supply.

"Your giving of things without the giving of yourselves is making people dependent on the rich foreigner. Many of our people are becoming lazy."

Quang didn't say so but we could not miss the further application. What he said about things could also apply to the giving of our advice, our culture, our religion. In this country already plagued with literally thousands of advisers, how could we further insult the self-confidence of the people by passing on a "better way of life" or "a superior religion"?

We climbed down the ladder out of Quang's room realizing we could not teach until we had learned; we could never advise until we had listened; we could not really give until we had first known the blessing of great need. And perhaps it was in listening and learning that we truly gave.

I could not help but think of the way of Jesus who spent His life in giving Himself—very seldom things—rather Himself.

Perhaps this was a lesson Paxmen would still have to learn. That the building of houses and barns, the gift of cows and chickens, the distribution of food and clothing, the proud turning over to national agencies of facilities and extension programs had missed the point of the lesson Jesus came to teach. The real gift, if it was given at all, lay in the way the Paxman gave of his self to people. And the only lasting monument of his effort is found in those who have learned from him to give of their selves to each other.

Perhaps after all, the Vietnamese have something to teach us. For they are learning lessons we have never been introduced to. In the refugee camps, for example.

One of the helpless groups caught in the clutches of this conflict are the refugees. Most of the refugees were made so by the continued Vietcong harassment in areas where control was disputed, by some military operation in the area or by the incessant and either careless or indiscriminate bombing by American air power.

And with this uprooted set of farmers, carpenters, and fishermen who have been forced to leave their homes and take up temporary residence in a refugee camp, we have the opportunity to share life. And particularly so with the numerous women and children.

When a person asks me what our work consists of, I look him squarely in the eye and try to catch his reason for asking. If his eyes are the wary eyes of a USAID official or the inquisitive eyes of a veteran program man or the searching evaluative eyes of a born administrator, I'm likely to reply that my job consists of camp improvement, digging wells, building latrines, erecting schoolrooms, planting gardens, digging drainage ditches, and teaching handicrafts to the disabled, the old, and the blind.

But if those questioning eyes sparkle with living and perhaps a certain joyous, foolish, youthful idealism, along with the gentle warmth of understanding, my reply may take on a different character.

What do we do here in Quang Ngai? Well, we equip ourselves with a few rudimentary tools like some facility in the Vietnamese language, a pair of sandals, a bicycle instead of a car, and a smile.

Then we ride to the refugee camp and stroll through the market to see what's for sale that morning, squat down and discuss prices with a gnarled old woman chewing betel nut, show a child the little homemade kaleidoscope we carry in our pocket, teach him how to play hopscotch, sit down on a bamboo bed and listen to an old farmer tell about his house, his rice harvest, and his oxen in his *que houng* of Thu Thinh. We'll also probably accept his invitation to stay for lunch even though we know we're gambling on a week of the "Hanoi hops."

Both answers could be quite correct. It just depends on the eyes.

Part of our work is also material distribution of different kinds. We enjoy sharing in this way but each time we do the old questions come up. Am I giving more by handing out a bundle of clothing or sitting on a bamboo bed listening?

If it is more blessed to give than to receive, it is certainly also more humbling to receive than to give. Giving of things without giving of oneself makes one proud. Receiving from a person who does not give himself creates resentment toward the giver. Giving that which has cost the giver nothing destroys the giver.

We just received a large shipment of commodities to be distributed at our discretion. I have no doubt that the persons who gave these clothes, or the money to buy school kits or health kits, or their time to prepare the shipment, have done it in sincerity and with concern. But now we face the challenge of placing these in a way that will really constitute a gift and not a hurt.

Should we select a needy community and make a mass distribution, risking the resentment that grows out of such a comparison between cultures? Should we select individual families who appear to have critical need for this specific gift and risk the reactions of those who don't receive? Should we step back and ask the Vietnamese to do the distribution and risk family or regional favoritism?

How shall we give? It's hard to know. Yet there must be some validity in the desire to share and some way for those who have, to share with those who have not.

Perhaps, as I said, the Vietnamese have something to teach us. A set of values that could be closer to the New Testament than our American way of life. An understanding about the transiency of things. An attitude toward time.

Life is to be lived—each moment. In the midst of war's clamor, Vietnam quietly teaches me that. It is a difficult lesson to learn for those of us nourished with the virtues of industriousness and achievement. We find it hard to accept the old man who sits at his table practicing Chinese calligraphy when he could be out cultivating a rice crop. We cannot understand very well why a man would not subject himself to a definite work schedule in a factory if this would mean a higher wage.

Yet, I'm learning, slowly, to find the bridges between cultures. Bridges which, hopefully, can bear the weight of mutual sharing and later mutual understanding.

There are other things I've learned, most painfully. Perhaps the most frustrating and enlightening and rewarding lessons I've learned in Vietnam have been about myself. I claim to be a pacifist but in a flare of impulse this morning I kicked Keo, our dog. I tell my Vietnamese friends we must seek the path of love and peace within this war situation. But this afternoon I gossiped about another unit member to a friend of mine.

Always learning. I feel guilty, having come to give, and instead receiving so much. So many have been my gracious teachers.

The workman who came this morning to beg help to acquire tin roofing, the little guy I sat beside in church who didn't seem to know any of the hymns because they had Western tunes, the exuberant province chief congratulating the Quaker couple upon their dedication of a Child Day Care Center, the uncommonly rotund female proprietor of the little side restaurant where we ate, the little fellows along the street playing marbles stopping long enough to "Hello, numbah one" the passing Americans—all of these contribute to the day. And each of these has taught me a part of his life. With Tennyson I feel "I am part of all I have met."

I am part also of each experience or sensation, each memory . . . bamboo shoots . . . muddy roads . . . overexposed film . . . U Thant . . . pomp and circumstance . . . cinnamon on rice porridge . . . Masiko . . . "thank you" not "tank you" . . . parents' pride . . . flat tire . . . birthday cake . . . busy blind hands . . . deprivation of things . . . bougainvillea . . . God with us . . . the mighty sky . . . Orion.

The memories also—"847 Vietcong dead, actual body count, probably several hundred more which were dragged away before the count." And the weapons, hundreds of them captured on display downtown in front of the city library. The prisoners also, 27 of them, Vietcong, spoils of war.

When I came on the scene scores of people were milling around looking at the weapons and just being caught up in the weird festivities of the occasion. Then they came, as I stood beside my bicycle, dirty, unkempt, poorly clothed, blindfolded, hands tied behind their backs, lines of these hunted beings were wired together to prevent escape. The armed guards—South Vietnamese-Americans—herded them up the street to what must have been their waiting cell and horrifying interrogation.

Memories and sensations crowd around one daily. The country is pulsing with life—hurried din of the marketplace, the eager bustle in crowded schools, the villages and the refugee camps, pulsing with life and reeking with death—the staccato bursts of gunfire, the deep and distant rumblings of a B-52 bomb load finding its mark and tearing the earth apart, the skyful of helicopters (right now there's a lot of fighting going on in Quang Ngai province).

But the memorable part, the really exciting part of Pax service is people.

Sometimes it's that person you pass on the street; sometimes it's the child reaching with his grubby hand to tug at your shirttail; sometimes it's the gnarled old man with a wispy beard who extends a bony hand to meet the Paxman who has come to visit his village.

And even more, it is with the other members of the unit that perhaps our most intensive, most demanding, and most rewarding relationships are cultivated. After living in the same house with five other people for months on end, one comes to perceive rather clearly one's threshold of tolerance. It is in this everyday laboratory that the Paxman is challenged to live the pacifism he professes. It is in the crucible of unit life that a man is melted, forged, shaped, and tempered. If any feeling of disenchantment with a unit member is allowed to go to seed, this will bring a harvest of bitterness and contempt. If any feeling of affinity with a unit member sparks into being, this may well develop into an intensively honest brotherhood relationship. It is in the inescapable "always" of unit living that the Paxman experiences the exhilaration of his Everests and the black despair of his valleys of Baca.

Vietnam waits at the crossroad where sanity and selfishness are fighting a battle for the soul of a nation. While its people, puzzled and frightened and numb with the regular crushing of hope, carry the burdens of war, the men of Pax stand beside them, not with glib answers but simply with the word of caring spoken by presence.

3 PAX AND MISSION

WHY PAX?

The real *why* of a man's decision often lies hidden beneath a thick fog of dubious rationale. Or is jostled into the background of conscious thought by conflicting drives. Or is lost in the busy clutter of daily activity.

To find that *why* and then, having found it to face it, demands a peculiar brand of courage not always a mark of men still in their teens or just barely moving into adulthood. Yet the men of Pax who crossed my path wielded a sharp knife of self-analysis as they searched their wanderings for the telltale footprints of motivation.

These footprints varied from a hazy outline to a sharply defined shape; from a pattering of tiny prints scattered across an adolescent past to one or two massive indentations pressed indelibly into a growing personality; from the hesitant, faltering step of wondering uncertainty to the long, bold stride of newly acquired independence. As the images of past decisions and actions flashed on the screen of memory, a refreshing honesty focused each image until there lay, clearly revealed, each mark of motivation in telling sequence.

For many, the image of Pax has been polished to a false but lustrous sheen by the touch of glamor in travel to distant lands, or by the whisper of noble service to deprived peoples, or even by the hint of condescension toward those whose patriotism leads them to share in violent and bloody cause. Certain honest men of Pax admitted they were dazzled, some almost blinded, by this luster shining on the path they had chosen.

Others conceded that Pax service offered an escape: from an affair of breaking hearts, from imperious parental domination, from a superficial set of values—or a postponement: of college major decisions, of vocational choice, of assuming the responsibilities of adult life outside the security of protective institutions—or an opportunity: for self-identification, for self-development, for self-direction.

Still others searched in vain for the shape of a motive. Instead, all they found was the happenstance of a Pax recruiter, or parental encouragement, or peer group decision, or the pressure of their next birthday.

Of course, for citizens or permanent residents of the United States, overriding every other possible motivation, in terms of immediacy at least, was the United States draft of manpower through procedures set up under Selective Service. Regardless of personal elements leading to a Pax service decision, there was always present the law of his country which required of a young man a period of service in the national interest.

So essentially, except for Canadians, each Paxman is conscript, caught in the mesh of defense planning but allowed to contribute his gift of patriotism through an approved form of alternative service. Within the alternative, options do exist and the conscript may make choices. In this sense of having chosen Pax, he is a volunteer for the rigors and demands and opportunities inherent in the Pax program. Yet, the U.S. Paxman is never allowed to forget the fact that his work is being done as a Selective Service obligation and that he is a conscripted representative of the United States.

However, within this context of obligatory fulfillment of a national statute, there exists a surprising flexibility. And it is precisely at this point that other factors begin to appear as motivations. Perhaps they cannot be seen correctly as motivations to service; rather as motivations to a quality of service issuing from a religious conditioning, a spiritual commitment, and a highly personal involvement in human need that plunges immensely beyond the provincial boundaries of obligation.

This involvement, intense and generous, marks many Paxmen and uncovers drives and dedication only slightly shaded by the draft requirement.

Peer example probably heads the list of motivating forces. Again and again, those in service and others out of service referred to contacts with former Paxmen as prime movers in the decision-making process.

Marvin Schrock, who did his service in West Pakistan says, "Early in the Pax program, when I was quite young, Ken Imhoff and Harold Neuman visited our community. They had just returned from Pax. I don't know where they served. I can't recall whether they had slides or not. Nor can I remember much of what they said. But the fact that they, as young men, had been able to do something worthwhile made a tremendous impression on me. I couldn't get over the revelation that ordinary persons, like these two, could make a significant contribution to people."

Interestingly, for many, hardships and sacrificial demands constituted the greatest challenge, rather than adventure or a change of scenery. Closely allied to this was the quick response to knowledge of human deprivation—the desire to serve where one was needed, almost desperately needed.

Roy Brenneman, Pax Algeria, said, "I wanted to be where my work would cost me something, where I could really give myself."

Paul Miller, Paxman from Nes Ammim in Israel, echoed Roy's comment: "I had quite a struggle deciding between the military and alternative service. Finally, I chose alternative service, partly because I had great difficulty justifying the violence of war but also partly because I was afraid my new Christian life wouldn't stand up against the temptations I knew I'd face in the army. But then I had trouble justifying what seemed like an escape. That was, until I heard of the Congo and the danger and hardships Paxmen faced there. Then I decided on Pax because it seemed to demand the kind of sacrificing I wanted to do."

Joe Haines, Paxman, went to Hebron Boys' School in Jordan. Later he returned to Beit-Jala (near Bethlehem) as administrator of the school program there. He says, "I was planning to make a career of service to people. From what I had heard, Pax looked like a good test of myself. I felt strongly that, wherever I went, I had to be needed badly; I wanted to do something useful, no matter what it would cost me."

Parental influence formed a third motivation. Some of the Paxmen were obviously careful in their selection of parents. Thus they were blessed with fathers and mothers who not only supported their decision to serve overseas but whose early training had been service-oriented.

Dale Linsenmeyer, Pax Greece, was very explicit: "My homelife influenced me greatly. Our home was always open to missionaries as well as nationals from other countries. I was encouraged to think of others. When I was 13, my parents sent me with several men to a mission station in Arizona. The two weeks spent there molded much of my life. When I came to service age, Pax was a natural."

Home, church, and school provided a context in which influences toward Pax could function. Sometimes, a transient personality touched the young man. But more often it was a steady, consistent, repetitive sharing of philosophy by those nearby. Or it was a challenge exemplified—father, mother, brother, pastor, teacher, classmate—which left its imprint and made the adolescent, in actual fact, a man of Pax. Not made in the sense of inanimate fabrication; rather, made in the sense of providing an atmosphere and a rationale within which the way of peace became the only sensible response.

Surprisingly, dogma by itself seemed to accomplish little. The potential Paxman noticed dogma, was aware of church doctrine, had been exposed to the peace position. And yet somehow, he resented the implication that ready-made reactions were required. Frequently, he rebelled. However, in the process of rebellion he often discovered reasons for faith which reflected the dogma he rejected but were totally his own because he consciously made them so.

This was true at two levels, perhaps most noticeably while the Paxer was deciding between military or alternative service. Sometimes that "decision" was made almost automatically because other options were never seriously considered. In other cases, a Paxman struggled through to the peace rationale during his service. But many times, more times than one would expect, 18-year-old men weighed the issues and made conscious, but often tortured decisions to give up the easy road of mass assimilation in the military machine; instead to stand more or less alone on an unpopular platform.

Having decided, then, on a I-O position (conscientious objection) and having received a I-W classification (a

CO in work program), he frequently floundered in his efforts to choose between domestic service (Civilian Peace Service—formerly known simply as I-W) and overseas Pax.

Without a doubt, many men in the domestic program match the Paxer in considered forethought, in depth of dedication, and in daily involvement with need. At the same time, a large number who eventually selected Pax did so because they felt strongly that their commitment to peace and service required more than they understood a domestic assignment included.

Comments like the following were not unusual; in fact, whenever the two forms of service came into focus together, such testimonies were almost normal. Whether they represent a knowledgeable and objective evaluation or a kind of service bias is difficult to say.

"I had the impression there was less challenge in domestic I-W."

Another Paxman wrote, "To be able to support a car and to be getting home every few weeks didn't seem like service to me, so I chose Pax."

Still another. "I knew I couldn't kill. But I also knew I couldn't accept an undemanding, perhaps even a comfortable or plush job while my buddies were giving up their lives in Vietnam. That's why I felt it had to be Pax for me."

A Bolivian Paxman said, "It was mostly spiritual motivation. This seemed the way to be Christian, most fully Christlike."

Or a Paxer who served in Algeria commented, "I knew a lot of fellows who came back from service. I sort of had the impression those who returned from overseas Pax were different from those returning from domestic service. Whether they went in with more or came out with more, I can't say. But I liked what I saw in returning Paxmen, so I volunteered for Pax."

Men of Pax show themselves human. All of them,

except the Canadians in the program, acknowledge the obligatory nature of service. Many of them concede the existence of crass and human motivations with varying degrees of strength. A few admit these crasser drives were all that drew them into Pax.

However, the majority of men interviewed were unanimous in their emphatic insistence that spiritual motivations were dominant, if not in the decision-making process, then almost certainly during the period of early adjustment to distance from the familiar, adjustment to a new culture, and adjustment to the demands of an assignment, sometimes ill defined and sometimes uncompromisingly rigid.

And where lack of experience of immaturity or a spiritual adolescence made difficult or impossible an in-service evaluation of motivation, the passing of years has sharpened insights. In this more intelligent introspection, accomplished long after the fact, the shaping force of outside influences is seen. And the molding together of both environmental and hereditary forces is recognized as the element compelling rejection of or response to values which have their roots in the way of life Christ exemplified.

For men of Pax, positive response has been the answer. *In the name of Christ* symbolizes their commitment. This has been the essential motivation.

FROM THEN UNTIL NOW

From birth, Pax has shown itself dynamic and alive. Thrust abruptly into pressing need, men of Pax responded with skill and dedication, forcing, just as abruptly, a growth in program to match both the needs they served and their own ready involvement.

From the beginning, these twins—need and resource—have conspired to maintain this growth. Perception, empathy, response, and relevance have driven the Pax program from one milestone to the next. Change and flexibility have marked each era and often have opened the door to constantly expanding opportunities.

Though moving from country to country, the essential character of Pax has remained constant. At the same time, the face and shape of Pax have reflected rapid shifts from infancy, through childhood and adolescence, to an early maturity. Now, in typical fashion, Pax points the finger at its parent and wonders out loud about teaching that parent some of the lessons youthful enthusiasm has learned.

Perhaps these are crucial days. And before Pax becomes fully institutionalized, settling into the ruts of maturity, it may yet shake the status quo sufficiently so that change and flexibility and significance may continue to mark its contribution.

The changes in Pax have taken place on several levels: philosophy, projects, and persons. The first two will be dealt with here and the third in the chapter following.

Already noted is the comment that the essential character of Pax has remained constant. Contrasted with this is the judgment that Pax philosophy has changed. Apparently contradictory, the two statements actually complement each other. They reflect on the one hand a well-placed objective, firmly anchored, and on the other hand, a fascinating flexibility in response that has kept Pax vibrantly alive.

The prophet Ezekiel describes a personal experience which characterizes the unchanging constant in Pax history, "Then I came to them of the captivity at Tela-bib, that dwelt by the river of Chebar, and I sat where they sat, and remained there astonished among them seven days" (Ezek. 3:15).

If any single characteristic identifies Pax, it would be simply the *being with* element. Again and again, the men of Pax have immersed themselves voluntarily in situations of need. Frequently, they admitted that their resources and skills seemed utterly inadequate. And yet, by some miracle of grace, the immediacy of their presence, the sincerity of their sharing, and the honesty of their attempts to understand became a resource. Sitting where they sat—just being with men and women in their need—constituted a gift so seldom given freely.

In all the years of Pax, this essential element has never been modified. But within this context of constancy there have been shifts, even shifts of philosophy. Basically, these changes have not been of quality but of understanding. Perhaps, to be most precise, one could say these have been changes in perception or insight.

This is illustrated best by reference to the Mennonite Central Committee, the Pax parent organization. Its earliest responses to need were characterized exclusively by relief measures: food and clothing, occasionally shelter. Later efforts were enlarged to include reconstruction. Still later, the rehabilitation of persons entered the circle of concerned planning. More recently, discussion about meeting the needs of the whole man has nudged both philosophy and policies in new directions.

Even though a comparative newcomer to the scene,

Pax has shared in each of these levels of service. Identified as stages, however, Pax entered the picture at the stage of reconstruction. Men of Pax today are involved in rehabilitation, as well as efforts to reach the total man, regardless of his need.

As noted earlier, perceptions of need have changed, have been enlarged. In consequence, philosophy of program has changed so that in the midst of a reassuring constancy there has been a dynamic flexibility.

Nowhere has this been more evident than in the tension between so-called social service and evangelism. As a relief and rehabilitation agency Mennonite Central Committee seemed to concentrate on material aspects of need. The early Paxmen followed in this tradition. Yet, in the first group there were those who questioned whether the Christian *should* give only bread. Before long these same men were asking whether the Christian *could* give only bread.

In the theological world, biases still exist which place Christian witness and humanitarian concern in opposition to each other. The one bias insists that the way to a man's heart—the seat of his spiritual affections—is through his stomach. The other bias, in effect says: Forget his stomach, just save his soul.

Men of Pax, offspring of peace churches, struggled with the realities of this conflict. And out of this struggle many of them concluded that a dichotomy of material and spiritual service was not only unrealistic, but also unscriptural. Giving "in the name of Christ" seems not to allow for such a drawing of lines. Following the example of Christ in His ministry to persons with need calls for service to the whole man—giving to every need.

J. D. Graber, former General Secretary of the Mennonite Board of Missions and Charities, writes, "Jesus apparently never attempted to rationalize the connection between service and witness . . . whenever

He saw need He met it, simply because it was according to His nature to do so. . . . If the church is the body of Christ upon earth . . . then she will also serve as Christ served. She will not need to have a formulated philosophy regarding the relationship between word and deed. She will meet human want as Jesus did."

Should the Christian give only bread? The real question is, *Can* the Christian give only bread? Given in the name of Christ, each act becomes a reflection of His concern for the whole man. Each reconciling word becomes a bridge to peace. Each humble sharing becomes a gift of His life to another.

Pax has exemplified this, perhaps largely because its administrators, though fixed firmly in purpose, have been flexible in their responses to need.

Another evidence of dynamic flexibility in program has been the changing image of Pax. From builder in Germany to plowman in Greece; from pulling Le-Tourneau heavy road-building equipment through the jungles of Peru to desk administration in West Pakistan; from ranging the islands of Indonesia in program direction to community development in Algeria; from involvement with refugees in Vietnam to being an ecclesiastical diplomat in Crete.

From unskilled hod carrier to highly skilled agricultural technician, the Paxman has adapted to the environment of need. In the early years, most of the work was manual with only an occasional demand for more professional skills. Recently, much of the program has called for men with academic or technical preparation.

However, even though program requirements have drawn increasingly on those with more preparation, the tradition of Pax that every man must be willing to do any job remains strong. And in turn this tradition is one of the strengths of Pax service.

Of course, the concrete evidence of this changing Pax image rests in the varied and changing nature of Pax projects.

In Hong Kong, Bruce Harvey exemplified versatility. A college graduate, Bruce assisted in the material aid program, carried responsibility for a feeding program, drove a truck hauling supplies, worked as coolie, office boy, and secretary in the Mennonite Central Committee office. Sometimes he worked alone; other times he had a Pax partner.

"Pax Paris, Inc." was the legend painted on a construction pillar late in 1966. Although the major emphasis in the early years of Pax had been building, the construction project in a suburb of the French capital marked something of a departure from the more recent program patterns.

The small Builders Unit in Paris, however, participated in a project of major significance. In a historic way, American Mennonite missionaries and the French Mennonite Church are cooperating with the Welfare Department of France in the development of a work program for retarded persons. One of only three such sheltered workshops in the entire country, the Paris project provides productive employment—assembling zippers, packaging of plastic items, leaflet assembly and packaging—for dozens of individuals between the ages of fifteen and thirty.

The Paris Pax unit is making possible expansion of this profoundly significant work, both in the city and at a country estate nearby.

In Peru, Royce Yoder worked as an auto mechanic. Royce had already fulfilled his two-year Selective Service obligation by the mid-fifties; nevertheless, he decided to enter Pax for a full term.

Tournavista, Royce's service location, lies several hundred miles from Lima, Peru. In return for a tract of jungle land, R. G. LeTourneau, of road-building equipment fame, agreed to build a road for the Peruvian government. Tournavista became the headquarters town of this project and home to a number of Paxmen. Some operated heavy equipment. Royce was assigned to maintain about a dozen vehicles—Army surplus six-by-sixes, Volkswagens, and GMC Carryalls.

Perhaps the Pax travel award, if there were such a designation, would go to Leslie Maust. A Paxer from Michigan, Leslie expected to spend his term working in agriculture on Halmahera, Indonesia. Instead, after a few short months, he found himself working with Church World Service in material aid distribution, project surveys and administration. His travels ranged throughout the two thousand inhabited islands which comprise Indonesia, spread along about three thousand miles of the equator between the Philippines and Australia, and as far afield as Bangkok, Hong Kong, and Tokyo.

But Leslie Maust was not the only Pax traveler, nor the only one whose assignment on the field took on unexpected proportions. David C. Bower left New York for East Pakistan where he planned to serve as an administrative assistant to the East Pakistan Christian Council Economic and Social Welfare Committee. However, a replacement for the retiring director of this committee did not arrive as scheduled, so David spent two years in the top administrative post.

As chief administrative officer, as well as Church World Service representative, David became responsible for the deployment of personnel, allocation of material resources, and general supervision of program. From his headquarters office in Dacca, the capital of East Pakistan, he also maintained liaison with the Pakistani government.

Aside from emergencies, the major effort was a feeding program, although some work was done as well in rehabilitation—finances for self-help projects, agricultural services, development of cooperatives.

After two years in East Pakistan, David moved to West Pakistan, to direct the Church World Service program most of the final year of his three-year term.

And so they serve: the Davids and Bruces and Leslies and Royces. With dedication and versatility. With routine application and sometimes with brilliance. With strong purpose and a willingness to adapt.

To be sure, not all Paxers adapt with equal facility. But there have been few instances of refusal to make valiant efforts. Men who have professional and clerical skills have learned construction where necessary. And some who had been only laborers or farmhands surprised themselves and others when they were pushed into and then willingly tackled administrative jobs.

The trail from then until now has brought Pax into the late 1960's with both gratification at the ground covered and excitement at what the current pioneers may find as they push toward tomorrow.

A new star of considerable promise appeared in the Pax sky on August 10, 1967. On that date five Paxmen landed at Kinshasa, Congo.

Of course, they were not the first. But, as representatives of the new Service Education Abroad (SEA) program, they came as frontiersmen to explore the possibilities of relating service to education in an overseas culture. SEA participants having completed at least one year of college can earn a full year of college credit during a 26-month service term.

While the major part of the term is spent in service, intensive academic experiences will mark the beginning, middle, and end of the period. Courses in African History, Contemporary Africa, African Cultures, Economic Development of Africa, and Religions of Africa will be offered at the Free University of the Congo. During the service term each man will carry an individual study project, as well as develop proficiency in the French language with the aid of a tutor.

The Council of Mennonite Colleges has worked out the program which was extended to Latin America in June 1968. This program may well broaden the Pax idea beyond its traditional form. Thus the new becomes an agent of further change.

And so, in the changing panorama across the Pax horizon new men, within new program patterns, take their places, committed to people, given to reconciliation, ready for any task. Paxmen still dig ditches or use hammers or drive truck. But many more of them are being placed in positions requiring preparation and specific kinds of experience. More of them are better trained when they enter service. And more of them probably attempt to relate their field assignments to vocational choices already made.

These facts do not detract from the extremely significant contributions made by Paxmen ever since 1951. Nor do they belittle one kind of work as opposed to another. But the facts of change in Pax assignments and responsibilities do highlight the flexibility of the program, the excellent adaptability of young men coming from a variety of backgrounds, as well as the great range of potential interest and service present in those who would serve their country as men of reconciliation and good will.

THE RISK IN SERVICE

No Paxman has entered service overseas without running a great risk. Not the risk of travel or flying shrapnel or hostile natives. Nor the risk of rioting mobs. Or the risk of snipers' bullets in burning ghettos. Rather, he runs the risk of being changed, and that greatly.

To be sure, a variety of physical dangers or difficult situations confront Paxmen in some countries. Where there is warfare, there is danger. Where internal rebellions tear a country apart, Paxmen may very well face death. Where countries are underdeveloped, health services may be inadequate and illness a threat. Primitive circumstances often force Paxmen to undergo abnormal hazards.

But the big risk men of Pax face is that their experiences will so change them, they will literally never be the same again.

Nor is this necessarily bad. However, the average person returning from overseas service, if he has responded at all to the challenges before him, has been forced to stretch himself courageously and become in short months a mature and responsible individual. How the Paxman responds to the stimulus of experience helps to determine his usefulness on the field and also his realization of the potential in himself. Ironically, the more completely he gives himself to the task at hand, the greater will be the changes and the more difficult will be his return to the culture from which he has come.

In other words, the greater his dedication, the greater risk he runs that change will set him at cross-purposes with many of the very individuals who applauded his decision to serve in this way.

The Paxmen themselves were quite vocal in their

comments regarding change. Perhaps the frankest self-revelation came from the Paxman who said bluntly, "I just matured; that's all there is to it. I grew up! I started thinking about life and I became aware of the world's needs. I doubt very much if I'd have grown in the same way or to the same degree had I stayed at home."

Another said, "I was different when I came back; the fellows I had left at home seemed different also, but not in the same way. For me, the process of maturation during my two years of service was the big thing."

A Paxman from Israel said, "We came in as boys and we left as men."

An Algerian Paxman testified, "Pax makes a man out of you real quick. You get on the plane and leave home, and that's it. You either grow up or you have problems."

An administrator commented, "Pax service produces real maturity. George Bernard Shaw said, 'Frequently in life my education has been interrupted by schooling.' Pax service is an education. Some of the Paxmen really worked others over. They knocked off rough edges and helped these fellows to reach adulthood."

Closely related to this was the entire process of self-discovery. One Paxman said, "This experience really changed my life. I was put in an atmosphere and into situations where I learned to know a great deal about myself."

A Paxman who served in Bolivia in considerable isolation said, "My period of service represented the first real confrontation with myself. I lived alone and I thought a great deal. Out of these thoughts came perceptions about myself that I probably could not have arrived at in any other way."

A Paxman from Greece wrote, "My service gave me a lot of self-confidence as a person."

A Kansas Paxman said during the course of his service, "The biggest change I have seen in myself lately is simply an understanding of myself, an accepting of myself, and a believing that God has accepted me as I am."

Another Paxman asked, "What changes did I find in my life? I think I lost some of my initial self-assurance after I discovered I didn't know as much as I thought I did. Even though I had graduated from college with good grades and a good sense of confidence, I discovered during my first months that this wasn't enough. Actually, the difficulties of that first month uncovered some things about myself that were necessary for me to know. This is really the beginning: if a Paxman can uncover his roots and find himself in the first months of service, this can make all the difference in the world."

Another area of obvious change was in spiritual perceptions. One Paxman said, after serving in Jordan for a period of time, "For me, it was quite a thing to leave a Christian community and come to a Muslim country. Out here I really learned to dig for myself. I discovered reasons for being a Christian that I hadn't known existed before."

A Paxman who served in Hong Kong said, "Pax made a tremendous spiritual contribution to my life. I had grown up in a Christian home. My childhood was spent in some of the best churches in the country. In a sense, it was easy to be good. During my years in college, I rather slid along spiritually, although externally I am sure I seemed to be a good Christian. In reality, it was the only life I knew.

"The day I graduated from college I was suddenly out from under all the academic pressure. And suddenly I was alone with myself. The undercurrent of uneasiness about my spiritual status, which before I had barely been able to identify, immediately came to the forefront. This is the way I went into service.

257

"During service I had to face myself and my spiritual background in a realistic way. Looking at the different religious customs of Hong Kong, it became perfectly obvious that people following these customs didn't necessarily believe what they were doing. With a rather startling shock I was forced to honesty and had to ask how much different this was on the American scene where the culture seems to be rather Christian.

"I began to face up to some pretty basic questions: Who is God? Does Christianity really make a difference? What does God expect of me? It was during this period of confrontation that I began to grow spiritually. I began to realize that one can do a lot of good things and do them conscientiously, without being spiritually mature. I also began to realize that one can have a large beautiful structure with no foundation—so busy doing good, acceptable things that there is no time for the basics of spiritual living."

A Congo Paxman said about his faith, "I never stopped to think much about my faith before I left. But in the middle of problems and facing situations in which I seemed to be beyond myself, I stopped to think more. In that context the whole experience of faith became a bit more personal."

For a number of Paxmen, these spiritual insights led to simple but significant changes in philosophy of life. One Paxman said, "I learned that I couldn't be a Christian without being a servant."

Another said, "I suddenly discovered that I had to serve other people and stop living for myself, if I really wanted to follow Christ."

After more than two years in Greece a mature Paxman, doing graduate work in the field of economics, said, "To be a Christian and to follow Christ is my main philosophy. I know that it sounds like a cliche, but I believe that I must be an ambassador for Christ."

The desire to help people represented another significant change. One Paxman testified, "I really didn't notice people before, even though I was around them all the time. But in Pax I discovered it is only as one develops friendships, relates to persons, and then helps them that life takes on any meaning."

Another Paxman who served in Europe and who is now a college professor said about his Pax experience, "Personally the timing of my Pax service was very good for me; it shook me out of the rut of self-interest into which I had fallen."

Another Paxman said, "I came to see people as much more important than things. To me this was a revelation."

Without a doubt the most vehement reactions with respect to change were reserved for comments about things—materialism. One Paxman said, "It took me four years to find out that happiness does not lie in things—in a car, in nice clothes, in a well-paying job. The whole experience of Pax has made me anti-materialistic."

From Indonesia, a Paxman writes, "The definition of necessities differs so greatly between the American viewpoint and the viewpoint found in some underdeveloped countries. I think I learned to question the American definition and learned to appreciate the simple life of the people I had come to serve. They taught me so much about values."

A Pax voice from Peru raises a basic question, "I wonder if it is possible to be so tied to materialism and still accomplish God's will?"

These are but a small percentage of a large number of telling comments about changes which took place in the lives of Paxmen in service overseas. A few words can hardly convey the deep feeling with which these sentences were uttered. Nor do they accomplish more than hint at the months of deep struggle while responses to new experiences were being hammered out and direction of life and purpose was being changed. Nor do they reflect the fear and the uncertainty that many of the men felt as they moved into the unknown of uncharted territory.

But change they did, from boys to men, from uncertain individuals to self-assured persons, from students with limited perceptions to knowledgeable searchers-after-truth, many of them conscious that they were in the midst of a profound learning experience.

These men, in new cultures, gradually began to see the selfishness of ethno-centrism. They developed vastly different perspectives regarding nationalism. They acquired a much broader view of the value of education and greater insight that enabled them to recognize when the process was actually taking place. They grew into a readiness to face problems courageously. They learned something about compassion fatigue and what it means to become calloused to need when one is confronted with crying desperate want day after day.

Sheltered until their service began, inexperienced Paxmen were forced to grapple with basic issues of faith. Though young in years, they began to see Christian service in a new light and began to develop their own concepts of how best to serve. They felt the urgency of the complex problem: how do you really help people to help themselves? They felt the chill of national reaction to foreign missionaries who were so busy administering programs they had no time to make friends with people. They struggled with the cynicism that comes from seeing "rice Christians" and the frustration that follows being identified with overseas Christians who were there to help "these poor people," without realizing that they probably needed more help themselves.

All of these sources and influences focused upon the young, untried Paxman, far from home for the first time. And in some cases, they produced serious traumatic reactions. But, significantly, in most cases, the boys became men. Men of Pax rose to the challenge and discovered in that courageous response a quick maturity far beyond their years.

It was during this period also that a great number made basic vocational decisions. Many of these decisions reflected drastic shifts in thinking. A Paxman who served in Germany and Greece said, "My life ambitions were changed. I had planned to be a farmer in a more or less closed and isolated Christian community. However, I was only in service a short time before I began to revise my plans and look for other ways in which I might respond to the needs of men."

A European administrator says, "In many cases, their future vocation became crystal clear because these men were out on the cutting edge of service. They were discovering what they could do and what they couldn't do. They began to realize their potential was far greater than they might have earlier suspected." The same administrator recognized that Pax service often results in drastic changes. In an orientation period he said to a group of them, "Some of you think you are coming for only two years. What you don't realize is that this may very well be only the beginning of a lifetime of this kind of service."

One of the pioneers of the Pax program said to me as he sat in the living room of the parish house next to his congregation, "You wouldn't be interviewing me here if it had not been for Pax. I went over to serve as a farmer and a cabinet builder. I expected to come home and be a farmer and a cabinet builder. Instead, I am a pastor."

No up-to-date and comprehensive study of vocational changes is available. However, Menno Wiebe, in April 1962, completed a study entitled "Effects of Foreign Experiences of Paxmen on Their Vocational and

Religious Outlook." Among other things he discovered, in the group studied, that almost half changed their occupational plans because of service in Pax. He discovered also that a great many Paxmen returned from their service to study, rather than to continue their previous occupation. A high percentage of these new students reflected a pronounced interest in the social area—another evidence of the shift from things to people.

Perhaps the most precise measure of change in the Paxman is the degree of adjustment required when he reenters his native culture. Of course, this is modified in part by the degree of maturity attained during the two- or three-year period of service. However, it was quite evident that those who appeared to have attained the greatest personal maturity seemed to be most out of step with the culture to which they were returning.

Their comments are graphic.

—In a sense we are lonely people when we get home. Very few have gone through similar experiences and people don't seem to have more than a superficial interest in what we did.

—For me the reentry adjustment was critical. I noticed that talk was so mundane, that the philosophies of those around me seemed so material. This resulted in a withdrawal from most people.

—When I got back to America I got the biggest shock of my life. I saw how rich America really was. I couldn't get over it.

—My reactions when I returned to North America from overseas service were the first nudge which started me thinking of going back into overseas service again. I got home to my church and heard them arguing over little things and I began to realize how utterly out of touch with the needs of the world these people were. That is when I began to feel personally responsible.

—I think having been in Pax has made me more uncomfortable than I would have been otherwise. I feel guilty because I am not meeting more needs. I have had a hard time adjusting to the grasping American way of life.

—I understand now why one of the returning Paxmen, before my service, seemed so different. He didn't fit in. But neither did I when I got back.

—When I got home I was appalled at the materialism. But I must admit that I have lost some of my earlier reaction. Being immersed in the culture here at home seems to blunt the edge of one's critical reaction.

—For me the reentry problem was great. I spent the first two weeks walking around in a daze, trying to find my bearings.

—Most congregations are not too sympathetic to the returning Paxman. He seems to be a bit of an oddball. Too often the returning young man finds himself asking questions of his fellow Christians that make them uncomfortable.

—I think I was bothered most by the people who had seemed to support my going. When I returned, the extent of their objective in life seemed to be their own families and their future security. I had a great deal of difficulty reconciling this with the apparent interest they took in my work while I was gone.

—The hardest adjustment for me when I came home was the availability of farms and the feeling of my parents that I must now settle down. For them this meant the traditional vocation.

—I suspect there is materialism in every country in which Paxmen served. However, here at home it seemed to reflect itself in crasser and more thoughtless ways.

—It seems now as if I will feel guilty the rest of my life. I can't just sit down here and forget what I have seen. That is simply impossible. The experience was good for me, but I suspect I will be uncomfortable in my luxury the rest of my life.

One of the reasons, of course, for the discomfort many Paxmen felt when they came home was that their comments and their questions became a conscience to their home communities, to their congregations, and to their own families. The nagging undercurrents of doubts about selfish ways of life rushed to the surface as returning Paxmen told of their experiences. And the plush affluence suddenly looked out of place. Because of this, entire communities sometimes set up walls of reaction against these who returned and became conscience to them. The Paxmen felt this acutely, having had their sensitivities honed during many months of close interaction with people with various kinds of need.

But the Paxmen themselves were also facing certain personal difficulties. Perhaps the greatest of these was a homesickness for the special brand of Pax culture in which they had been living. This represented somewhat of a comfortable limbo—neither home nor foreign in character. It was an atmosphere which accommodated the rebellion of youth but also provided a kind of necessary security.

Another element, closely related, is the radical shift a Paxman faces as he moves from a situation in which the outer reaches of his potential are being challenged, into a situation where he and his gifts seem to be relatively unimportant. Especially has this been true of those Paxmen who have been thrust into positions of considerable responsibility and come home to find themselves a tiny cog in a large wheel or an unnamed student on a campus or the forgotten person returning to a community where all of his former friends are in graduate school or are married and have their first child.

These and many more are the risks of service. But

in assuming the risk, the Paxman has stepped out into an experience which generally has enlarged his vision, has extended his potential, and in a very real way has led to a degree of personal fulfillment that would not otherwise have been possible.

This is why Paxmen continue to accept the risk.

4 PAX IN HISTORY

"It was agreed that we recommend to the MCC Executive Committee that further effort should be made to open to our young men opportunities for civilian service of the greatest possible significance and relevance to human need and suffering resulting from modern warfare."

This recommendation by the Peace Section Executive Committee to its parent body, Mennonite Central Committee, was acted upon March 17, 1951. "Executive Secretary, Orie O. Miller, presented a proposal to set up a separate program of service for IV-E men to be called Pax Services."

Recently retired, Miller reminisces. "One day early that spring I was traveling on the train. The Builders Unit for Germany had already been authorized. This represented a second-mile kind of peace service for many of the men accepted for the first group. They had already served in Civilian Public Service fulfilling their Selective Service obligation but were offering a plus peace service.

"I tried to think of a word that would symbolize the idea these fellows were putting into practice. The

Latin word for peace—Pax—came to me. The committee approved it and Pax was born."

A number of influences led to the birth of this child now past its seventeenth birthday. One of these has been mentioned already: the experiences of Civilian Public Service men. At a time when there was still considerable public scorn and antagonism to their position, almost 6,000 Mennonites and Brethren in Christ men elected CPS* as a Christian alternative to war. They worked in sanitation projects, forestry and fire-fighting services, conservation camps and mental hospitals.

For some, the years of early manhood given up to these activities seemed a futile waste. But for many, the years of voluntary servitude in CPS opened up new vocational horizons and service opportunities.

Especially was this true in state mental institutions. Here, the men who served, as well as pastors and theologians back home, suddenly discovered in practice a positive and graphic illustration of the love ethic

*(A distinction should be made here between two uses of the term, CPS. During World War II and since, in historical documents, CPS has stood for Civilian Public Service—referring to the alternative service option open to, or the actual work done by, conscientious objectors.

Since 1951, when the draft of CO's began again, these men have been known as I-W's and their work designated simply as the I-W program. Actually I-W is a Selective Service classification for I-O men assigned to an approved alternative service work program—a I-O at work. This Selective Service classification was appropriated for a program name.

In 1967, among some of the church groups involved, the term Civilian Peace Service was chosen to cover the I-W category of men working in domestic programs. The abbreviation, CPS, should not be confused with the traditional Civilian Public Service, although the classification of men to which it refers is essentially the same.

Against this background, one further clarification is in order. As has been noted, I-W represents a Selective Service classification for men designated I-O—conscientious objectors—assigned to alternative service work. For Mennonites, Pax is the program designation for I-W men working overseas and Civilian Peace Service the program designation for I-W men working on the domestic scene.)

that had so long been limited largely to a negative, wartime application.

Of course, the entire program had issued from a concern to reflect the way of love. CPS men were placed in hospitals because both the government and the church considered service there to be significant. However, it seems clear now that the full impact of this significance struck Mennonite and related peace churches only in retrospect.

CO attendants challenged the primitive custodial patterns. They struggled to change conditions that were far less than satisfactory. In patient care they discovered that gentle love, respect, and a compassionate concern for the sick person could literally bring about miracles of healing.

Not only CPS men but an entire church began to see this kind of positive action as a truer reflection of Christian love than dogmatic doctrinal position or the passive holding of policies so representative of much peace church response in previous periods of conflict.

The way of love was seen with new and pervasive insight, not primarily as a negation of force, but in the context of service as a way of life, a pattern for living.

A second earlier influence had also left its mark on church thought. Mennonites have frequently been refugees. Hounded at times by national and ecclesiastical authorities, they knew the suffering that flight and uncertainty brought to people. Thus, their response of compassionate interest in the plight of others, caught in the same or similar straits, can be understood.

One of these periods of response to need fell in 1920. Reports of famine in Russia reached Mennonites early that year. On July 13, representatives of several North American Mennonite bodies met to begin work on a plan which would bring help to famine-plagued

Mennonites still in Russia. On July 27, a provisional central organization was set up to carry out this relief mission. The new agency was called Mennonite Central Committee and represented seven Mennonite conferences and relief organizations.

On October 6, 1920, two American relief workers, Orie Miller and Clayton Kratz, arrived in Russia. At that time the Ukraine was torn by civil war. Kratz was never heard from again. But relief work to Mennonite communities in that region continued through 1927.

In MCC, Mennonite and Brethren in Christ groups found a single channel for mutual concerns. Although of common ethnic origin, various immigrations had created a variety of streams of experience and thought. These were tempered and shaped by exposure to several different European cultures. Thus by the time successive waves of immigrants reached the new world, enough differences existed to constitute walls of separation.

The formation of MCC marked a significant step back into a closer relationship with each other.

From its inception, Mennonite Central Committee has actively sought to serve in areas of great need. The earliest contributions were limited to relief and material aid. But increasingly, the churches supporting MCC have seen that to maintain a dichotomy of service and evangelism is unscriptural. And, although MCC is still known as a relief agency, its workers serve around the world "in the name of Christ" trying to meet every kind of need, ministering to make men whole.

This agency has reflected simply the Mennonite tradition of serving in times and places of need. In its administration of the wartime CPS program, MCC leaders became acutely aware of both great human needs and untapped resources hidden in the church. Demands for help came from quarters where not war but other forces had caused striking devastation of human spirits. With its constituent groups, it developed the concept of voluntary service—actually an extension of its earliest relief efforts.

By 1950 voluntary service was firmly fixed in Mennonite thought as a pattern of sharing with others.

A third stream of influence flowed from summer student work camp tours in Europe. Originally sponsored by the Council of Mennonite and Affiliated Colleges in 1946 the tours were set up: "(1) to study conditions and life in Europe, among Mennonites and others, and (2) to make a contribution to postwar rehabilitation by a period of voluntary service."

By 1948 this program had grown to include short-term construction and repair projects. In the summer of 1950 six summer work projects were set up, including refugee housing in Donaueschingen, Darmstadt, and Westhofen in Germany; a church building at Kiel, Germany; a youth center called Agape for the Waldensian church in Italy; and a center for the French Mennonites at Belfort, France. In each of these projects North American and European youth participated.

At Espelkamp near Bielefeld, in the British zone of Germany, a unit was planned and set up on a continuing basis. This former munitions factory was being remodeled by Evangelisches Hilfswerk into a Christian community for refugees.

One of the Americans who went to Espelkamp as a VS worker was Cal Redekop. Shortly he was called to Frankfurt to assist Paul Peachey, director of European MCC.

At the same time, some of the Americans serving in the summer voluntary service caravans were asking for permission to serve on a year-round basis. Redekop and Peachey discussed the idea and Redekop was given the assignment to develop a voluntary service program to make this possible. Even though conscientious objectors were still draft-exempt at that time, Redekop wrote MCC headquarters suggesting that European Voluntary Service projects might provide opportunity for American men to do alternative service.

Finally a reply came from Orie Miller saying the request was approved and twenty men would be sent on an experimental building program. The men arrived in Rotterdam on April 1, 1951.

And Pax became a reality.

These men represented pioneers of a hardy stripe. Not only were they all volunteers, since at this time conscientious objectors were being deferred and there were no CO conscripts. But some had already fulfilled their draft obligation during World War II. In addition, they were paying $900 for the privilege of doing one year of hard labor.

For some years preceding, MCC had sponsored a trainee program. Properly qualified young Mennonites from Europe were given two six-month work assignments in North American Mennonite communities. Income from their work covered transportation costs and a minimal monthly allowance.

C. L. Graber, one of the early commissioners who helped to pioneer overseas youth service, suggested there might be young men from the United States who would like to serve in Europe in the same tradition, but going one step further and paying for their own transportation and maintenance as a gift to European refugees.

So a plan was proposed whereby each man provided his own support at the rate of $75 per month, or arranged to have it provided. This figure covered travel, room, board, preparatory, and administrative expenses, as well as a personal allowance of $10 monthly.

Later, a pattern of support assistance was worked out in which parents, friends, or congregations could provide for part or all of the $900 per year amount. When costs rose, this amount was increased to $90 per month or $1,080 for each year of service.

Pax qualifications have not been harsh, but they have been designed to eliminate mere adventurers. And they also screen out all except those whose personal lives can make a contribution to both unit and community contacts.

In order to qualify for service in the Pax program a young man must have the following qualifications:

Qualifications For MCC Personnel

1. Personal acceptance of Jesus Christ as Savior and Lord.

2. Active membership in a Christian church.

3. Prepared to participate in Christian witness in both word and deed, with commitment to a ministry of Christian nonresistance and reconciliation.

4. Readiness to participate in the religious, educational, and social program of the church, community, and MCC team, where the person is assigned.

5. Emotionally and physically qualified to cope with new and diverse demands of work, responsibility, and adjustments involved in cross-cultural assignments.

6. Willing to abstain from the use of tobacco and alcoholic beverages.

7. Respectful toward the convictions of others, understanding of differing customs and religions, and cooperative with the administration in carrying out the total program.

8. Vocationally competent to fulfill the job expectation and grow into expanding assignments.

In its first year, Pax did not represent service for draft-age men. Although change in the law and a draft for CO's seemed imminent, the first groups of men had no assurance that any part of their service would be acceptable for the fulfillment of their probable draft obligation.

The first peacetime Selective Service law was passed by Congress in 1940. From 1940 to 1947 MCC, at the request of Mennonite and Brethren in Christ churches, administered the CPS program. In 1948 the Draft Act provided deferment for conscientious objectors.

At the same time church leaders urged draft-age young men to volunteer for church service programs. Many did in spite of the fact they might later be called by Selective Service to fulfill draft obligations if and when the law would change.

That change took place on June 19, 1951, when the Universal Military Training and Service Act was passed and became law. Under this act, the draft age was lowered to 18 1/2, the term of service extended to 24 months, and the draft itself extended to 1955.

Under this act also, the conscientious objector was no longer deferred but, in lieu of induction into the armed forces, could "be ordered by his local board, subject to such regulations as the President may prescribe, to perform . . . such civilian work contributing to the maintenance of the national health, safety, or interest as the local board may deem appropriate."

Class I-A was established as the category of persons available for military service. Class I-A-O was set up for CO's available for civilian work contributing to the maintenance of the national health, safety, or interest. Class I-W designated CO's actually performing such work.

By December 1951, MCC took official action designating Pax as the overseas I-W program. On July 1,

1952, the Selective Service pattern began operation and men already in Pax service were then officially recognized as fulfilling their two-year draft obligation.

True to the Latin term, Pax grew quickly into a dynamic and aggressive effort to find and express a positive reflection of the peace position. The service-for-peace idea was perhaps best stated by Orie Miller when he told Paxmen at Backnang, "Pax is a new concept in Christian mission." Someone else wrote, "The practical demonstration of a positive alternative to military conflict is still one of the outstanding contributions to the Pax program."

The essential character of Pax has never changed. However, there have been changes. At its inception, Pax represented a distinct program, separately budgeted and administered. But by 1956, it became clear that field service for Mennonite Central Committee could not be sharply delineated and that, in the context of need, Paxmen and other volunteers always worked side by side, unmindful of Stateside designations. So separate field administrative procedures were phased out and by 1964, when Pax budget was merged with regular overseas budget, Pax ceased to be a separately identified program.

In turn, Pax grew into a recruitment procedure utilizing I-W men for overseas service. For some, this shift has seemed to be a traumatic denial of the original vision. For others, Pax today is more vibrantly alive than ever, for now Pax is not so much program as persons. The story of Pax is no longer a tale of statistics, neat categories of projects, an outline of policies, or a recounting of administrative decision. But rather, the story of Pax is the story of men—of a man—being with people in need and responding to that need with every resource at his disposal.

Within the context of military conscription, Christian young men have found in Pax a new and exciting outlet for service. Apart from that context, Pax overseas service was not essentially different, in motivation or result, from the Christian's call to follow Christ elsewhere—wherever destitution of spirit or body had reduced persons to need. But within that context, every routine act took on special meaning. In Pax, men found a structure within which they could escape the negativism of refusal and contribute positively to reconciliation and peace.

Much of this is reflected in the stated purpose of the Pax program:

1. To assist in projects that offer opportunities to alleviate human need and tensions in various parts of the world.

2. To provide an opportunity for a positive Christian witness by the individual in the unit.

3. To provide opportunities for self-development.

4. To promote international good will and understanding by working with citizens of other countries in a spirit of brotherly love.

5. To bring to the church constituency a greater consciousness and fuller realization of the suffering and hopelessness found in the world thus helping Americans to be better stewards of their spiritual opportunities and abundance of material wealth.

These objectives parallel, in their essence, the awakened concerns among Mennonites in North America. Until the turn of the century, many Mennonites found all of their time and energy consumed putting down roots in a new environment. Fear also, a residue of persecution and refugee wanderings, blocked involvement.

Yet, again and again, those same experiences gave birth to compassion and led to response whenever human need pushed its way into their isolated circles of awareness.

When this happened, and unfortunately usually only

then, Mennonites turned to each other. They seemed to feel that response to need demanded joint effort even though in worship and community and education their badly splintered image was maintained, a seemingly sacred but actually distorted trust.

Crises once came separately. Now they blend into one another, a sort of permanent crisis. Thus a temporary expedient to make possible cooperative service has become a way of life. Today 14 Mennonite, Brethren in Christ, and related groups comprise the constituency of MCC. Together they are beginning to find a reality for their faith which for many decades in North America was distracted by divisions and had lost its vitality.

Their doctrine of love, based on the New Testament and the life of Christ, has become for some a way of living. Where before love tended to mean nonresistance and nonparticipation in war it has now matured to mean a service of love to the needy and a service of reconciliation for all men. Where before historical and doctrinal splinterings denied the very ethic they promoted, Mennonites are now beginning to find brotherhood among themselves in a historic but still limited confirmation of the teachings they have proclaimed. And where before misplaced zeal and an attitude of fear kept faith hidden in ethnic isolation, today there is healthy interest in the affairs of men. This has led to increased exposure to the needs of men with a consequent relevant involvement.

Pax has had no small part to play in this unfolding drama.

An outgrowth of the New Testament ethic of love, as well as of the later Anabaptist application, Pax in these decades has helped bring to flower what for centuries was buried in European traditions, New World quaintness, and massive misunderstandings.

Until now, Pax has been known as an overseas alternative service for young men who prefer committing themselves to conciliatory programs rather than to destruction and alienation. Perhaps it is time that the insights gained by the young men in Pax be shared more widely as the essence of Pax—being with people in need—begins to reach beyond those caught by Selective Service. Perhaps it is time for the churches supporting Pax to accept more fully for themselves the pattern of living and serving that their sons have pioneered.

Pax has served well to identify and shape an idea put into flesh by American Christian conscripts. But it would seem the day has come when the core of that idea must find life and expression among more than Christian conscripts and a few dedicated youth volunteers. Or the so-called peace churches may find the idea has reverted to theory and Pax is only a Latin word.

Appendix I Paxmen According to Country

June 1	1951	1952	1953	1954	1955	1956	1957
Germany	28	39	58	69	60	50	43
Greece		5	14	11	11	12	8
Austria					8	6	9
France			1	1	1	7	2
Belgium						1	
Switzerland		1					
Holland			9	1	2	2	1
Paraguay			1	1	7	10	11
Algeria						9	9
Peru				10	8	6	6
Nepal						2	5
Indonesia						2	4
Korea			2	7	4	2	2
Jordan		5	7	7	5		2
Egypt			2				
Morocco							
Vietnam							2
Brazil							
Liberia							
Chile							
Hong Kong							
Pakistan							
Thailand							
Congo							
Crete							
Bolivia							
British Honduras							
India							
Burundi							
Israel							
West Pakistan							
East Pakistan							
Nigeria							
Mexico+							
Madagascar							
Zambia							
Yugoslavia							
Dominican Republic+							
Haiti+							
TOTALS	28	50	94	107	106	109	104

+Program administration changed from voluntary service to overseas services
*In French study.

1958	1959	1960	1961	1962	1963	1964	1965	1966	1967	1968
29	25	16	16	11	10	9	6	8	5	4
8	7	15	11	10	6	6	7			
10	8	7	12	9				1	1	1
2			2			4	2	4	6	2
1							*6	*9		*1
3	2	3	3	4	3	2	1	1	1	1
1										
12	10	6	7	6			1	1		
7			2	12	14	14	9	11	10	5
5	5	2	3							
6	7	7	6	4	3	4	4	6	4	4
5	5	2	4	4	5	7	4	2		
3	5	4	6	5	4	5	4	3	2	2
3	2	2	3	3	3	2	3	3	2	3
1	1	3	2	2	2		2	4	3	3
4	3	3	1	1	1	1	3	13	15	12
						2		2	6	6
	5	5	4	1			2			
		1								
		2	2	2	2	2	1	3		
		2	2	3	3					
		2	2	2						
		5	6	8	8	9	14	15	25	22
			1					4	4	4
			2	4	7	9	6	12	17	18
			2	2						
			3	3	2	3	3	8	4	4
				2	3	2	1	1	2	1
					2	4	5	4		
						3	4	5	4	5
						1			1	
								2	2	2
									8	7
									1	1
									2	2
									2	2
									2	2
									9	9
100	85	87	102	98	78	89	88	122	138	123

in 1967.

APPENDIX II Paxmen According to Conference and Denomination

June 1	1951	1952	1953	1954	1955
Mennonite Church	21	32	54	52	50
General Conference	5	7	22	35	30
Brethren in Christ	1	2	7	4	3
Conservative Mennonite		1		5	7
Mennonite Brethren				5	8
Evangelical Mennonite Brethren			1	3	3
Krimmer Mennonite Brethren				1	
Conservative Amish Mennonite		5	7		
Old Order Amish Mennonite		2	1		1
Old Order Wisler Mennonite					1
Independent		1			2
Presbyterian					1
Friends			2	2	
Church of Christ					
Baptist					
Evangelical Mennonite Church					
Old Order Mennonite Church	1				
Beachy Amish Mennonite					
Congregational					
Lancaster Conference					
Evangelical Mennonite Mission Church					
United Christian					
TOTALS	28	50	94	107	106

1956	1957	1958	1959	1960	1961	1962	1963	1964	1965	1966	1967	1968
58	56	60	51	38	45	48	39	47	45	64	70	64
24	24	23	24	33	36	31	24	24	20	30	41	38
5	7	7	2	3	1		1	3	2	2	1	1
8	4	3	5	6	7	7	5	7	5	7	6	5
6	5	1			2	1	1	2	4	5	8	7
1		1	1			1			1	1	1	1
	1											
1	1	1						1	1	1		
1												
1	1	1			1	2	1					
2	1									1	1	
1	1									3	5	4
1	1											
									2			
					1	3	4			1	1	
	1	1										
	1	2	2									
				1	1							
				5	5	3	3	5	7	6	3	2
				1	3	2						
											1	1
109	104	100	85	87	102	98	78	89	88	122	138	123

APPENDIX III Paxmen in Service 1951-1968

Name	State of Residence
Ackerman, Robert Wayne	Denbigh, Virginia
Adrian, Peter	Rosemary, Alberta
Aeschbacher, Kenyon Roy	Versailles, Missouri
Albrecht, Emanuel, Jr.	Pigeon, Michigan
Amstutz, Jon George	Goshen, Indiana
Amstutz, Mahlon Dale	Orrville, Ohio
Amstutz, Stuart	Apple Creek, Ohio
Andres, Homer	N. Newton, Kansas
Arn, John Willard, Jr.	N. Newton, Kansas
Auernheimer, Robert Bruce	N. Newton, Kansas
Babcock, William	Pekin, Illinois
Bachman, Stanley	Rock Falls, Illinois
Bailey, Kenneth	Upland, California
Barkman, Kenneth John	Steinbach, Manitoba
Bartel, Dick D.	Meade, Kansas
Bartow, David	Goshen, Indiana
Basinger, Doyle Edison	Dalton, Ohio
Bauman, Floyd	Waterloo, Ontario
Bauman, Roy	Waterloo, Ontario
Beachey, Nevin Allen	Greenwood, Delaware
Beachey, Alvin Ray	Kalona, Iowa
Beachy, Daniel	Hartville, Ohio
Beachy, Elmer E.	Goshen, Indiana
Beachy, Ken	Wayland, Iowa
Beattie, Challen Brown	Summit, New Jersey
Beck, Roger	Archbold, Ohio
Becker, Arlowe	Omaha, Nebraska
Becker, Bruce	Kitchener, Ontario
Beittel, William Fox	Beloit, Wisconsin
Bender, Gerald W.	Mt. Joy, Pennsylvania
Bender, Lowell	Bittinger, Maryland
Bender, Marcus Emery	Nampa, Idaho
Bergey, Ted Weston	Doylestown, Pennsylvania
Bert, Daniel	Newburg, Pennsylvania

282

Country of Service	Beginning Date Month and Year	No. of Years of Service
Congo	6/14/67	
Europe	10/5/59	8/15/61—2
Algeria	2/7/66	5/7/68—2
Germany	6/25/56	6/25/58—2
Europe	4/14/59	5/1/61—2
Holland	7/9/52	10/13/54—2
West Pakistan	8/31/66	
Europe	9/12/57	9/12/59—2
Europe	9/13/60	9/10/62—2
Germany	7/6/54	9/25/56—2
Morocco	3/25/58	10/14/60—2
Austria	4/22/58	4/19/60—2
Israel	9/25/64	8/21/66—2
Jerusalem	8/18/61	4/30/64—3
Europe	4/26/61	8/15/63—2
Hong Kong	10/1/61	8/24/64—3
Germany	7/18/53	7/25/55—2
Paraguay	8/20/56	1/21/59—3
Korea	3/29/60	4/28/63—3
Germany	7/6/54	7/10/56—2
Nigeria	7/6/66	
Algeria	1/9/62	2/3/64—2
Congo	11/9/65	2/8/68—3
Algeria	2/7/66	5/7/68—2
Germany	7/27/55	7/27/57—2
Greece	4/23/64	7/23/66—2
Congo	7/6/66	4/3/68—2
Paraguay	11/14/60	7/18/63—3
France	7/8/53	7/7/55—2
Europe	9/12/57	9/12/59—2
Europe	2/11/61	2/16/63—2
Congo	6/14/67	
Germany	6/25/56	9/23/58—2
Germany, Austria	7/8/58	12/30/58
Greece	12/30/58	7/20/60—2

Bert, Harry Donald	Newburg, Pennsylvania
Bert, John S., Jr.	Newburg, Pennsylvania
Bertsche, John David	Flanagan, Illinois
Besse, James Lee	Oberlin, Ohio
Beyeler, Carl	Waynesboro, Virginia
Beyeler, Robert	Wooster, Ohio
Birky, Howard	Shickley, Nebraska
Bitikofer, Merle Frederick	Salem, Oregon
Bixel, David Aaron	Bluffton, Ohio
Bixler, James Leslie	Kidron, Ohio
Bixler, Vernice Nevin	Apple Creek, Ohio
Bock, Victor	Winnipeg, Manitoba
Boller, Gary Dean	Kalona, Iowa
Bontrager, Bill	Topeka, Indiana
Bontrager, Daniel	Hartville, Ohio
Bontrager, Dennis	Akron, New York
Bontrager, Elmer	Hartville, Ohio
Bontrager, Melvin	Middlebury, Indiana
Bontrager, Wilbur Duane	Darien Center, New York
Borntrager, Ervin J.	Millersburg, Indiana
Borntrager, Wesley	Bloomfield, Montana
Boshart, Bruce Alton	Cucamonga, California
Boshart, Harold Lyle	Mannsville, New York
Boshart, Richard Scott	Goshen, Indiana
Bower, David Clark	Boyertown, Pennsylvania
Bowman, Ivan Earl	Ephrata, Pennsylvania
Bowman, James E.	Harrisonburg, Virginia
Boyer, Paul Samuel	Upland, California
Brandt, Merlin Pete	Rickreall, Oregon
Braun, Gordon A.	Altona, Manitoba
Braun, Tony (Anton)	Winnipeg, Manitoba
Breneman, David	Lancaster, Pennsylvania
Breneman, John Roy	Willow St., Pennsylvania
Brenneman, Clair Y.	Wellman, Iowa
Brenneman, Clifford	Creston, Montana
Brenneman, Merle Dean	Kalona, Iowa
Brown, Gordon Edward	Steinbach, Manitoba
Brooks, Allen D.	Goshen, Indiana

Peru	7/1/54	6/30/56—2
Algeria	7/15/64	11/15/66—2
Germany	7/27/55	1/12/56—1
Germany	7/27/55	9/14/57—2
Germany	3/30/55	6/ /56
Algeria	6/ /56	8/28/57—2
Germany	7/8/58	7/13/60—2
Germany	7/8/58	7/16/60—2
Europe	7/15/61	8/15/63—2
Jordan	10/10/54	12/ /56—2
Germany	7/9/52	9/10/54—2
Germany	7/6/54	9/20/56—2
Nepal	8/13/63	8/11/66—3
Germany	7/1/65	8/11/67—2
Congo	7/6/66	
France	2/7/66	2/6/68—2
Algeria	2/13/65	5/17/67—2
Paraguay	2/6/61	12/11/63—2
Germany	7/8/58	8/11/60—2
Congo	10/30/64	12/8/66—3
Israel	9/25/64	8/25/66—2
Europe	11/10/61	11/22/63—2
Paraguay	7/1/54	7/ /56—2
Germany	7/27/55	7/18/57—2
Germany, Austria	7/23/59	7/24/61—2
E. Pakistan	7/12/63	6/22/66—3
Germany	7/13/53	8/22/55—2
Vietnam	4/27/66	
Germany	7/27/55	7/27/57—2
Brazil	3/29/67	
Europe	7/15/64	6/15/66—2
Paraguay	8/1/58	2/28/60—2
Bolivia	2/28/60	11/12/60—2
Nepal	4/23/64	10/22/67—3
Algeria	7/1/65	2/5/68—3
Paraguay	11/12/55	11/14/57—2
Germany	7/13/53	7/18/55—2
Europe	9/13/60	9/15/62—2
Switzerland	7/7/67	
Europe	9/13/60	9/26/62—2

Brubaker, Benjamin	Mt. Joy, Pennsylvania
Brubaker, John D.	Elizabethtown, Pennsylvania
Buller, Kenneth H.	Mt. Lake, Minnesota
Burkholder, David L.	Harrisonburg, Virginia
Burkholder, Howard R.	White Cloud, Michigan
Busenitz, Roger	Newton, Kansas
Buskirk, Philip James	Brutus, Michigan
Byler, Ellsworth	West Liberty, Ohio
Campbell, Harold E.	Crimora, Virginia
Cender, Milton Lavern	Dewey, Illinois
Claassen, Richard A.	Beatrice, Nebraska
Claassen, Virgil	Whitewater, Kansas
Clemens, Paul	Lansdale, Pennsylvania
Conrad, Carl Jacob	Smithville, Ohio
Conrad, Mark Edwin	Hesston, Kansas
Cross, Vernon Jay	Middlebury, Indiana
Crow, Dana Lee	Monclova, Ohio
Dahl, Alvin H.	Yarrow, British Columbia
Davidhizar, Ronald	Wakarusa, Indiana
Davis, Kenneth	Mechanicsburg, Pennsylvania
DeCamp, John	Wooster, Ohio
Deckert, Loren Dwane	N. Newton, Kansas
Delagrange, Paul E.	Woodburn, Indiana
Derkson, Peter	Taber, Alberta
Detwiler, Sheldon Len	Hesston, Kansas
Dewarle, Gary James	Saskatoon, Saskatchewan
Dick, Eugene Henry	North Dakota
Dick, James Richard	Mountain Lake, Minnesota
Dick, Kenneth Ray	Lynwood, Washington
Dietzel, Cleason S.	Pigeon, Michigan
Dintaman, Philip	Lagrange, Indiana
Dintaman, Walter	Edmore, Michigan
Dirksen, Murl Owen	Flagstaff, Arizona
Driedger, Arthur	Wheatley, Ontario
Driedger, John V.	Leamington, Ontario
Driver, Daniel	Dayton, Virginia
Duerksen, Harding Jerroll	Canton, Kansas
Dyck, Abraham David	Alberta

Europe	4/23/57	4/23/59—2
Europe	11/10/60	12/1/62—2
Peru	6/22/58	10/15/60—2
Europe	3/23/57	3/27/59—2
Korea	10/19/53	9/18/56—3
Congo	10/12/66	
Europe	4/23/57	4/21/59—2
Germany	3/31/60	10/13/62—2
Congo	2/7/66	
Germany	7/13/53	9/16/55—2
Germany	4/9/54	11/5/56—2
Paraguay	4/22/58	4/22/60—2
Nepal	9/12/59	9/11/62—3
Germany	11/25/52	11/25/54—2
Germany	7/6/54	9/26/56—2
Europe	4/22/60	6/1/62—2
Germany	9/12/57	9/12/59—2
Congo	7/1/65	2/5/68—3
Europe	11/16/62	5/15/65—3
Europe	9/12/57	9/16/59—2
Germany	9/8/56	9/23/58—2
Germany	7/6/57	10/16/59—2
Liberia	8/22/58	11/19/60—2
Germany	7/6/57	7/22/59—2
Jordan	7/22/61	8/31/63—2
Vietnam	9/16/65	9/10/67—2
Korea	11/30/61	11/30/64—3
Bolivia	7/7/67	
Nepal	12/1/67	
Germany	7/6/57	7/6/59—2
Indonesia	2/14/62	2/11/65—3
Germany	11/25/52	11/25/54—2
Yugoslavia	9/6/67	
Germany	11/20/56	2/7/59—3
Europe	11/10/60	11/8/62—2
Holland	10/1/52	10/9/54—2
Korea	2/10/62	3/9/65—3
Bolivia	5/14/63	4/30/65—2

Dyck, Gerald Paul	N. Newton, Kansas
Dyck, Raymond Lee	N. Newton, Kansas
Eash, Dale	Goshen, Indiana
Eash, Loren	Goshen, Indiana
Ebersole, Gabriel	Middletown, Pennsylvania
Ebersole, Willard G.	Warren, Illinois
Ediger, Billy Gene	Inman, Kansas
Ediger, George Roland	N. Newton, Kansas
Ediger, Marlow Richard	Inman, Kansas
Ediger, N. Max	North Newton, Kansas
Ediger, Robert D.	Hillsboro, Kansas
Eigsti, James	Buda, Illinois
Eisenbeis, Larry Dean	Marion, South Dakota
Eitzen, Gordon	Mountain Lake, Minnesota
Enns, Bruce	Winnipeg, Manitoba
Enns, Karl	Waterloo, Ontario
Ens, Peter	Carrot River, Saskatchewan
Ensz, Charles	Beatrice, Nebraska
Epp, Dale Lee	Henderson, Nebraska
Epp, Gary	Omaha, Nebraska
Epp, John E.	Whitewater, Kansas
Epp, La Moine Richard	N. Newton, Kansas
Epp, Wayne Dale	N. Newton, Kansas
Erb, Emanuel	Berlin, Ohio
Erb, Kenneth W.	Casselton, North Dakota
Esch, Dwight C.	Hesston, Kansas
Esch, Phillip Charles	Phoenix, Arizona
Eshleman, Roger David	Greencastle, Pennsylvania
Ewy, Virgil Ray	Kingman, Kansas
Eyer, John Robert	Elizabethtown, Pennsylvania
Eyster, Delbert Ray	Grantham, Pennsylvania
Falb, Marion	Orrville, Ohio
Fast, George	Rosenfeld, Manitoba
Fast, Henry R.	Kindersley, Saskatchewan
Fast, Martin	Frazer, Montana
Fast, Walter	Winnipeg, Manitoba
Flaming, Melvin Dean	Manhattan, Kansas

288

Thailand	9/17/60	8/1/63—3
Europe	7/21/62	12/14/65—3
Germany	3/23/57	3/27/59—2
Nigeria	7/6/66	
Morocco	12/ /59	7/26/60—1
Peru	7/1/54	11/5/55—2
Europe	9/13/60	9/26/62—2
Peru	4/1/55	11/26/56—1 1/2
Jordan	10/1/52	10/1/54—2
Burundi	7/6/66	
Paraguay	8/20/56	8/20/58—2
Germany	6/25/56	10/14/58—2
Germany	7/13/53	10/25/55—2
Europe	4/22/58	4/22/60—2
Jordan	7/17/64	5/31/66—2
Germany	5/5/61	5/7/63—2
Europe	7/23/63	7/28/65—2
Germany	6/25/56	6/25/58—2
Congo	9/6/67	
Congo	7/14/64	7/9/66—2
Hong Kong	10/23/58	10/31/61—3
Germany	7/6/54	7/18/56—2
Germany	8/20/55	8/28/57—2
Paraguay	10/5/59	10/5/62—3
Bolivia	7/6/66	
Europe	9/13/60	10/16/62—2
Bolivia	7/7/67	
Algeria	6/14/67	
Peru	4/1/55	3/27/57—2
Germany	7/13/53	7/25/55—2
Europe	9/18/63	10/2/65—2
Liberia	8/22/58	8/23/60—2
Germany	9/13/58	11/3/58
Switzerland	11/3/58	10/3/60—2
Europe	9/29/61	9/29/63—2
Jordan	7/7/65	7/6/67—2
Peru	6/10/57	3/3/59—2
Europe	7/21/62	6/20/65—3

289

Fly, Maurice L.	Schwenksville, Pennsylvania
Forrester, Beryl	Woodville, New York
Franz, Ronald E.	Omaha, Nebraska
Freed, Everett Ray	Wakarusa, Indiana
Frey, John Kurvin	Conestoga, Pennsylvania
Frey, Norman Eugene	Rensselaer, Indiana
Frey, Vernon Andrew	N. Newton, Kansas
Freyenberger, Gerald	Wayland, Iowa
Friesen, Gilbert	Mt. Lake, Minnesota
Friesen, Marlyn G.	Henderson, Nebraska
Friesen, Randal	Seattle, Washington
Fry, Paul	Goshen, Indiana
Fulmer, Rich	Perkasie, Pennsylvania
Funk, Jake W.	Manitoba
Garboden, James L.	Geneva, Indiana
Gehman, Wm. Henry	Morwood, Pennsylvania
Geiser, Alfred	Apple Creek, Ohio
Geiser, Ernest William	Apple Creek, Ohio
Geiser, Wilson Chester	Apple Creek, Ohio
Geissinger, Cordell Marlin	Zionsville, Pennsylvania
Gerber, Daniel D.	Dalton, Ohio
Gerber, David R.	Smithville, Ohio
Gerber, Frederick John	Dalton, Ohio
Gerber, Gene Arthur	Walnut Creek, Ohio
Gerber, Harry Dean	Dalton, Ohio
Gerber, Marlin Eugene	Bluffton, Ohio
Gerber, Robert	Leesburg, Indiana
Gerber, Stanley	Walnut Creek, Ohio
Gerber, Stephen L.	Apple Creek, Ohio
Gillis, John Floyd	Peyton, Colorado
Gingerich, Daniel	Alpha, Minnesota
Gingerich, David F.	Chappell, Nebraska
Gingerich, Gary Edward	Au Gres, Michigan
Gingerich, Loren Lee	Hicksville, Ohio
Gingerich, Peter Daniel	Uniontown, Ohio
Gingrich, Byron	Albany, Oregon
Glick, Ervie	Minot, North Dakota
Goering, James Alfred	Peabody, Kansas
Goering, Lonnie G.	Moundridge, Kansas

Morocco	4/27/66	
Germany	3/31/60	3/31/62—2
Congo	11/16/66	12/15/67—1
Germany	9/8/56	10/14/58—2
Germany	7/13/53	7/18/55—2
Europe	4/22/58	4/22/60—2
Jordan	10/10/54	11/ /56—2
Europe	6/10/59	7/13/61—2
Europe	9/13/60	11/15/62—2
Liberia	8/16/60	8/12/62—2
Congo	9/4/65	12/3/67—2
Peru	7/1/54	11/5/55—1
Bolivia	7/28/66	
Paraguay	7/1/54	7/ /56—2
Morocco	4/27/66	
Germany	3/30/55	10/3/57—2
Korea	9/6/67	
Germany	3/30/55	8/21/57—2
Germany	11/25/52	11/25/54—2
Indonesia	9/19/62	8/20/65—3
Vietnam	8/ /61	
Europe	7/14/60	8/10/62—2
Europe	8/16/61	8/15/63—2
Europe	7/21/62	7/22/64—2
Germany	7/9/52	9/10/54—2
Germany	7/27/55	2/27/58—3
Korea	9/18/57	5/30/60—3
Europe	9/12/59	9/30/61—2
Europe	11/16/62	5/15/65—3
Peru	6/29/59	9/6/60—1
Bolivia	8/17/64	11/16/66—2
Europe	3/23/57	7/2/59—2
Bolivia	7/ /61	7/10/63—2
Liberia	8/22/58	8/23/60—2
Germany	7/27/55	9/2/57—2
Bolivia	4/21/66	
Europe	9/13/60	9/14/62—2
Germany	7/9/52	7/30/54—2
Congo	11/11/64	12/8/66—2

291

Goering, Lowell J.	Moundridge, Kansas
Goertzen, John David	Henderson, Nebraska
Good, Edwin Paul	Nampa, Idaho
Good, Glen	Kouts, Indiana
Good, Harley D.	Harrisonburg, Virginia
Good, James Arthur	San Pierre, Indiana
Good, Leland	Fisher, Illinois
Good, Loren Conrad	Fisher, Illinois
Good, Nelson Henry	Elida, Ohio
Good, Robert Marvin	Kouts, Indiana
Goossen, Ervin Ray	Hillsboro, Kansas
Graber, Cal Carl	Bluffton, Ohio
Graber, Kenneth Lee	Archbold, Ohio
Graber, Laverne	Freeman, South Dakota
Graber, Richard D.	Goshen, Indiana
Grasse, Warren Landis	Chalfont, Pennsylvania
Gregory, Fred	Star, Idaho
Groff, Harold	Colorado Springs, Colorado
Groff, J. Lester	Lancaster, Pennsylvania
Grove, Lorne	Ringwood, Ontario
Hager, Lamar	Perkasie, Pennsylvania
Haines, Joseph	West Milton, Ohio
Hamm, Harold John	DeWitt, Nebraska
Hamscher, Paul Marcus	Walnut Creek, Ohio
Handrich, Donovan Bruch	Fairview, Michigan
Harder, Arnold Arlee	Mt. Lake, Minnesota
Harder, Daniel	Mt. Lake, Minnesota
Harder, Gordon	N. Newton, Kansas
Harder, Leroy	Butterfield, Minnesota
Harder, Martin	Swift Current, Saskatchewan
Harder, Peter	Harrison Lake, British Columbia
Harms, Charles	Clinton, Oklahoma
Harms, Harry Albert	Kitchener, Ontario
Harnish, Paul Miller	Lancaster, Pennsylvania
Hartman, Dean DeVere	Wakarusa, Indiana
Hartman, Dwight	Elida, Ohio
Hartzler, Donald Richard	Bellefontaine, Ohio
Hartzler, Joseph T.	Belleville, Pennsylvania
Harvey, Bruce	Malvern, Pennsylvania

Germany	9/12/57	9/12/59—2
Bolivia	7/8/63	7/8/65—2
Germany	7/6/54	7/17/56—2
Germany	6/25/56	10/14/58—2
Greece	6/12/52	10/25/55—3
Europe	4/22/58	4/22/60—2
Vietnam	8/29/58	9/10/61—3
Switzerland	9/5/62	9/2/64—2
Europe	9/13/60	9/14/62—2
Germany	6/25/56	6/25/58—2
Congo	9/5/62	9/4/64—2
Germany	7/6/54	9/ /56—2
Bolivia	2/11/63	2/10/65—2
Paraguay	8/20/56	8/20/58—2
Germany, Algeria	7/6/54	8/22/56—2
Europe	4/22/60	10/29/63—3
Vietnam	8/31/66	
Europe	7/15/64	7/14/66—2
Jordan	11/30/59	12/9/61—2
India	4/23/64	4/22/67—3
Europe	4/22/60	8/23/63—3
Jordan	7/27/59	7/31/61—2
Germany	6/25/56	6/25/58—2
Europe	4/22/58	4/22/60—2
Nepal	4/23/64	5/5/67—3
Pakistan	2/6/60	2/6/63—3
Europe	4/22/58	4/22/60—2
Indonesia	9/12/59	9/12/62—3
Congo	7/12/61	7/31/63—2
Europe	7/14/60	9/14/62—2
Paraguay	8/20/56	8/20/58—2
Crete	8/31/66	
Korea	1/30/54	2/ /57—3
Germany	7/23/59	12/31/61—2
Germany	11/23/55	4/29/58—3
Europe	7/23/63	7/20/65—2
Germany	6/25/56	10/6/58—2
Algeria	2/5/64	5/12/66—2
Hong Kong	8/28/63	8/27/66—3

Headings, Mark	E. Lansing, Michigan
Hedrich, Donald S.	Lansdale, Pennsylvania
Heisey, Chester R.	Elizabethtown, Pennsylvania
Herr, David, Jr.	East Earl, Pennsylvania
Herr, John Henry	Lancaster, Pennsylvania
Herschberger, David	Harrison, Arkansas
Hershberger, Calvin	Kansas City, Kansas
Hershberger, Garth	Wellman, Iowa
Hershberger, Jerrold	Wellman, Iowa
Hershberger, Paul F.	Goshen, Indiana
Hershberger, Richard Lee	N. Judson, Indiana
Hershey, Clyde Kenneth	Bird in Hand, Pennsylvania
Hershey, Gaius	Troy, Ohio
Hertzler, Maurice E.	Mechanicsburg, Pennsylvania
Hertzler, Truman Ray	Elverson, Pennsylvania
Hertzler, Wallace Leroy	Denbigh, Virginia
Hess, Richard	Mt. Joy, Pennsylvania
Hess, Roy N.	Lancaster, Pennsylvania
Hiebert, Johnny Leroy	Hillsboro, Kansas
Hiebert, Leroy Vernon	Elbing, Kansas
Hiebert, Pete	Winkler, Manitoba
High, Herbert H.	Lancaster, Pennsylvania
Histand, Robert A.	Doylestown, Pennsylvania
Hochstedler, Calvin Dean	Kalona, Iowa
Hochstedler, Eli	Nashville, Indiana
Hochstedler, Keith	Wellman, Iowa
Hochstedler, Kenneth	Wellman, Iowa
Hochstetler, Alan	Nappanee, Indiana
Hochstetler, Leslie Ray	Kalona, Iowa
Hochstetler, Otis Edward	Goshen, Indiana
Hochstetler, Paul Edwin	Goshen, Indiana
Hoefel, Gary	Odessa, Washington
Hoeppner, Abram	Windygate, Manitoba
Hofer, George	Bridgewater, South Dakota
Holdeman, Ivan	Denver, Colorado
Hollingshead, Jean Paul	Moorestown, New Jersey
Hooley, Carl Walter	Elkhart, Indiana
Hoover, Albert	Troy, Ohio
Hoover, Edgar	Detroit, Kansas

Europe	9/12/57	9/12/59—2
Congo	10/30/60	10/30/62—2
Germany	7/13/53	1/31/56—3
Europe	4/30/63	5/1/65—2
Israel	12/28/65	12/27/67—2
Germany	11/20/56	11/26/58—2
Germany	7/8/58	8/20/60—2
Germany	6/25/56	1/4/59—3
France	11/13/65	11/12/67—2
Germany	7/6/54	8/22/56—2
Paraguay	8/1/58	7/12/59—1
Germany	7/23/59	9/30/61—2
Weierhof, Germany	7/15/64	8/9/66—2
Indonesia	6/19/57	1/16/61—3
Germany	7/13/53	9/16/55—2
Peru	4/15/56	4/15/58—2
Germany	3/19/56	4/29/58—2
Europe	9/12/57	9/12/59—2
Germany	3/19/56	3/28/58—2
Germany	7/13/53	9/16/55—2
India	9/3/66	
Congo	7/6/66	
Europe	7/14/60	1/18/63—3
Europe	11/16/62	11/24/64—2
Bolivia	7/3/65	10/2/67—2
Germany	7/8/58	7/13/60—2
Algeria	1/12/57	9/4/59—2
Vietnam	8/29/58	8/31/61—3
Germany	7/27/55	9/25/56—1
Austria	7/24/58	8/3/60—2
Korea	11/30/61	11/29/64—3
Berlin	1/5/67	
India	8/18/64	9/15/67—3
Europe	6/10/59	4/25/60
Morocco	4/25/60	7/13/61—2
Greece	8/22/51	8/19/53—2
Germany	12/1/51	3/15/54—3
Paraguay	7/1/54	7/1/56—2
Indonesia	10/25/56	10/25/59—3
Indonesia	10/25/56	10/25/59—3

Hoover, Jared O.	Detroit, Kansas
Hoover, Robert Lee	Denver, Pennsylvania
Horst, Allen	South English, Iowa
Horst, Elvin, Jr.	Seville, Ohio
Horst, Otho	Clear Spring, Maryland
Hostetler, Albert Glenn	Massillon, Ohio
Hostetler, Dalton Clark	Harper, Kansas
Hostetler, Edwin Ray	Kalona, Iowa
Hostetler, Meredith Wade	Indianapolis, Indiana
Hostetter, Douglas	Harrisonburg, Virginia
Hostetter, James Geib	Elizabethtown, Pennsylvania
Huebert, Johnny H.	Henderson, Nebraska
Hunsberger, Arlis	Telford, Pennsylvania
Hunsberger, Merrill	Goshen, Indiana
Hurst, Carl Daniel	Goshen, Indiana
Imhoff, Kenneth Wayne	Washington, Illinois
Isaac, Marvin	Meade, Kansas
Jantzen, Carl Raymond	Beatrice, Nebraska
Jantzen, Ernest J.	Plymouth, Nebraska
Jantzen, John Edgar	Plymouth, Nebraska
Jantzi, Gerald H.	Marilla, New York
Jantzi, Glendon C.	Adams, New York
Jantzi, Gerald	Wood River, Nebraska
Janz, Gerhard	Rosthern, Saskatchewan
Janzen, Kenneth Duane	Henderson, Nebraska
Johns, Joseph	Centerville, Pennsylvania
Jones, David C.	Schwenksville, Pennsylvania
Jost, Howard	Hillsboro, Kansas
Juhnke, James	Lehigh, Kansas
Kamp, Stanley	Orrville, Ohio
Kanagy, Max Earl	Goshen, Indiana
Kasper, Arlo	Hutchinson, Kansas
Kauffman, Carl	Haven, Kansas
Kauffman, Dale Forest	W. Liberty, Ohio

Europe	9/12/59	9/13/61—2
Israel	10/14/63	12/2/65—2
Congo	7/14/60	7/14/62—2
Peru	4/15/56	4/15/58—2
Germany	3/19/56	11/ /56
Nepal	11/ /56	5/25/59—3
Germany	7/6/57	12/17/59—2
Germany	7/27/55	
Vienna	8/24/56	9/8/57—2
Germany	10/1/52	11/6/54—2
Germany	7/27/55	7/27/57—2
Vietnam	6/7/66	
Germany	7/13/53	10/25/55—2
Paraguay	8/20/56	8/20/58—2
Germany	3/30/55	10/3/57—2
Hong Kong	9/17/60	8/9/63—3
Germany	6/25/56	
Indo-China	2/2/57	8/ /59—3
Germany & Egypt	11/25/52	11/28/54—2
Europe	9/21/62	9/5/64—2
Germany	7/13/53	11/1/53
Iraq	11/1/53	5/1/56—3
Europe	9/12/57	9/12/59—2
Germany	7/6/54	1/4/57—3
Congo	2/7/66	5/6/68—2
Jordan	8/10/53	8/28/55—2
Germany	9/8/56	10/4/58—2
Germany	3/31/60	3/27/62—2
Congo	6/14/67	
Liberia	8/22/58	8/23/60—2
France	2/8/66	2/6/68—2
India	7/5/66	
Germany	7/8/58	7/13/60—2
Nepal	5/5/61	5/4/64—3
Europe	6/21/62	9/28/64—2
Germany	7/27/55	10/15/57—2
Hong Kong	8/17/64	9/1/67—3
Jordan	8/10/53	9/16/55—2

Kauffman, Duane	Haven, Kansas
Kauffman, Elton	Minot, North Dakota
Kauffman, Ervin Jacob	Kalispell, Montana
Kauffman, John Jay	Iowa City, Iowa
Kauffman, John Kurtz	Parkesburg, Pennsylvania
Kauffman, Loren Paul	Clarkesville, Michigan
Kauffman, Merrill	Fairview, Michigan
Kauffman, Richard Dean	Middlebury, Indiana
Kauffman, Wayne	Minot, North Dakota
Kaufman, Allen	Fredericksburg, Ohio
Kaufman, Kenneth	N. Newton, Kansas
Kaufman, Wendell Dee	Moundridge, Kansas
Kaufman, Harold	Danvers, Illinois
Keefer, Kenneth	Halifax, Pennsylvania
Kehl, Harvey	New Dundee, Ontario
Keim, Albert N.	Uniontown, Ohio
Keim, Wayne Joseph	Bay Port, Michigan
Kennel, Leonard Elam	Gap, Pennsylvania
Kennel, Paul Charles	Lancaster, Pennsylvania
King, Daniel Wayne	Waynesboro, Virginia
King, Forrest D.	Scottdale, Pennsylvania
King, John	Detroit Lakes, Michigan
King, John Mark	Conrath, Wisconsin
King, Kenneth	Indianapolis, Indiana
Kipfer, Reynold	Kitchener, Ontario
Kirkwood, Ronald Gene	Nappanee, Indiana
Kisamore, Glenn Galen	Hatfield, Pennsylvania
Kissel, Paul Nyce	Souderton, Pennsylvania
Klaassen, Erwin	Weatherford, Oklahoma
Klassen, Marvin P.	Mt. Lake, Minnesota
Klassen, Corney	Vineland, Ontario
Klassen, John Martin	Homewood, Manitoba
Klassen, Loyal	Mt. Lake, Minnesota
Klassen, Waldemar	Edmonton, Alberta
Klassen, William Herbert	Newton, Kansas
Kolb, Lester	Spring City, Pennsylvania
Konrad, Herman	Abbotsford, British Columbia
Kooker, Harley	Harleysville, Pennsylvania

Jordan	10/12/66	
Algeria	7/1/65	10/2/67—2
Bolivia	7/7/61	7/10/63—2
Paraguay	3/31/60	3/7/63—3
Germany	7/27/55	7/27/57—2
Germany	3/31/60	4/16/62—2
Europe	9/12/59	4/14/62—3
Crete	9/22/61	9/22/63—2
Paraguay	3/30/60	3/7/63—3
Germany	3/19/56	4/13/57—1
Amsterdam	7/6/54	7/9/56—2
Europe	9/29/61	9/29/63—2
Jordan	10/10/54	12/ /56—2
Vietnam	4/27/66	
Nepal	10/5/59	10/5/62—3
Germany	7/27/55	7/27/57—2
Vietnam	9/6/67	
Germany	7/13/53	7/25/55—2
Vietnam	2/7/66	
Morocco	8/17/64	2/15/67—3
Germany	7/27/55	
Vienna	8/24/56	7/27/57—2
India	7/7/67	11/12/67
Germany	10/1/52	10/19/54—2
Germany	7/8/58	
Greece	10/30/58	8/3/60—2
Germany	11/20/56	12/7/58—2
Jordan	6/22/52	6/22/54—2
Germany	5/30/55	10/17/57—2
Germany	9/12/57	9/21/61—4
Europe	9/29/61	9/23/63—2
Paraguay	9/12/59	10/4/61—2
Europe	2/11/61	2/16/63—2
Europe	9/13/60	8/28/62—2
Germany	7/6/54	10/31/56—2
Bolivia	10/16/59	8/20/60—1
Germany	7/13/53	7/20/55—2
Congo	5/26/65	8/25/67—2
Paraguay	8/20/56	9/12/58—2
Vietnam	7/25/66	

Koop, Alfred Walter	St. Catharines, Ontario
Kratz, John	Souderton, Pennsylvania
Krehbiel, Randolph	Moundridge, Kansas
Kremer, Ronnie Ray	Milford, Nebraska
Kroeker, Glen	Henderson, Nebraska
Kroeker, Harold Wayne	Henderson, Nebraska
Kropf, Dale Eugene	Albany, Oregon
Kulp, David	Telford, Pennsylvania
Kurtz, Don	Roanoke, Virginia
Kurtz, Eugene	Pocomoke, Maryland
Kurtz, Wayne	Fleetwood, Pennsylvania
Lambright, James	Lagrange, Indiana
Lambright, Richard Dean	Lagrange, Indiana
Lambright, Robert Dean	Lagrange, Indiana
Landes, Richard	Fountainville, Pennsylvania
Landis, Howard	Souderton, Pennsylvania
Landis, Ira Snavely	Strasburg, Pennsylvania
Landis, John Robert	Lancaster, Pennsylvania
Landis, Joseph Groff	Harleysville, Pennsylvania
Landis, Larry Shertzer	Lancaster, Pennsylvania
Landis, Roy Stoner	Blooming Glen, Pennsylvania
Lantz, Omar S.	Gap, Pennsylvania
Lapp, Omar James	Gap, Pennsylvania
Lapp, Wayne A.	Columbia Falls, Montana
Lauver, Marcus	Scottdale, Pennsylvania
Leatherman, Bruce Howard	Pipersville, Pennsylvania
Leder, Willis Roy	Freeman, South Dakota
LeFevre, Elwin Noah	Sterling, Illinois
Lehman, David S.	Apple Creek, Ohio
Lehman, Junior E.	Apple Creek, Ohio
Lehman, Peter	Lititz, Pennsylvania
Leichty, Norman	Wayland, Iowa
Lind, Loren Jay	Salem, Oregon
Linsenmyer, Dale	Beatrice, Nebraska
Linsenmyer, Dean Alan	Beatrice, Nebraska
Litwiller, Allen Dean	Delavan, Illinois

Bolivia	3/29/67	
Paraguay	4/22/58	6/15/60—2
Algeria	9/4/65	11/22/67—2
Congo	4/17/62	4/16/64—2
France	1/3/68	
Germany	7/13/53	6/23/55—2
Congo	6/14/67	
Europe	9/29/61	9/29/63—2
Congo	8/12/64	9/12/66—2
Europe	4/23/56	4/23/59—3
Greece	7/15/64	7/11/66—2
Germany	3/19/56	
Austria	7/19/56	
Greece	8/28/56	4/23/57—1
Germany	7/27/55	7/27/57—2
Germany	7/27/55	7/27/57—2
Pakistan	5/5/62	3/1/65—3
Greece	3/24/51	3/19/54—3
Europe	9/29/61	9/29/63—2
Europe	9/29/61	9/29/63—2
Berlin	7/7/67	
Congo	8/ /61	8/21/63—2
Germany	9/12/57	9/4/59—2
Korea	8/30/54	3/2/55—1
Germany	3/30/55	3/30/57—2
Germany	3/9/54	
Algeria		4/5/56—2
Pakistan	2/6/60	2/16/63—3
Europe	7/23/63	7/28/65—2
Germany	3/24/53	3/23/55—2
Germany	7/13/53	11/12/55—2
Germany	7/8/58	6/6/60—2
Germany	3/20/51	8/18/54—3
Germany	9/15/65	9/14/67—2
Europe	4/14/59	4/11/61—2
Germany	7/6/57	7/6/59—2
Europe	4/14/59	4/19/61—2
Congo	7/6/66	
Korea	3/7/59	3/7/62—3

301

Loewen, John	Reedley, California
Loewen, Victor	Morris, Manitoba
Long, Jay Lyndale	Souderton, Pennsylvania
Longenecker, Robert	Ashley, Michigan
Mack, Jesse E.	Collegeville, Pennsylvania
Martin, Earl S.	New Holland, Pennsylvania
Martin, Harvey W.	Ephrata, Pennsylvania
Martin, Kenneth	Elmira, Ontario
Martin, Luke Sauder	New Holland, Pennsylvania
Martin, Mark B.	Elizabethtown, Pennsylvania
Martin, Ronald Jay	Lafayette, Indiana
Mast, Amos	Thomas, Oklahoma
Mast, Ora	Lovington, Illinois
Maust, Gale Elmer	Bay Port, Michigan
Maust, Leslie Edward	Bay Port, Michigan
Maust, Wilbur	Pigeon, Michigan
Messer, Silas III	Nashville, Indiana
Miller, Arlen Dale	Wellman, Iowa
Miller, Charles P.	Conneautville, Pennsylvania
Miller, Dennis	Manson, Iowa
Miller, Duane Keith	Wellman, Iowa
Miller, Eldon R.	Middlebury, Indiana
Miller, Eugene Alfred	Henderson, Nebraska
Miller, Harold	Wellman, Iowa
Miller, J. Mark	Bally, Pennsylvania
Miller, James	Uniontown, Ohio
Miller, John Wendell	Vestaburg, Michigan
Miller, Leon Keith	Hydro, Oklahoma
Miller, Lloyd P.	Nappanee, Indiana
Miller, Lyle Jacob	Kalona, Iowa
Miller, Martin Robert	Harrisonburg, Virginia
Miller, Paul Donavon	Hanston, Kansas
Miller, Raymond Roy	Wooster, Ohio
Miller, Samuel	Arcola, Illinois
Mininger, John Mark	Thompson, Pennsylvania
Mininger, Ron	Elkhart, Indiana
Mishler, Fritz	Eugene, Oregon

Europe	3/30/60	9/14/62—2
Congo	9/5/62	11/19/64—2
Europe	11/10/61	11/9/63—2
Algeria	1/26/67	
Germany	7/6/57	7/2/59—2
Vietnam	2/7/66	
Morocco	3/25/58	7/8/60—2
West Pakistan	7/17/64	7/22/67—3
Germany	7/6/54	10/31/56—2
Congo	7/23/65	10/22/67—2
Brazil	9/10/64	3/9/67—3
Europe	4/23/57	4/21/59—2
Germany	9/13/58	
Austria	3/16/59	9/13/60
Congo	10/30/60	10/19/61—3
Zambia	9/14/67	
Indonesia	2/16/63	4/30/66—3
Germany	6/25/56	6/28/58—2
Germany	7/13/53	4/7/55—2
Germany	7/6/54	10/22/56—2
Germany	7/6/54	8/25/56—2
Indonesia	2/16/63	2/15/66—3
Europe	11/16/62	11/6/64—2
Bolivia	4/21/66	
Germany	7/6/57	7/6/58—1
Germany	7/27/55	7/27/57—2
Korea	11/12/65	
Nepal	8/29/58	8/29/61—3
Congo	6/14/67	
Bolivia	7/7/67	
Korea	3/28/57	5/30/60—3
Europe	9/21/62	10/14/65—3
Bolivia	7/7/67	
Israel	2/7/66	4/1/68—2
Germany	7/9/52	10/9/54—2
Germany	8/14/67	
Congo	2/7/66	5/6/68—2
Congo	1/4/66	
Germany	6/25/56	7/5/58—2

303

Moser, Millard Earl	Berne, Indiana
Moyer, Harry Robert III	Perkasie, Pennsylvania
Moyer, Marvin Stover	Goshen, Indiana
Moyer, Robert Glenn	Perkasie, Pennsylvania
Mueller, Harold Victor	Bell, California
Mullet, Gary	Kalona, Iowa
Myers, Paul Edward	New Paris, Indiana
Myers, Wilson	Doylestown, Pennsylvania
Nafziger, Gary	Kalona, Iowa
Nafziger, Leslie J.	Wauseon, Ohio
Neuenschwander, John	Dalton, Ohio
Neuenschwander, Sherman	Dalton, Ohio
Neufeld, Alfred	Laird, Saskatchewan
Neufeld, Gerhard	Vancouver, British Columbia
Neufeld, Johann Hans	Carrot River, Saskatchewan
Neufeld, Waldo	Margaret, Manitoba
Neufeldt, Alfred Waldo	Laird, Saskatchewan
Neufeldt, Harold	Inman, Kansas
Neufeldt, Peter W.	Laird, Saskatchewan
Neumann, Harold R.	Metamora, Illinois
Newcomer, David	Portland, Oregon
Newkirk, Jonathan	Yorba Linda, California
Nice, William Moyer	Harleysville, Pennsylvania
Nickel, Rodney	Omaha, Nebraska
Nickel, Stanley	Mountain Lake, Minnesota
Nisely, David Eugene	Sturgis, Michigan
Nissley, Harold Miller	Elizabethtown, Pennsylvania
Nitzche, Jerry	Bancroft, Nebraska
Nofziger, Roger D.	Goshen, Indiana
Nofziger, William	Wauseon, Ohio
Nussbaum, Curtis	Apple Creek, Ohio
Nussbaum, Kenneth Leroy	Apple Creek, Ohio
Oesch, Don	Kalispell, Montana
Ott, David H.	Long Island, New York
Palmer, Ronald	Portland, Oregon
Peachey, David Jonathan	Belleville, Pennsylvania

Germany	7/13/53	9/16/55—2
Peru	6/10/57	6/10/59—2
Germany	5/30/55	5/21/57—2
Germany	9/12/57	9/12/59—2
Germany	7/6/54	7/17/56—2
Algeria	11/9/65	2/8/68—3
Europe	9/13/60	9/13/63—3
Germany	5/30/55	5/21/57—2
France	2/7/66	2/6/68—2
Paraguay	8/1/60	6/25/63—3
Liberia	8/22/58	8/23/60—2
Europe	11/13/65	11/12/67—2
Germany	8/1/60	12/10/61—1
India	7/6/66	
Europe	8/16/63	7/28/65—2
Liberia	11/12/60	12/21/62—2
Switzerland	8/25/60	12/31/61—1
Bolivia	7/8/63	7/8/65—2
Europe	9/21/62	9/2/64—2
Germany	11/25/52	3/24/54
Jordan	3/25/54	11/26/54—2
Berlin	7/8/65	7/7/67—2
Vietnam	8/31/66	4/29/68—2
Europe	4/30/63	4/19/66—3
Peru	7/12/60	7/10/62—2
Congo	10/12/66	
Bolivia	8/17/64	11/16/66—2
Germany	3/19/56	3/11/58—2
Nepal	8/13/63	10/20/66—3
Germany	3/30/55	4/23/57—2
Peru	7/1/54	6/30/56—2
Algeria	10/4/60	5/22/63—3
Germany	5/30/55	6/26/57—2
Europe	4/22/58	4/22/60—2
Jordan	8/3/65	8/2/67—2
Bolivia	10/12/66	
Germany	7/6/55	7/6/56—1

Penner, Abe Peter	Giroux, Manitoba
Penner, Dietrich Peter	Houston, British Columbia
Penner, Harold Peter	Winnipeg, Manitoba
Penner, Maurice	Newton, Kansas
Penner, Melvin W.	Henderson, Nebraska
Penner, Orlando Leroy	Hillsboro, Kansas
Penner, Rodney Dwight	Durham, Kansas
Peters, James Faus	Manheim, Pennsylvania
Peters, Joe LaVerne	Aurora, Nebraska
Peters, Leron	Henderson, Nebraska
Peters, Ronald D.	Henderson, Nebraska
Petkau, Harold Walter	Morden, Manitoba
Pfile, Elton Eugene	Freeport, Illinois
Phillips, Stephen	Ottsville, Pennsylvania
Plank, Clyde D.	South Webster, Ohio
Plummer, James Riley	Kingston, Ontario
Preheim, Gayle Orlo	Freeman, South Dakota
Quiring, Lynn Henry	Weatherford, Oklahoma
Ramer, Richard Wayne	Goshen, Indiana
Ramseyer, Woodrow	Baden, Ontario
Raser, John Rudolph	Iowa
Ratzlaff, Edwin Ben	Mt. Lake, Minnesota
Ratzlaff, Gary Dean	Omaha, Nebraska
Ratzlaff, Robert	Moundridge, Kansas
Regier, Larry	Henderson, Nebraska
Reichert, Lamar	Bremen, Indiana
Reimer, Don	Saskatoon, Saskatchewan
Reimer, Edward D.	Fresno, California
Reimer, Gorden	Steinbach, Manitoba
Rempel, Alfred	N. Battlefield, Saskatchewan
Rempel, Alvin George	Rosthern, Saskatchewan
Renno, Harry	Belleville, Pennsylvania
Ressler, Donald	Orrville, Ohio
Richer, Allen	Wauseon, Ohio
Riehl, Menno S.	Ronks, Pennsylvania
Rohrer, Daniel G.	Ronks, Pennsylvania

Burundi	9/19/60	5/18/64—2
Germany	8/ /61	8/15/63—2
India	8/31/66	
Indonesia	9/12/59	9/12/62—3
Congo	9/4/62	
Europe	11/16/62	5/15/65—3
Europe	9/12/57	9/12/59—2
Peru	4/15/56	4/15/58—2
Congo	8/31/66	
Germany	9/12/57	9/12/59—2
Congo	9/5/62	8/25/64—2
British Honduras	11/8/61	11/7/63—2
Germany	7/27/55	7/27/57—2
Germany	9/ /56	9/ /58—2
Congo	7/1/65	11/25/67—2
Paraguay	8/ /58	8/1/60—2
Vietnam	8/31/66	
West Pakistan	9/6/67	
Peru	2/6/61	2/6/63—2
Korea	4/12/54	1/10/56—2
Germany	7/27/55	7/27/57—2
Paraguay	7/1/54	7/ /56—2
Congo	7/11/61	7/31/63—2
Bolivia	1/3/68	
Liberia	8/16/60	8/12/62—2
Germany	6/27/55	11/10/58—3
Europe	8/16/61	8/15/63—2
Germany	7/29/65	8/15/67—2
Europe	7/15/61	3/28/63—2
Switzerland	9/14/65	9/21/67—2
Germany	7/6/57	7/2/59—2
Morocco	3/20/68	
Germany	6/25/56	10/6/58—2
France	4/27/66	6/1/68—2
Germany	4/26/60	3/31/62—2
Germany	7/23/59	
Luxembourg	2/1/60	
Germany	6/13/60	
Luxembourg	7/18/60	
Greece	10/4/60	7/20/61—2

Rohrer, Myron	Seville, Ohio
Ross, Truman Kenneth	Comins, Michigan
Roth, Arnold G.	Wayland, Iowa
Roth, Cloy Eugene	Milford, Nebraska
Roth, Dan	Orrtanna, Pennsylvania
Roth, Herbert	Stryker, Ohio
Roth, Philip Arthur	Orrtanna, Pennsylvania
Roupp, Albert Allen	Elkhart, Indiana
Rounds, Stephen Pike	Exeter, New Hampshire
Rudy, Willis	Baden, Ontario
Rupp, Marlin Paul	Wauseon, Ohio
Rupp, William W.	Morenci, Michigan
Sandoz, Jerry Eugene	Newberg, Oregon
Sauder, Charles	Archbold, Ohio
Sauder, Richard	New Holland, Pennsylvania
Schertz, Edward Jay	Lowpoint, Illinois
Schertz, Wayne	Flanagan, Illinois
Schierling, Donald D.	N. Newton, Kansas
Schlabach, Isaac E.	Apple Creek, Ohio
Schlegel, Donald Clark	Toronto, Ontario
Schmidt, Allen	Marion, South Dakota
Schmidt, Archie	Walton, Kansas
Schmidt, Earl Richard	Rosthern, Saskatchewan
Schmidt, John Russell	Newton, Kansas
Schmidt, Melvin Dean	New Haven, Connecticut
Schmidt, Orville Dale	Chicago, Illinois
Schmidt, Richard Allen	Emporia, Kansas
Schmidt, Wesley Eugene	Newton, Kansas
Schmucker, Walter W.	Archbold, Ohio
Schrag, Dwayne	Newton, Kansas
Schrag, Marlin	Omaha, Nebraska
Schrag, Robert Menno	Newton, Kansas
Schrock, David	Millersburg, Indiana
Schrock, Elwood	Glen Flora, Wisconsin
Schrock, Herman Devon	Mishawaka, Indiana
Schrock, Jacob William	Kalona, Iowa

Europe	4/17/62	7/28/65—3
Congo	4/27/66	
Greece	4/4/51	7/9/54—3
Peru	7/1/54	12/31/55—1
Korea	8/29/58	3/7/62—4
Germany	3/19/56	3/11/58—2
Paraguay	7/1/54	7/1/56—2
Germany	3/24/51	6/1/54—3
Greece	12/1/52	12/1/54—2
Nepal	8/28/58	8/29/61—3
Crete	4/27/66	5/15/68—2
Paraguay	4/18/60	3/3/63—3
Vietnam	8/31/66	
Germany	9/12/57	9/4/59—2
Congo	7/14/64	7/10/66—2
Brazil	9/10/64	3/9/67—3
Germany	11/20/56	1/19/59—3
Germany	7/6/54	1/4/57—3
Germany	11/25/52	11/25/54—2
Europe	7/15/61	7/22/63—2
Germany	9/13/58	9/12/60—2
Bolivia	3/20/68	
Germany	5/30/55	
Nepal	9/ /56	5/17/58—3
Bolivia	7/3/65	10/2/67—2
Indonesia	8/7/59	2/2/63—4
Germany	8/20/55	4/2/58—3
Paraguay	7/13/53	9/ /55—2
Paraguay	9/18/65	9/17/67—2
Germany	3/19/56	9/23/58—2
Europe	7/14/60	7/8/63—3
Germany	7/8/58	7/13/60—2
Germany	7/6/54	7/17/56—2
Europe	11/16/62	11/24/64—2
Bolivia	7/28/66	
Germany	3/24/53	
Greece	1/ /54	3/24/55—2
Germany	5/30/55	
Algeria		10/ /56—1

309

Schrock, Stanley	Roanoke, Illinois
Schroeder, Clarence	American Falls, Idaho
Schroeder, Wesley	Collinsville, Oklahoma
Shaak, Robert John	Saskatchewan
Shank, John Franklin	Broadway, Virginia
Shantz, Kenneth	Waterloo, Ontario
Shearer, John Irvin	Scottdale, Pennsylvania
Shelly, Alton Myers	Columbus, Ohio
Shelly, Ralph Myers	East Greenville, Pennsylvania
Shenk, Douglas	Elida, Ohio
Shetler, David Allen	Scotts Mill, Oregon
Shetler, Dean Ray	Hollsopple, Pennsylvania
Shetler, Stanley Eugene	Blountstown, Florida
Short, Dale	Archbold, Ohio
Short, Denzel Ray	West Unity, Ohio
Short, Donald Lee	Archbold, Ohio
Short, James Lowell	Stryker, Ohio
Short, Larry Walter	Wauseon, Ohio
Short, Wayne	Archbold, Ohio
Showalter, Glen E.	Broadway, Virginia
Siemens, Arthur	Tuxedo, Winnipeg
Slabaugh, Glenn Jay	Bremen, Indiana
Slotter, J. F.	Souderton, Pennsylvania
Smeltzer, Carl Leslie	Elkhart, Indiana
Smeltzer, Walter Edward	Elkhart, Indiana
Smucker, Marcus G.	Bronx, New York
Snyder, Howard	Hesston, Kansas
Snyder, Jon	Canby, Oregon
Snyder, Melvin Merle	La Junta, Colorado
Sommers, Clell Eugene	Louisville, Ohio
Sommers, Leon Henry	Cochranton, Pennsylvania
Springer, Merle E.	Saybrook, Illinois
Stalter, Leland Ray	Chenoa, Illinois
Stauffer, James	Lancaster, Pennsylvania
Stauffer, Lamar Eugene	Lancaster, Pennsylvania
Stauffer, Norman Clair	Goshen, Indiana

310

Europe	8/12/63	8/24/65—2
Germany	3/24/53	3/23/55—2
Congo	10/12/66	
Thailand	9/17/60	3/24/63—3
Germany	9/22/53	8/6/54—1
India	7/17/64	7/27/67—3
Germany	7/27/55	11/24/57—2
Germany	7/27/55	7/27/57—2
Germany	7/13/53	
Greece	1/ /54	10/25/55—2
Europe	9/12/57	9/12/59—2
Bolivia	7/7/67	
Germany	11/25/52	11/24/54—2
Yugoslavia	9/6/67	
Germany	7/27/55	7/27/57—2
Germany	8/14/52	1/ /54
Greece	1/ /54	10/25/55—3
Germany	6/12/52	7/5/54—2
Germany	3/30/55	4/23/57—2
Morocco	7/15/64	10/18/66—2
Crete	3/20/68	
Europe	2/11/61	2/16/63—2
Bolivia	5/14/63	4/30/65—2
Liberia	11/12/60	4/26/63—3
Korea	9/30/62	12/17/65—3
Germany	7/6/54	9/ /56—2
Germany	7/13/53	1/25/56—3
Germany	7/13/53	9/16/55—2
Europe	9/12/57	9/12/59—2
Congo	11/12/63	12/22/65—2
Germany	7/9/52	7/5/54—2
Algeria	6/14/67	
Korea	11/20/64	12/5/68—4
Korea	9/30/54	3/2/55—1
Paraguay	4/22/58	4/22/60—2
Germany	7/6/54	
Greece	10/ /55	12/13/57—3
Germany	7/6/54	
Greece		1/4/57—3
Europe	9/12/57	9/12/59—2

Stauffer, Sanford R.	Elverson, Pennsylvania
Stayrook, Miller	Johnstown, Pennsylvania
Steckly, George Edwin	Albany, Oregon
Steffer, Ernest David	Apple Creek, Ohio
Steiner, Clayton	Apple Creek, Ohio
Steiner, Richard Lee	Dalton, Ohio
Steiner, Robert L.	Bluffton, Ohio
Stemen, James Arthur	Goshen, Indiana
Stichter, Kenneth Eugene	Goshen, Indiana
Stichter, Ralph	Nappanee, Indiana
Stoltzfus, Mast	Elverson, Pennsylvania
Stoltzfus, Stephen S.	Elverson, Pennsylvania
Stover, Samuel L.	Perkasie, Pennsylvania
Stuckey, Paul Eugene	Archbold, Ohio
Stucky, John Gary	Moundridge, Kansas
Stucky, Willard Lee	McPherson, Kansas
Stutzman, Allen Linford	Ronan, Montana
Stutzman, Ronald Dean	Corry, Pennsylvania
Stutzmann, Dennis	Corry, Pennsylvania
Suderman, Abe	Vienna, Austria
Suderman, Donald James	Hillsboro, Kansas
Suderman, Peter Ernest	Port Edward, British Columbia
Suderman, John Jacob	Goshen, Indiana
Sutter, Elton E.	Delavan, Illinois
Swartz, Robert L.	Detroit, Michigan
Swartzendruber, Duane	Princeton, Illinois
Swartzendruber, Edwin	Minier, Illinois
Swartzendruber, J. Paul	Kalona, Iowa
Swartzendruber, William L.	Kalona, Iowa
Thiessen, Aldon Dean	Henderson, Nebraska
Thiessen, Jacob Werner	Saskatoon, Saskatchewan
Thiessen, Jake Donald	Austin, Manitoba
Tiessen, Henry	Winkler, Manitoba
Toews, Ernest Carl	Ruthven, Ontario
Toews, John W.	Sardis, British Columbia
Toews, Peter	Homewood, Manitoba
Troyer, Aden Dale	Sugarcreek, Ohio

Vietnam	4/27/66	
Jordan	6/24/52	8/4/54—2
Germany	3/24/53	3/24/55—2
Germany	3/9/54	4/14/56—2
Algeria	1/4/61	5/2/63—2
Madagascar	1/5/67	
Germany	7/6/54	8/25/56—2
Germany	7/27/55	7/27/57—2
Nepal	11/4/57	10/25/60—3
Peru	8/4/58	7/1/60—2
Germany	7/27/55	
Austria		4/22/59—4
Peru	3/30/55	11/ /56—1
Jordan	10/1/52	9/30/54—2
Germany	3/19/56	4/2/58—2
Congo	8/31/66	
Greece	1/19/51	3/19/54—3
Zambia	9/6/67	
Europe	11/16/62	5/15/65—3
Congo	10/12/66	
Congo	8/15/60	7/14/62—2
Brazil	9/6/67	
Vienna	7/7/66	
Germany	7/6/54	7/10/56—2
Korea	3/7/59	3/7/62—3
Peru	6/10/57	5/19/58—1
Germany	6/25/56	
Indo-China	9/ /56	8/ /59—3
Peru	6/29/59	7/7/61—2
Bolivia	7/8/63	7/7/65—2
Germany	10/1/52	11/6/54—2
Germany	10/1/52	10/9/54—2
India	8/15/61	6/27/64—3
British Honduras	4/25/61	6/5/63—2
India	11/7/64	5/27/68—3 1/2
Europe	10/5/59	10/13/61—2
Congo	11/11/64	2/11/67—3
Congo	11/19/61	11/1/63—2
Europe	4/26/61	4/20/64—3

313

Troyer, Albert Lynn	Wellman, Iowa
Troyer, Arthur Gerald	Syracuse, Indiana
Troyer, Daniel, Jr.	Wooster, Ohio
Troyer, Floyd	Goshen, Indiana
Troyer, Lyle Kay	Meadows, Illinois
Unger, Gilbert Peter	Giroux, Manitoba
Unrau, John	Aldergrove, British Columbia
Unrau, Robert Rempel	Wichita, Kansas
Unruh, Anton Melvin	Hillsboro, Kansas
Unruh, Lavern J.	Wheaton, Illinois
Unruh, Paul Willard	N. Newton, Kansas
Unternahrer, Norman	Wayland, Iowa
Unzicker, Donald R.	Roanoke, Illinois
VanPelt, Willard	Columbiana, Ohio
von Gunten, Kenneth	Berne, Indiana
von Gunten, Roger	Berne, Indiana
Voth, Donald	Omaha, Nebraska
Voth, Irvin D.	Newton, Kansas
Voth, Roy Henry	Newton, Kansas
Wadel, Mark Nathan	Shippensburg, Pennsylvania
Wagler, Richard Lee	Jeffersonville, Ohio
Walters, Gordon	Etna Green, Indiana
Waltner, Philip	Harley, South Dakota
Warkentine, Eldon H.	Mt. Lake, Minnesota
Waybill, Nelson Noel	White Cloud, Michigan
Weaver, Dale	New Holland, Pennsylvania
Weaver, Edwin I.	Uniontown, Ohio
Weaver, Harold Lee	Collegeville, Pennsylvania
Weaver, Mark	Macon, Mississippi
Weaver, Robert M.	Gap, Pennsylvania
Weaver, Stanley Leroy	Lima, Ohio

Paraguay	4/22/58	4/22/60—2
Germany	7/8/58	9/26/58
Germany	11/25/52	12/3/54—2
Peru	2/6/61	2/6/63—2
Korea	7/9/64	8/15/67—3
Burundi	9/19/62	5/8/64—2
West Pakistan	8/3/65	
Europe	11/10/60	11/ /62—2
Germany	10/1/52	10/9/54—2
Jordan	9/18/54	2/28/57—3
West Pakistan	12/3/65	
Bolivia	2/10/65	
Europe	9/21/62	9/15/64—2
Germany	3/23/57	4/21/59—2
Europe	9/12/59	
Greece	1/29/60	
Germany	3/21/60	
Agape-Verlag	6/3/61	9/30/61—4
Germany	11/20/56	12/7/58—2
Vietnam	8/29/58	8/8/61—3
Jordan	10/10/54	11/ /56—2
Germany	3/30/55	4/23/57—2
Germany	7/8/58	
Austria	8/15/58	
Germany	11/3/58	9/23/60—2
Greece	2/7/66	
Germany	9/13/58	10/30/61—3
Europe	4/23/57	4/21/59—2
Korea	10/10/53	6/3/55—2
Germany	7/9/52	10/9/54—2
Germany	10/10/58	10/11/60—2
Germany	7/8/58	8/11/60—2
Nepal	9/13/60	7/25/63—3
Congo	11/11/64	11/14/66—2
Germany	7/6/54	
Algeria		9/18/56—2
Jordan	10/27/62	9/7/64—2

Weaver, Wilmer	Hartville, Ohio
Weber, Edward James	Kitchener, Ontario
Weber, John Robert	Kitchener, Ontario
Wedel, Clarence Herman	Burns, Kansas
Wedel, Galen Silas	Moundridge, Kansas
Weitkamp, Gary Richard	Los Angeles, California
Wenger, James Alvin	Hesston, Kansas
Wenger, John Elwood	Wayland, Iowa
Wenger, Marion Roy	Elkhart, Indiana
Wengert, Paul A., Jr.	Smoketown, Pennsylvania
Whittaker, Milton Dwaine	Westfield, Indiana
Wiebe, Delbert	Whitewater, Kansas
Wiebe, Delmer	Whitewater, Kansas
Wiebe, Gary Edward	Huron, South Dakota
Wiebe, Herb	Abbotsford, British Columbia
Wiebe, Menno	Mt. Lehman, British Columbia
Wiebe, Roger A.	Filley, Nebraska
Wingerd, Eldon Simon	Ramona, Kansas
Witmer, Enos James	Salem, Ohio
Witmer, Owen	Salem, Ohio
Wyse, Donald G.	Archbold, Ohio
Wyse, Harold Dean	Archbold, Ohio
Wyse, John Dean	Archbold, Ohio
Wyse, Paul Monroe	Broadway, Virginia
Wyse, Sanford Jay	Archbold, Ohio
Yoder, Charles Dean	Millersburg, Indiana
Yoder, Daniel Keith	Wellman, Iowa
Yoder, David Jay	Springs, Pennsylvania
Yoder, Edward Wayne	Hartville, Ohio
Yoder, Ezra	Kalona, Iowa
Yoder, John Lester	Belleville, Pennsylvania
Yoder, Joseph Benjamin	Belleville, Pennsylvania
Yoder, Kenneth Leo	Grantsville, Maryland
Yoder, Kenyon D.	Goshen, Indiana
Yoder, Kermit	Goshen, Indiana

Europe	2/11/61	2/16/63—2
Germany	11/20/56	8/31/60—4
India	8/15/61	7/15/64—3
Germany	11/25/52	11/25/54—2
Nepal	8/31/66	
Europe	9/13/60	11/8/62—2
Bolivia	7/6/66	
Germany	3/19/56	3/18/58—2
Germany	6/12/52	7/27/54—2
Germany	9/12/57	9/12/59—2
Bolivia	1/5/67	
Paraguay	9/13/57	9/13/59—2
Paraguay	9/13/57	9/13/59—2
Bolivia	7/7/67	
Germany	3/19/56	3/19/58—2
Paraguay	11/12/55	11/14/57—2
Brazil	3/29/67	
Germany	7/13/53	9/16/55—2
Nepal	10/28/57	11/4/60—3
Peru	4/1/55	4/15/57—2
Germany	6/12/52	7/27/54—2
Nepal	10/28/57	12/15/60—3
Germany	7/6/54	
Algeria	7/ /56	12/13/56—2
Peru	4/1/55	4/15/57—2
Congo	9/6/67	
Germany	7/13/53	10/25/55—2
Paraguay	8/1/58	11/5/60—2
Germany	7/13/53	
Greece		1/21/56—3
Europe	6/10/59	7/13/61—2
Paraguay	9/13/57	9/13/59—2
Europe	9/29/61	9/29/63—2
Germany	3/9/54	4/5/56—2
Espelkamp	4/23/55	11/20/58—3
Algeria	7/15/64	10/14/66—2
Germany	7/8/58	
Amsterdam	9/2/58	
Greece	7/2/59	8/24/60—2

Yoder, L. Douglas	West Liberty, Ohio
Yoder, Lee Sharp	Belleville, Pennsylvania
Yoder, Leon	Goshen, Indiana
Yoder, Lester S.	Elverson, Pennsylvania
Yoder, Myron Sanford	Sarasota, Florida
Yoder, Robert D.	Kalona, Iowa
Yoder, Roger J.	Elkhart, Indiana
Yoder, Roger Lee	Wakarusa, Indiana
Yoder, Ronald D.	Goshen, Indiana
Yoder, Royce	Elkhart, Indiana
Yoder, Wilbur	Goshen, Indiana
Yoder, William L.	Topeka, Indiana
Yordy, James Walter	Chicago, Illinois
Yost, Russel S.	Newton, Kansas
Yutzy, Valentine	Plain City, Ohio
Zacharias, Rodney C.	Halbstadt, Manitoba
Zehr, Alvin J.	Croghan, New York
Zehr, Dean Richard	Rantoul, Illinois
Zimmerman, Harry Bucher	Malvern, Pennsylvania
Zook, Benuel	Womelsdorf, Pennsylvania
Zook, Ira T., Jr.	La Tour, Missouri
Zuercher, Herman Nevin	Wooster, Ohio

Morocco	7/14/66	
Germany	7/13/53	10/25/55—2
Indonesia	9/18/63	9/17/66—3
Germany	7/13/53	7/25/55—2
Germany	7/6/54	7/10/56—2
Nepal	7/6/66	
Europe	7/23/63	7/28/65—2
Europe	3/30/62	3/29/64—2
Europe	7/ /61	8/15/63—2
Peru	6/22/58	10/15/60—2
Germany	3/23/57	9/12/59—2
Holland	3/24/51	4/3/54—3
Germany	10/1/52	10/10/54—2
Algeria	9/4/65	12/21/67—2
Korea	1/19/54	2/7/57—3
Congo	8/31/66	
Germany	11/25/52	11/25/54—2
Germany	11/25/52	1/ /54
Greece	1/ /54	10/25/55—3
Europe	4/23/57	4/21/59—2
Nepal	1/5/67	
Germany	7/27/55	
Greece	8/28/56	11/4/57—2
Europe	4/14/59	4/4/61—2

Total number of men who served in MCC Pax, as of June 1, 1968: 674

319